CW01653968

GATE D5

Part two

James Ally

For Lucas.

You have no idea how hard it is to be here without you.

I wish you could read it.

Before it all begins,
Before you understand,
The only way,
I must walk away.

Before we awake in the morning,
And we have breakfast together,
Before...
I must walk away.

Before the years pass by,
Health and beauty slip away,
Before you bow your head over my grave,
Please, let me walk away.

James Ally

Contents

1. Lie

Amsterdam, July 2018

The nurse briskly made her way through the winding hospital corridor, the darkest corners of which were bathed in cold fluorescent lights. At the end of the hall, outside the doctor's office, she grabbed the doorknob and took a deep breath.

'Doctor, she's already here. She's arrived.'

'Great.'

A short man with a grey beard and the stature of an officer rose from his desk. He closed his briefcase with one hand and with the other grabbed a mug of half-finished coffee, sipping it loudly. He scanned the desk, but he must have decided that none of the documents were useful because he followed the nurse empty-handed.

As he passed the patients' rooms, the doctor greeted the other employees moving through the corridors with a nod, although this politeness was just a reflex.

When they reached the second floor, the doctor opened the door to the conference room, where he found a woman standing by the window. She turned to face them the moment they walked in.

'Dan Visser,' he said. 'We spoke on the phone.' He approached her, extending his hand.

As she offered hers in return, his gaze lingered on her ring – a green stone braided with silver, exactly like her necklace.

'Tracy Richardson,' she said, squeezing his hand. 'How is he feeling?'

'Let's sit down.' He pointed at a chair.

'Two weeks ago, the patient passed out at the airport in Amsterdam, and we have been struggling to get through to him since he woke up. We diagnosed derealisation, which may result from the previously diagnosed anxiety-depressive disorder. We prescribed him Diazepam, which he tolerates well. He's calmed down. From the information I have obtained from his husband, the patient has reported suffering from a similar condition in the past when, as I understand, you worked with him. His husband suggested locking the room where he is currently staying for safety reasons. He gave us your contact details.'

'This is unnecessary. The patient hasn't put himself or any other person at risk.'

'I understand.' The doctor paused, as if searching for something in his mind.

'When can I see him?'

'If you're ready, now. The nurse will take you.' He rose from the desk. 'I have added you to our central register and given you unrestricted access to the patient. Your office is waiting. If you need anything, please report it to the staff or come directly to me. I'm in room thirty-eight, first floor.'

'Great, thank you.'

Tracy got up, and a few moments later, she followed the nurse, clutching her purse tightly to her chest. Her serious face remained cold and focused, but her eyes scanned the walls around her. Would she be able to reach Tom? Would he recognise her? Would he react at all? These thoughts didn't leave her for a moment, and she almost tripped over her own feet, nearly missing one of the turns. She ran a hand through her hair and slowed her footsteps. The nurse smiled at her, but the tension didn't leave Tracy's face.

They stopped at the last door at the end of a corridor that stretched for miles. For some time, the nurse fumbled with a bunch of keys, the metallic sound echoing. Tracy waited, perfectly still.

When the door opened, she spotted a man lying on a roughly made bed. He didn't even move when the nurse stood aside to let Tracy, who had to stop herself from rushing into the room, through.

'You can go back to your duties. I don't expect any problems,' she said to the nurse, then stepped forward.

Tom lay facing the barred window.

'Tom?' She said his name calmly.

Each step she took gradually revealed the image of the man she could barely recognise. His pale face was first to emerge, partially obscured by his tousled fringe and reddened eyes, releasing a whispering stream of tears that hid discreetly in the pillow.

When she stopped before him, she tried to find in the faded man some scrap of the life she remembered from their last meeting.

*

The sound of the door opening meant that someone would force me to speak again, but I just wanted to remain silent.

'Tom?'

A familiar, soothing voice reached my ears, followed by approaching footsteps. As she drew close, I involuntarily opened my mouth, but no words came out. My voice was hiding somewhere deep inside me. I wasn't sure if it was a dream. Hallucinations? A vision?

‘Tom? Do you recognise me?’ She sat down next to me.

I scanned her face, locating her gaze.

‘I came the second I found out you were here. Will you tell me what happened?’

Desperation clasped my throat, squeezing more tears out of my eyes. I was frightened that they had sent her to take the letters from me, so I pressed them tighter to my chest. Only then did she notice, but instead of reaching for them, she found my gaze again.

‘Tom, I spoke to the doctor, and I know you fainted at the airport. I suspect something more happened, right? Something that made you escape into silence. I wish you could tell me about it.’

She waited a long time for my answer, her eyes peaceful and patient. I wanted to tell her everything, but not a single word found its way out of my throat. Tracy took some tissues from her purse and gently wiped away my tears.

‘Tom, I’m here for you. I have a room next door. I’ll be here all the time. Rest now, and I’ll check on you tomorrow.’

My body didn’t even flinch while I listened to her footsteps fading. Moments after she left, a nurse gave me some medicine. I felt the soluble-plastic capsules in my mouth, making me drowsy with sleep.

Recognising the sounds of yearning, I didn’t fight my drooping eyelids; I just surrendered to them, feeling the bliss holding my hand and leading me into an unreal world.

First – his voice. A warm whisper. As if everything we talked about was always our secret. Then his scent, making me slow my breaths so I could inhale it deeper.

‘We’re already late,’ Lucas whispered, snuggling against my back in the bathroom.

‘You realise it’s your fault.’ I smiled as I looked in the mirror and buttoned my shirt.

‘I know, but my only excuse is that I love you.’ He started kissing the nape of my neck passionately.

‘Oh no! Don’t start that again!’ I laughed, pushing him away. ‘Emma will be furious if we’re any later than we already are.’

*

When I opened my eyes, the rays of sun coming in through the large window illuminated the paper plate left on the table. Was Tracy just an image from a dream? And if not, how did she find me?

All I could hear was my breathing as more questions filled my mind. Why? Why did Chris do this to me?

I jumped at the sound of knocking. I waited, unsure if I had misheard it, but the knocking continued more clearly, and a moment later, Tracy opened the door. I shifted on the bed, and she took that as permission to come in. She looked tired, as if she had just arrived after an all-night flight.

‘Good morning, Tom,’ she said, turning the chair at the breakfast table in my direction. She sat down and smoothed her skirt. She studied my face before she repeated the same words.

I wanted to reply but found my throat even drier than the day before. I opened and closed my mouth like a fish desperate for water.

‘I’ll help you.’ She reached for the plate. ‘You must eat to gain strength.’

She tore off a small piece of cheese baguette and brought it to my lips. A sense of relief came over me, and I realised that someone had taken over something for me for the first time in a long time. I opened my mouth, allowing Tracy to feed me. With every small bite, a sense of trust came closer, eventually sitting comfortably between us. I stopped after a few bites. Tracy waited a moment, making sure I wasn't hungry anymore, then went over to the window and opened it. Fresh air entered my nostrils.

Later she came back for lunch and dinner. She tried to talk to me. I could see her lips move, but I heard only the muffled sounds, which became clearer until I could hear her last sentence.

'Tom, if you're ready to talk, know that I'm here; you don't have to worry about anything. Remember that.'

After dinner, she gave me drugs that gradually stole reality, dragging my mind into a deep sleep. Harry ran towards me, shouting something. At first, it was difficult to hear his voice, but after a while, the cry became clearer and more desperate.

'Daddy... Don't leave me...'

I woke up in a cold sweat. I stared into the darkness of the room, trying to pierce through it. My gaze landed on the barred window. I had been here the whole time.

I leaned clumsily against the edge of the bed. I took a deep breath, then another, as if checking I could still breathe. *Daddy...* His voice kept calling me. He was waiting for me, and I was here, useless.

I couldn't let him down again. Not now. Not after what he'd been through at the airport.

Harry's face grew clearer before my eyes. I had no right to run away. I had to fight for him.

The next morning I recognised her by the footsteps. She approached, treading lightly as if afraid to disturb the silence.

'How are you feeling today, Tom?'

As she sat down in the chair next to me, I opened my mouth, but only a faint rustle came out, and my throat immediately went dry.

She smiled and poured me some tea. When she placed the mug on the cupboard next to me, I could smell the scent of fresh strawberries, as if she'd picked them from a forest outside.

'I smuggled you something.' She winked at me.

My mind began to run towards her, holding the dormant words in my hands, careful not to drop them. They were waking up, and as I slowly opened my mouth, I managed to get them out one by one.

*

Mum took the cake out of the fridge. Our eyes flickered conspiratorially, checking if Harry was anywhere close. He could never sit still for long, with one small exception – he loved books before he could even read, so while we were preparing for the celebration, Chris took him to the office, where he let him look through our bookshelf. This gave me a chance to decorate the cake with nine candles. I was inserting the last one when I heard Harry's small feet running towards the kitchen. I exchanged scared looks with Mum, then hid the cake behind my back without thinking.

'Honey, we had a deal. You don't come near the kitchen until Grandma has finished preparing the surprise.'

He couldn't catch his breath from excitement. I saw the book in his hands.

'What's that?'

Harry immediately handed it to me. I glanced at the cover, and a shiver ran down my spine.

'Daddy, in this town, people travel in boats! Do you know where it is?'

I nodded uncertainly.

Almost three years had passed, but every time I had to fly somewhere, I chose flights away from Amsterdam, even though I knew I would have to face the demons of my past sooner or later.

'Could we go there sometime?' He looked at me pleadingly.

I was stunned, but seeing the jumping fireflies in his eyes, I wanted to fulfil his wish.

'Anytime you want,' I heard myself say.

After ceremonially blowing out the candles in the living room, Harry ran excitedly from gift to gift, shouting in delight between bites of cake. Mum and Chris laughed as he impatiently ripped the wrapping paper and opened the boxes and bags. I couldn't stop thinking about Amsterdam. The streets we walked and the cheese museum, where Lucas put a small piece of Dutch delicacy in my mouth. I shook my head and closed my eyes tight. When I opened them, Mum was standing in front of me.

'Everything all right?'

'Yeah, I'm just a little tired,' I said, and hugged her.

'I'm going to put Harry to bed now. He's starting to fall asleep,' Mum whispered.

After Harry was asleep and Mum had returned to her room, I started tidying up the living room. I was picking up the plates from the table when Chris appeared.

'Do you really want to go back there after everything?' I heard the irritation in his voice, and I decided to ignore it.

'I don't know what you're talking about.' I carried some plates to the kitchen and returned to the living room to grab more.

'Tom, please.' He followed me as I did a second round but stopped me at the door this time.

'Chris, Harry wants to take a boat ride through the canals of Amsterdam. What's wrong with that? Was I supposed to tell him he can't?'

'That's not the point.'

'What is it then?'

'I just don't want you to go there.'

'Will you explain why?' I kept my gaze on him.

He fell silent, his cheek tightening from clenching his teeth.

'Chris, it's just a trip—'

'A trip?' he interrupted. 'Have you forgotten what happened there?'

'I haven't forgotten, but I will not hide from it for the rest of my life.'

'I'm asking you—'

'Harry should be exploring the world, not sitting locked in his room playing computer games all day.' I started loading the dishes into the dishwasher.

'But I don't agree, do you understand?' He turned on his heel and walked out. I closed my eyes. I should have discussed it with him before agreeing, but there was no time. Harry put me on the spot. And it was his birthday.

I finished cleaning the kitchen and, a little hesitantly, made my way upstairs to our bedroom. Chris sat on the bed, clearly upset. I stood in the doorway.

'I'm sorry. I don't know what got into me.' I sat down next to him, reaching for his hand. 'Let's all go together. We'll have a great trip.'

'Tom, I'm never going there,' he said coldly, staring straight ahead.

'But why? Because of me?' I squeezed his hand tighter. 'I'm sorry.'

'Not because of you. It's because of what happened. You don't even know how scared I was thinking that I might have lost you forever.'

'Chris, it's in the past, and we can't live with it forever. We have to face it.'

'That I didn't throw the book away either. I could have prevented this,' he said, ignoring my words completely.

'Chris, please.'

But he remained silent, focused.

For the next few days, I struggled to accept my decision, but every time I saw Harry, who never parted with the book, I just wanted to grab him, run out of the house and drive straight to the airport. I hoped that Chris would finally give in, but he acted as if the subject had never been brought up. I didn't know what to do.

*

After a week, I decided to try again. He was doing something in the garage when I walked in.

'Can we go back to the topic of the trip?'

'You know my opinion. It won't change,' he said, stern.

'If you don't want to go, can I go with Harry?'

He fell silent again. I held my breath, my heart beating hard, waiting for his verdict.

'Do what you want,' he said casually without looking at me.

From then on, Chris punished me with silence. Before leaving for work, he kissed Harry and gave me a cold goodbye.

‘Is Dad mad at you because of our trip? Maybe we should go another time?’ Harry asked one day.

‘No, he has a lot of work on and is very tired. He’d love to go with us, but they won’t give him leave now. We will take photos and record videos for him. It’ll be fun.’

There was a smile on Harry’s face again. I booked a hotel room for three in case Chris changed his mind. I couldn’t mute the memories of the buzz at the airport and the smell of croissants which were now returning to me. They warmed my heart.

Two weeks after Harry’s birthday, we flew to Amsterdam. Until the last night together, I tried to persuade Chris to join us, but he remained unmoved.

After checking in at Newcastle Airport, we sat at the gate. Harry sat on my lap and wrapped his arms around me, resting his head on my chest before falling asleep. I looked around. A couple was trying to cram more stuff into their carry-on suitcases, small kids were running around their stressed-out parents, and small columns of pilots and flight attendants marched through the airport. I kept glancing at Harry, but he was missing it all. His warmth enveloped me like a blanket. Like him, I wanted to fall asleep peacefully, only to wake up once we landed.

After the boarding announcement, I kissed Harry on the forehead, gently waking him up. I put him on the floor and reached for our suitcase. He looked around, a little drowsily, and squeezed my hand tightly. A few seconds later, we headed towards the plane.

The flight attendant who welcomed us on board smiled and gave Harry a lollipop, which made him hug me tighter.

'Harry, what do we say?' I whispered, stroking his head. He blushed delightfully before whispering, 'Thank you.'

This time he answered in English, although he often liked to joke using Polish words that had become somewhat of our secret code.

As I passed Gate 11F, I looked over my shoulder. Now a girl with red hair was sitting there, clutching her husband's or boyfriend's hand. If things had gone differently, we'd probably be sitting there right now with Lucas, flying to Warsaw for our anniversary.

We took our seats a few rows behind her. Harry stared out of the window, hypnotised. He couldn't understand how such huge machines could rise in a moment, but this vision didn't scare him; rather, it aroused an ecstasy similar to that which first-time pilots must feel.

'Daddy, when are we leaving?' he asked.

'As soon as all the passengers are seated. Patience,' I chuckled.

It was a nervous laugh, but Harry didn't seem to notice.

Ten minutes later, we were up in the air. Throughout the flight, Harry kept his eyes on the window, glancing from time to time at the flight attendants delivering snacks and drinks. His eyes sparkled with excitement, and the sight touched my heart.

The landing was smooth. As the first passengers rose from their seats, Harry instinctively did the same. I grabbed his hand.

'Just a minute, darling,' I mumbled. My throat was dry even though I had drunk a whole bottle of water during the flight. I looked out the window. I'd come back here after all. Time shrank as if not a year had passed since we met. I fought with the hope of seeing him again.

Harry shifted in his seat. I slowly got up, and we joined the other passengers as they disembarked.

As we moved along the glass-walled corridor, Harry squeezed my hand while scanning the space around him. The rays of the sun touched our faces. When we approached the exit, I switched my phone on. Chris hadn't left a single message. With each step, my heart beat faster. I swallowed, only for my throat to dry out again. Images of me walking down the hall with my suitcase and Lucas greeting me with a smile flashed through my mind.

'Daddy.' Harry tightened his grip.

'Sorry, Daddy was just thinking of something. What did you say?' I looked into his hungry, adventurous eyes.

'Where are we going?'

'We're about to enter the hallway. It's huge, so you can easily get lost. Don't let go of my hand even for a second, OK?'

'OK.'

A few moments later, I stopped and looked at the pillar and the empty place next to it, where a red rose lay. Flowers had been left in various parts of the airport in tribute to the victims of the attack. There were more of them along the next wall, and a golden plaque on which was engraved the inscription *We have not forgotten you.* I felt tightness in my chest.

We moved on, and simultaneously, the sun's rays filtering through the windows spilt onto the floor. It was as if he was giving me a sign, saying, *Hello, I'm here with you.*

I glanced at Harry, who was looking around, greedily taking in the whole airport. At one point, he stared at the huge window before pulling me towards it.

'Daddy, look at all those planes!' Jumping up, he pointed at the planes parked on the tarmac.

I smiled. Maybe he'd be a pilot one day? 'Would you like to see the airport briefly before we leave?' I squatted in front of him.

'Yes!' His blue eyes shone like sapphires in a jewellery store.

Although the memories of Lucas's presence in this place touched me with sadness, at the same time, I felt indescribable peace and gratitude for the moments I had spent here. I couldn't have returned to this airport today if it weren't for the therapy.

'First, I'll take you to my favourite coffee shop, and we'll buy some cakes, my little traveller.'

'I want chocolate!' he cried.

Fervently, with its small hands, love was hugging me with joyful eyes. I closed my eyes as I felt the touch of an angel sent for me in this cold and empty world.

I stopped outside Café Chocolate. The familiar smell of chocolate wafted in the air, and I realised that the cookies I had tried so many times were displayed in glass cases where Harry had glued his nose, and time seemed to have skipped this place.

We approached the table, and I couldn't calm the thoughts that kept me under the illusion that in a moment we would see Lucas emerge from the depths of the café to greet us. He ducks in front of Harry and introduces himself, then hugs him tightly.

We took our seats, right next to the window. A moment later, the waiter appeared, but his face was unfamiliar. I placed my order. Harry sat next to me, looking around, and my eyes involuntarily rested on the empty seat in front of me. I imagined Lucas sitting here with us now, smiling and talking about his day, while we disappeared from the real world for a moment, engrossed in his stories.

When the waiter brought our order, I asked for a knife. He was surprised but complied with my request. I cut the croissants in half, our tradition. I swapped halves with Harry, although they were no different from each other. Lucas had said it was like sharing the halves of our hearts. Harry observed this carefully.

'Daddy, why did you cut them?'

'Because this is how I give you half of my heart, showing how much I love you.' I stroked his head. His eyes filled with the purest and most immaculate love, enduring and selfless.

'Then I'll give you my half as well.' He quickly placed a piece of croissant on my plate.

I kissed my son and smiled at seeing his chocolate-smeared face. When we were done, I paid the bill, and Harry dashed out, searching for his next airport adventure. As I left the table, I looked at the empty seat again.

'I wish you could meet Harry. You'd love him,' I whispered as I left the café.

Harry was pulling my hand, and I was laughing because he had absolutely no idea where he was going. Just outside Gate D5, I stopped. Flashes of memories greeted me, evoking wistful sounds.

'What are you doing?'

'Let me...' Lucas grabbed the handle of my suitcase.

I felt a stronger pull. Harry was shaking my hand.

'Daddy, this corridor is endless.'

'Yes?' I laughed. 'Wait, honey, let's go in here for a moment.' I gestured towards the gate.

We took our seats in the last row. Harry's face showed concern, as if we were going back home.

'Daddy, there's nothing here.'

'This place is very special to me, sweetie.' I wanted to tell him everything, but he was too young for it. 'I used to spend time here with my friend.'

'Did you have fun?'

'Yes, we played games, cards, read books and talked.'

'And where is he now?'

How to explain this to a child? What should I say?

'My friend...'

I wanted to say his name, but something stopped me. I had so little left of him that even his name was an intimate keepsake that I held deep in my heart. I looked away. All around us, the passengers on the next flight were taking their seats.

'Did you know that one day every soul will go to heaven? When the time comes, it flies high, high...'

'And the angel flies with her, holding her hand?'

I looked at Harry. This little boy understood more than other children, and yet I wanted so much to protect him from the truth.

'Yes, they fly together to heaven.'

Harry's mouth dropped open.

'My friend just flew there, and you know what? He might be looking down on us now. It is possible.'

Harry lifted his head and waved at the ceiling, and I involuntarily did the same. I thought of Lucas seeing us now. I smiled and grabbed Harry in my arms, hugging him tightly.

'Daddy, I'm thirsty.'

'All right, wait here. I'll go and get something from over there.' I pointed at the vending machine.

A moment later, I was inserting a coin, and the sound of it rolling echoed into the depths of the machine, which then noisily spat out two bottles of water. I remembered when Lucas tried to shake something out of the same machine. He put the coins in, and the machine gurgled, but no bottle popped out. He looked around to ensure no one was watching, then kicked it vigorously several times. The machine started, and a moment later, we were squeezing two bottles of water in our hands, grinning like teenagers.

I grabbed the bottle, turned towards Harry and froze. He wasn't alone. A man was squatting in front of my son, handing him something wrapped in a paper bag. What the hell? I ran towards them, pushing away the people lining up at the adjacent gate.

'What are you doing?' I tugged at his shoulder.

The man slowly got up and turned around to face me. His wide auburn eyes sent a strong shiver through me. My heart froze. Impossible... but... Lucas opened his mouth, but no words came out. I struggled to breathe, and I felt the strong beating of my heart in my temples. Darkness enveloped me.

*

'And what happened to Harry?' Tracy asked.

I lowered my head, struggling to hold back tears. I could only imagine a crying child who thought I had left him forever.

'Chris came and took him home. Harry must be distraught now that he hasn't seen Amsterdam. I failed him.'

I saw Tracy take a moment to gather her thoughts so she could play her thankless part.

'Tom... Lucas died in the explosion. You know that.' There was disappointment in her voice, which told me that she thought the therapy had failed entirely.

I turned to the cupboard and fished out a bundle of letters from the drawer. I passed the first one to her. She seemed confused.

'Come on, open it.' I gestured at the envelope.

'Where did you get it from?' She turned the letter over in her hand, scrutinising it.

'Lucas passed it to me through one of the nurses. Chris banned him from seeing me. He's alive,' I said confidently.

Tracy took her glasses out of her purse, wiped them with a tissue and slowly slid the letter out of the envelope. She did it gently, as if the paper would break into a million pieces. She opened the page folded in half, and her eyes began to trace the lines.

My love,

I'm writing to you because my therapist suggested it would help me, although she knows fully that you will not be able to answer me. I would like to join you so much, but here they lock you up in a psychiatric ward just for having thoughts like that. It's been six months since I lost you. I feel your presence every time I remember our last evening. They give me drugs, but they don't work. They can't erase you from my mind or heart. I don't have the strength to get out of bed and start the day. At work, they think I'm depressed because of the explosion. I want to hug you and fall asleep in your arms. You know what? You'd say I'm crazy, but I think I made a year's supply of your strawberry tea. When I brew it, it feels like you're here, sitting on the sofa, smiling at me. I'm so sorry I didn't get to you in time. You were left alone when that wall collapsing took you away from me. You died, and I wasn't there with you, but wherever you are, I love you and will never stop. I have to finish – tears are smudging the letters. Maybe tomorrow will be a better day.

Yours,

Lucas

Tracy looked up. I saw a throbbing disorientation in her eyes. She was trying to understand what she had just read, as I had when I first saw the letter.

'Read on.' I handed her another. 'You'll like this one.' I couldn't stop the anger tinged with irony spilling out of me.

She hesitantly opened the envelope and slid out the letter.

Dearest,

I remember when my sister brought me a new phone at the hospital. My old one and my wallet went missing somewhere in the rubble at the airport. I called you immediately, and my heartbeat sped up when I heard it ring. I was waiting eagerly to hear your voice, but instead, an unfamiliar male voice picked up. Your husband, I later learned. I asked him about you, and he told me you passed away the night before. I couldn't speak. My breath blocked my throat, and I didn't want your husband to hear me cry. My phone fell out of my hands, and I lost connection when it dropped on the floor. The next day I called again to ask where the funeral would be, but he didn't want me there. He said I'd done enough harm to his family and that I should never call again. I respected his will. Sorry, I can't write anything more today.

Yours,

Lucas

Horror shone from Tracy's eyes, and the stone mask slipped from her face.

'Do you still think I've lost my mind?' I passed her another letter.

She didn't answer.

Dearest,

Today I was at the airport. They've rebuilt everything. You would like it. I was sitting at our gate. I visit it often. Did you know that once I met that big female athlete who wanted to buy all the croissants back then? I bought them at the airport and ate them in our last row. People leave flowers in places where they lost their loved ones. I leave you a rose under our pillar. I visit this place with Emma and Sven. They miss you, too. Sometimes I feel like you're about to come out of the bridge into the corridor, and I'll be able to see you again. I know I should stop, but I can't. I have therapy tomorrow, but I don't know why I'm going. I don't need therapy; I only need you.

Yours,

Lucas

'There are many more letters,' I said.

'Tom, I don't know what to say. This... this changes everything...'

'You have to help me!' I grabbed her hand. 'I only have you.'

'What do you want me to do?'

'Help Lucas get here, if only for a moment. Please.' My eyes teared up.

For the next few moments, the only sound that could be heard in my room was her heavy breathing.

'Wait.' She jumped up from her chair. 'Be right back.'

*

She had failed him. Focused on Tom, she hadn't seen the threat lurking in Chris. A plan began to form in her mind. She approached the nurse waiting in the corridor like a guard.

'Who has access to the patient other than the doctor?'

'Only me,' the nurse replied immediately.

'The patient in that room' – Tracy pointed – 'he's received some letters. Do you know anything about it?'

The nurse lowered her head, hiding her flushed face.

'It was me,' she whispered. 'The man who gave them to me, he was crying, and kneeling in front of me. I couldn't... I couldn't say no. Will you report it?' She looked up in fear.

'Do you have his details?'

'No, but this poor guy comes here daily and stays in the waiting room until evening.'

'Is he here now?'

'Probably.'

'I want you to take me to him.'

The nurse hesitated for a split second, nodded, and started towards the waiting room.

'You won't report it?' the nurse asked when they got into the lift. She pressed the button for the ground floor.

'Don't worry. You won't lose your job.'

When they arrived, the nurse used her card to open the glass door. On the other side, dozens of people were waiting. Tracy entered the rows of seats and, like a sniffer dog, searched them one by one, hoping to catch the face Tom had described to her so many times in the past.

'He's there.' The nurse pointed to a man dozing against the wall with his head resting on his hand. As she approached him, Tracy leaned down and touched his shoulder.

'Lucas?'

He opened his reddened eyes. His pale face revealed fatigue, and the first grey streaks could be seen in his raven-black hair. He sprang to his feet.

'What's happening?' He looked scared.

'My name is Tracy Richardson. I'm Tom's therapist. Please come with us.'

'You won't kick me out.' He sat down again and turned to face the opposite direction. 'I'll keep coming back until you let me see Tom!' Anger twisted his face.

'Calm down; nobody's kicking you out.' Tracy held out her hand and looked warmly into his eyes. 'Please, trust me.'

The image drawn with Tom's stories now confronted reality, but instead of the smile she had heard so much about, she saw only sadness and hurt.

'Where do you want to take me?' Lucas scanned the room.

'I'll explain everything in a moment. Please, come with us.'

Tentatively, he stood up. He exchanged looks with the nurse, and she nodded reassuringly. He lowered his head and followed them out.

'You'll see Tom in a minute,' Tracy announced once they were back in the lift and the nurse had pressed the button.

Lucas shuddered and looked at her in disbelief. He was silent for a long time, probably thinking it was a trap to get rid of him.

'But you must know Tom is not well,' Tracy continued. 'I'm not going to hide my hope that meeting with him could change that.'

It must have hit him then that he was really about to see Tom, because his facial expression changed dramatically. His pupils widened, and light came back to his eyes. His mouth moved slightly in an attempt to smile.

'Thank you,' he choked out shakily.

They got off the lift and continued down the labyrinthine corridor. When they reached the doors at the end, Tracy and the nurse stopped. Lucas caught up with them, then, unsure where to stand, positioned himself awkwardly next to Tracy.

'I have to warn you that Tom has been on strong medication since he arrived, which can make him lethargic and lacking energy. If you feel it's too much for him, call me immediately. I'll be outside. I'm not sure what might happen, but I think your presence will improve his condition.'

'I see.'

'You can go in now,' Tracy said. 'We'll wait here.'

'Thank you, thank you so much.' Tears filled his eyes.

He took a deep breath and turned the doorknob with a trembling hand. The second Lucas saw Tom sitting on the bed, tear-stained joy tightened his throat, and without thinking, he let his legs lead him towards his beloved.

*

At the sound of the door opening, I turned over. I was sure Tracy was coming back, but when my eyes met his, I froze. I parted my lips, but not a single word came out. Lucas covered his mouth with his hand, and tears began to flow simultaneously from our cheeks between large gulps of air. He took small, timid steps towards me. He was shaking, and my heart quivered, unsure of the moment's reality.

We stared at each other for a long time as he sat beside me. He had lost weight, and his pale face bore months of sleepless nights. He extended his hand, and I hesitantly placed mine in it. He took me in his arms. His warmth pierced me like it always had in the past. We couldn't stop crying, our sobs merging into a single sound. After a long time, he looked at me painfully and gently wiped the tears off my cheeks.

'Tom... I'm not crazy, am I? Say something.'

'I don't know. Maybe I'm crazy... Maybe we're not here at all...' I studied his face with my fingertips.

Lucas closed his eyes, and we hugged again, freezing in silence and shielding the sound of our breaths from the world.

'Will you take me out of here?' I whispered.

'Immediately.' He stood up.

'Wait.' I grabbed his hand. 'You have to know something. A lot has changed. I have a son.'

He came back and sat next to me again.

‘I know.’ He smiled. ‘Harry is a brilliant boy.’

I looked at him in surprise.

‘I talked to him while we were waiting for the ambulance. He even sounds like you.’ He chuckled. ‘I’m not going anywhere.’ He stroked my cheek. ‘Let me just talk to Tracy.’

All I could hear from the hallway were the distorted sounds of Lucas and Tracy speaking, but at some point, they became clearer.

‘I’ll do whatever it takes. Please, trust me. I know you don’t know me—’

‘If I didn’t know you,’ she interrupted, ‘we wouldn’t be talking right now.’

Lucas fell silent.

‘Get him out of here before Chris finds out.’

‘Here’s my phone number and address.’ I saw him hand her a piece of paper through the half-open door. The whole time I felt dizzy with thoughts like fireworks exploding in my head. What would happen now? Chris would never let me go. What if he used Harry to keep me? What should I do?

‘Sign this, please.’ Lucas returned after a while. He was clutching a document. ‘It will help us get you out of here. Tracy will take you over as a patient, and I’ll take you home.’

‘And Harry?’

‘It will be the first thing we discuss once we get home.’

I nodded. I signed the document, and he immediately passed it to Tracy, who stood in the doorway, looking at us with motherly gentleness.

I felt too weak to stand, so Lucas arranged a wheelchair and pushed me to a taxi. I still couldn't believe this was happening. I kept turning my head and glancing at him to ensure he was really there. Every time, he caught my gaze and returned it with the smile I loved so much.

He helped me to his apartment. As we entered, I stumbled through the doorway, but Lucas held me, and I felt safe.

The smell of a vanilla candle wafted through the hallway. A projection of memories from my last visit began to slide before my eyes. We went inside, but he kept holding my hand tight as if he was afraid of losing me.

'Are you hungry?' he asked in an undertone.

I shook my head.

'Then I'll make you your favourite tea; I have a lot of it.' He smiled, then led me into the living room and helped me to the sofa. I felt its familiar softness that had once welcomed us the last night we spent together.

He let go of my hand slowly, then walked towards the kitchen, occasionally turning to me.

'Be here when I get back, please.'

'I will.' A pleasant warmth enveloped me.

I scanned the room. It matched everything I remembered. A leaky window through which the wind peeked and slightly moved the curtain. The desk on which our photo still stood, and rolls of projects piled up from a metal basket next to it.

Lucas returned a moment later with two mugs of tea in his hands.

'I'm here.' He placed them on the table, sat next to me, and as he took my hand, I was struck by sadness, remembering how much had been taken from us.

'How have you been coping?' Not for a second did he avert his eyes.

For a moment, I felt like we had gone back in time and it was that special night again, and the events after that never happened. I wanted to fool my mind for as long as possible, but I couldn't.

'It was a nightmare.' I looked down. 'I remember waking up in a hospital, asking about you, but no one knew anything. Chris came and took me home, and after a few days, I got a visit from a police officer. He wanted me to identify some people in the photos from the airport, but you weren't among them.'

I closed my eyes and took a deep breath as the despair flooded back.

'Then the policeman took out a wallet covered in blood. He opened it and showed me the photo of the two of us. He said they found it in the remains of the bodies from the blast. I couldn't... I broke down.'

I lowered my eyes and fell silent. Lucas stroked my hand. I looked at him.

'Chris was trying to help me.' I sounded like I was justifying myself. 'That's how I ended up at Tracy's. Without her, I wouldn't be here now. I thought about joining you so many times... It would have been easier.'

'I'm glad you didn't.' He brought my hand to his lips and kissed it.

'Tracy put me under hypnosis so I could say goodbye to you. It helped a lot, but I never forgot you. Therapy has rebuilt my marriage, although it has never been the same. We created something new, and I was learning to love someone who has changed...'

He lowered his voice. 'Do you love him?'

'I thought so. Now I see the lies he fed me to rebuild everything.'

I gazed out of the window.

'You know, when I saw you at the airport—'

'I thought I was hallucinating,' he interrupted. 'Then you fell, and your son cried terribly. He didn't know what happened to you. I hugged him and promised him that everything would be OK. Later, a policewoman showed up and took Harry to the station.'

'Thank you for being with him.'

'He's a sweet baby. Will you tell me about him?'

'Would you like me to?'

'I would, very much.'

2. Harry

After the end of therapy, my life regained its former balance. Chris showered me with love and acceptance that flowed from him like a waterfall. I bathed in it and allowed it to rebuild our relationship, which, at that point, seemed perfect. I remember the joy in his mother's eyes as we sat in the garden, where Chris wrapped me in a blanket and kissed me. She said she was so proud that I had survived everything and was happy she could see us together now.

Our daily dinners became something special, too. Chris carefully set the table, adding small, pleasing decorations. Sometimes it was a freshly cut rose floating in a bowl full of water alongside two tea lights. Other times, he would scatter chamomile flowers on our plates or place small bouquets of wildflowers to decorate the napkins. I was delighted with his transformation. From a caterpillar, he became a beautiful butterfly that spread its wings over us, shining brightly.

During one of our dinners, Chris suddenly got up, straightened his shirt and took out of the cabinet the best wine he kept for special occasions. He opened it with vigour and began to fill our glasses, clearly satisfied with something.

'Tom,' he began as he sat down, 'I'd like to return to a topic I've avoided for a long time.'

'Yes?' I stopped chewing, my mouth half full.

'Lately, I've been wondering what it would be like if we were parents.' His joyful gaze lingered on me.

The fork slipped out of my hand and fell on the table, staining the tablecloth with leftovers. I looked first at the fork and then at Chris.

'There could be three of us sitting here,' he continued.

I looked at the empty chair next to me, and my mind began to awaken a dormant desire, visualising a boy with a mouth full of food smiling at me.

'Tom?'

'Are you sure?' I looked at him. 'This will change a lot in our lives.'

'I think it's a great idea,' he replied quickly, although, for a split second, I sensed some uncertainty.

'How come you've changed your mind?'

'I think it's time for the next stage in our lives. You've always wanted it, and I want to make you happy.' He smiled.

I wasn't sure if he was serious or if he was offering me a momentary hope that he would take away at the next opportunity. Regardless of his intentions, my desire curiously peeked out, like a child revealing part of his face behind the door. Fighting with it, I decided to wait. I didn't say a word for days, holding out for Chris to initiate another conversation.

It was a Friday, and I was tidying the utility room when he suddenly appeared behind me.

'What are you doing?' I twitched when he hugged me.

'Honey, I'm worried. You haven't said anything about my proposal for several days now. Don't you want it anymore?' I felt his warm breath on the back of my neck.

'I wonder if we're ready for this.' I turned to him. 'Our lives will change irrevocably.'

'I know, but I want this for us. After everything that's happened, I'm sure there's nothing we can't handle.' He grabbed my hands. 'I've already spoken to the adoption director. If you agree, I'll arrange the meeting.'

'You surprise me.' I looked into his proud eyes.

A week later, we were getting ready to see the director of the adoption agency.

After we were dressed and washed, Chris went to the garage, and I stopped in front of the window and watched the wind play with the tree branches for a while. The sight always calmed me down. I was tired after spending the night researching adoption materials and the questions that might come up in the initial interview. After a few minutes, I heard the door opening.

'Are you nervous?' Chris came over and hugged me.

'A little bit.'

'It'll be OK.' He kissed me. 'I'll wait in the car.'

We were standing in front of the director's office an hour later. Multiple layers of white paint on the door prevented it from closing completely. I hesitated for a moment. *Does Chris know what he's doing?* But when I glanced at him, his smile seemed to promise something new in our lives, something I longed for.

He knocked on the door and we walked in. The woman behind the desk lifted her head, and her smile embraced us with empathy. She was a little over sixty. A graphite jacket revealed a cream blouse, and two strands of her otherwise tightly arranged hair hung loose. Behind her, children's drawings decorated the walls.

'Here we are,' Chris announced as he let me through the door.

'Hello.' She pointed at the two chairs before her desk. 'My name is Julie Miller.'

'Tom Anderson.' My voice rustled in my mouth, stressed. Chris sat down and grabbed my hand. I sat next to him.

'Chris has told me a lot about you. I heard you were a carer for your sister. It's a tremendous experience; it puts you on a par with a parent.' She smiled.

'That's probably too big of a word.' My cheeks began to burn.

'Let's just get straight to the point. Why do you want to become parents?'

Prepared for the question, the words poured out of me, although I doubted either of them could tell I was speaking from memory. I really believed in everything I said.

'I've been thinking about it for a long time, and now my husband and I have got to where we share our desires.

'Being a parent is the greatest privilege. It makes you a superhero, someone special and irreplaceable to someone who needs and looks up to you. You can give your child inspiration and teach them about the world, but the greatest gift that comes with it is being able to be with your child when he experiences both joy and pain. Just the thought of becoming a parent... I believe I could be a good parent, but sometimes these huge emotions also make me afraid that we will repeat my parents' mistakes.'

'Fear is normal. It motivates us to keep getting better,' said Julie. 'Tell me more about how you see yourself as a parent.'

'It seems that a life shared with a child is about more than gifts and the most elaborate entertainment, although it is incredibly tough to resist. It is, above all, a safe home, a present and unconditionally loving parent who listens to the child's needs. They offer them their time, patience and love, struggling with the first emotions and questions to which we often do not know the answers.'

I paused, and Chris immediately filled the silence.

'We have huge amounts of feelings that we would like to share. It would be a great happiness for us if we were chosen.'

Julie's smile seemed cautious, as if she were dividing it into small portions. I wanted our answers to satisfy her expectations, but as time went by, my sense of doubt increased.

'I must point out that these children have experienced many issues due to abandonment. Most of them face complicated emotions. A new home might trigger the fear of sudden change, which in the past meant abandonment. Caring for a child always requires a lot of attention, commitment and love from the parent, but it might be even more important in this case. These children need a safe and stable home. Your task will be to befriend the fears they carry inside them.'

My familiar fear of abandonment pierced my heart.

'We're aware of that,' I replied without waiting for another question.

'I have a great sense of responsibility towards these children.' She looked at us sharply. 'That's why it's my job to find them the best parents. Of course, when that happens, parents can count on my support. Do you know what the whole process looks like?' Her gaze landed on Chris, and her smile disappeared completely. I could see in her face the reflection of the parent who had come to give back the adopted child because, once again, she couldn't calm down at night after another nightmare, like a store-bought product.

'It wouldn't hurt to remind us; we wouldn't want to miss anything.' He clenched his hands together, his skin bluish.

'So, first, you submit the required documents; I sent you the list via email.'

'We have them with us,' I replied.

'Great. The committee will look at the documents and then ask you to attend an interview. You'll be assigned a process supervisor, who will answer all your questions and prepare you for your new life. Then you will go through the parenting course. If you pass all the required steps and the committee approves your application, we will start looking for a child for you and sign the adoption papers, making sure everything complies with our regulations. The whole procedure can take up to a year, but there have been cases of earlier adoptions.'

'We understand.'

On the way back, the smile never left my face. The doubts had disappeared completely, and I was focused only on starting the whole process as soon as possible. Chris didn't say much in the car, but occasionally, he asked practical questions to which I already knew the answers.

'Which of the rooms will we use for the child?'

'The one next to ours; we need to be close if he wakes up at night.'

'And where will the office be?' Chris momentarily took his eyes off the road and glanced at me.

'We'll move it downstairs,' I replied without thinking.

'And a school?'

'We'll find something in Workington or Whitehaven.'

Chris laughed, and I frowned at him.

'What's so funny?'

'I see that you already have a detailed plan of everything, including the colour of the walls and furniture in the room.'

'Is that wrong?'

'No, no! It's why I love you.' He put his hand on my knee.

We spent the next two weeks preparing the house for the process supervisor's visit. We rearranged every room, sometimes changing the decor entirely. I was surprised by Chris's involvement. He pointed out things we could improve, moved furniture around and took some days off to help me paint the walls. Since we had made the decision, I felt he was ready to be a parent for the first time. Even if he had some fears, he hid them well.

Finally, our process supervisor showed up. She asked many questions. Where did we work? Did we argue? What were our weekends like? What did we eat? Did we consume alcohol or drugs? Division of responsibilities at home? Guests? She even asked us about all the car fines we'd ever received. At one point, she looked at us as if she was about to ask us about our sex life. If she had, I'd probably have burned up with embarrassment.

Later, she monitored every nook and cranny of our house with special attention paid to the future nursery. Throughout her visit, I was tense and felt tight in my stomach. Her visit was not helpful at all. 'We'll be in touch,' she said as she left.

I sat exhausted on the sofa. Trying to escape negative thoughts, I started to imagine how I would decorate our child's room. Child. I repeated the word several times, and a new emotion overtook me. Wallpaper with spaceships or maybe some cars? An oak bed by the window with a soft mattress that gives the impression of a downy cloud? Next to it a desk, a command centre with a computer and speakers for gaming. But wasn't it too early? I didn't know when children started playing games. In the garden, we would attach a swing to the branches of our apple tree, and we would need to buy a third bicycle so that our son could ride with us on trips.

I desperately struggled to contain my excitement, and the moment Chris fell asleep, I slipped into the office. I took the tape out of the drawer and measured the whole room. As soon as morning arrived, I began browsing the internet for the perfect furniture. However, after a few minutes, I gave up. It dawned on me that it was too early. I spent the whole day trying to distract myself from the visions of the failed adoption process, yet over and over, I kept going through the questions the process supervisor had asked. What exactly did I say when she asked if Chris did the dishes? Was I nervous when she mentioned that some people go out more than us?

The next day I decided to call Sue.

'Hello, Tom! How are you? I was just about to call you. I haven't heard from you for a week!'

'We've been a little busy, Mum.'

'Everything all right?'

I walked over to the window. Chris was pulling the lawnmower out of the garage.

'Mum, Chris and I... we've decided to adopt.'

'Really? That's wonderful news. Why didn't you call sooner? Jesus, I'm going to be a grandma!' she shouted happily into the receiver.

'We're done talking, and we're starting the process.'

'I'm so happy! Now your life will change radically. You'll see.'

'Mum, nothing is certain yet.' I was beginning to regret the phone call. Although her uncontrollable happiness mirrored mine, I was worried it would overwhelm Chris, who could still change his mind.

'I know it will work. I can feel it.'

After talking to Sue, I felt more confident. As if I had been waiting for her approval and confirmation that we were doing the right thing. It gave me the strength to go on.

Every day when Chris left for work, I searched the internet for information about adoption and all the problems we could face. I was in a trance. I went on forums and into chat rooms, talking to people who had already gone through the process. I wanted to know everything and be the best at it.

A month later, we were scheduled for the parenting course. I woke up excited an hour before the alarm clock rang. I got out of bed, trying not to wake Chris up, even though my whole body trembled joyfully. I went to the kitchen, turned my favourite radio station on and set about preparing breakfast. I sang along to most of the songs Heart played that morning, even though I usually enjoyed them in silence. I moved to the music, desperately trying to shake off the impatience twisting my insides, but the moment I saw Chris walk into the kitchen, my joy began to melt like butter in a hot frying pan. His face was serious, grim, as if something horrible had happened.

'Good morning,' he barely murmured, and sat at the table.

'Are you OK?' I placed a portion of scrambled eggs on his plate.

'I don't feel like being judged by strangers all day.' He began to butter the toast. 'Did you see how the process supervisor analysed everything we did? Do you remember the questions she asked us? I'm sure it will be even worse now.'

I sighed. Like a patient parent, I drew out my motivational speech.

'I understand. It's inconvenient, but imagine it's training like you do at work sometimes. New people come and you have to show them around. You don't judge them, right? You just want to make it easier for them.' I heaped a portion onto my plate and sat down to face him.

'I don't know...'

'We're in this together.' I put my hand on his arm. 'Remember?'

'Yes.' He sighed heavily.

'It'll be fine, you'll see.'

The impatience never left, but once we got in the car, I said a final farewell to any traces of joy I had tried to spark while in the kitchen – every attempt I made to remind Chris that we were doing it because we wanted to failed completely. Our journey to Workington was silent and tense.

The course was held at the hospital. I suddenly felt exposed as I sat in a room with large windows. I looked around and counted twelve other couples, and yet, we were the only same-sex couple, which made me worry about whether the other participants would accept us. I stole a glance at their faces, and seeing the same fear and confusion in them that I felt made me more confident.

A moment later, the door opened and a short round man walked in with enough confidence to feed all those who'd come here.

'Hello, everyone. My name is Toby Natt, and I'm the parenting course instructor.' He reached for a chair and placed it in the middle of the room. 'The course is designed to prepare you for difficult situations; trust me, they will happen sooner than you expect. You have to be ready for anything.

Although I won't give you simple solutions, you can apply them to everything. Each situation is unique. Every child is different. We're not taking shortcuts here. I might make suggestions and share what has worked in similar cases, but it's up to you to decide what works best for you.'

Some participants nodded shyly, and I glanced at Chris to see his reaction. His face hadn't changed much since we got out of the car. I returned my gaze to Toby.

'We will be acting out some scenes, which some of you might find difficult as they tend to trigger certain emotions. However, you won't come across anything you wouldn't see as a parent. My aim is to help you prepare. There are no mistakes here. We're simply learning something all of our parents should have learned anyway.'

A wave of nervous laughter followed his words. Toby smiled. He had seen it all before, I reassured myself, and smiled back at him.

'So let's not waste time. I'd like to ask our first couple to join me in the centre here.'

The silence dropped so heavily that I almost held my breath. Not a single person moved, and I, like many others, averted my eyes like a student avoiding the teacher's searching gaze. Toby scanned the name tags pinned to our shirts.

'How about Tom and Chris? Please, don't be afraid! It's just an exercise.'

I looked at Chris, who had lost all colour from his face. I took a deep breath, stood up and offered him my hand.

'Let's give them a round of applause.' Toby started clapping, and the others joined in.

We stopped in the middle of the room, all eyes studying us with great interest. I looked down at my shoes. While Chris swallowed hard, Toby quickly stepped between us.

'I'll put you in a scene. Your child pushed a classmate who fell to the floor and hurt his knee. The teacher called you to school and informed you about the incident. You went home with your child, and now you're trying to talk to him. I will be the child. Are you trying for a boy or a girl?'

'A boy,' I mumbled.

'Great, then I'm your son. Here we go.'

Toby sat down in a chair with his arms folded, and a grimace of disappointment and resentment shifted his face.

'Did you do it?' Chris said.

'It wasn't me!' Toby shouted.

'But that kid didn't hurt his own knee.'

'It wasn't me!' Toby screamed so loudly that Chris jumped.

He raised his voice. 'Who did it then, if not you?'

'I don't want to talk to you!' Toby yelled, and pushed Chris, who was leaning over him, away. 'You're not my father!'

'Lucky you, you little brat!'

A shiver ran down my spine. I took a step forward as if to protect Toby.

'Stop!' Toby called. His voice had returned to normal, and the calmness with which he shifted between roles impressed me greatly. Was this something he had learned as a father? I expected him to say a few words to Chris, but he turned towards me instead. 'Now, the same scene with you, Tom. Here we go.'

He retook his position in the chair, and I exchanged glances with Chris as I approached him.

'Son, you're safe here.' I put my hand gently his shoulder. 'We love you and want to know what happened.'

'It wasn't me! Leave me alone! You are not my father!' Toby screamed.

I took a deep breath and, closing my eyes, let it out slowly.

'Honey, no one is judging you. We just want to know what happened. If we don't know the truth, we can't protect you. Come on, I'll make you your favourite toast, and you can tell us everything.'

'Stop!' Toby called. 'Tom, great! Well done!'

The parents smiled and clapped. I looked at Chris, worried that this situation had upset him further. When the applause died down, Toby walked over to him.

'Chris, I understand that the situation was uncomfortable. Everyone was looking at you, and it didn't help that you had to perform in front of strangers. However, you can't afford to have that reaction with your future child. What he'll need is love and understanding. You can't respond to his aggression with aggression because that will stop the two of you from reaching any agreement. You need to activate a more empathetic approach. I know it's hard, but that's what we're here to learn. You can go back to your seats. Who wants to go next?' He looked around.

The journey home was as quiet as the drive to Workington had been. Occasionally, I glanced at Chris, but his eyes never left the road. I was preparing a stronger motivational speech in my head, aware that he might refuse to join me the next day.

At home, the atmosphere stayed the same, and not knowing how to start a conversation, I began looking through files from work, although there was not a single task that I had left unfinished. I hoped Chris would find a way to deal with his reluctance, but he remained silent. I even considered calling Sue, but when evening came, I counted to three in my head and dared to start a conversation.

'Chris, what's going on?' I asked. He was sitting in the living room with the remote control in front of the TV.

'Nothing,' he grunted.

'Is it because of the course?' I joined him on the sofa. 'It's our first time. Don't worry about it. Those exercises are supposed to prepare us for difficult situations.' I took his hand, but he shook me off immediately.

'We all make mistakes,' I said. 'Please talk to me.'

'If you insist.' He shifted. 'I'm not sure if we made the right decision.'

'What are you talking about?'

'We've been through so much. Now, everything's back to normal for the first time in ages, and we've decided to do something that might ruin it again. Don't get me wrong, I'm not saying we shouldn't do it at all, but maybe it's not time yet.'

'Not time? Chris, we're almost at the end of the road, and you want to turn around? It was your idea!'

'Because I wanted to give you something you've always dreamed of, but now I realise it might be beyond me.'

I took a deep breath and, in my mind, reached for everything I'd read about parenting. I knew it was OK to have doubts. Just because I had none didn't mean Chris was saying anything wrong.

‘You’re scared; it’s natural. I understand.’ I managed to calm my voice. ‘We’re in this together; I’ll help you.’

‘It’s late.’ He got up from the sofa and reached out his hand. ‘Let’s go to sleep. It’s been a long day.’

I reasoned that maybe he was stressed out from work or just embarrassed that everyone was watching our every step. I didn’t want to pressure him, but deep down, I felt a sense of uneasiness growing. I decided to give him some time and space for the next course to sort things out. We both went back to our daily activities as if nothing had happened. But we ate our meals in silence. I was afraid to ask what was on his mind.

A few days later, I attempted the conversation again, over breakfast. I placed a plate with an omelette before him and sat beside him.

‘Chris. I know this course is stressing you out.’ I stroked his back. ‘I don’t feel comfortable about it either, but it will be over soon, and we won’t have to go back there. Ever again. Can you hold on a little longer?’ I tried to find his gaze.

He didn’t respond for a while but then looked at me. Fear of what he was about to say gripped me, and I froze in silence.

‘I’ll do it because I love you,’ he said, and kissed me.

I was overwhelmed with doubt that he hadn’t made a fully informed decision, and if that was the case, could we be good parents? Would we be able to give the child as much love as he needed? What if we couldn’t? Would it be the responsible decision for our child? Or was it all too soon and we should have waited?

But Chris was capable of love. I knew that once he met our child, he would do his best to give him everything he needed. I felt it.

After breakfast, we got in the car to go to our second workshop. I enjoyed learning new things, like that training does not help us change a child's behaviour. It's to change ourselves, and that will make the child learn something special from us, something that will make them a great person.

During the course, Chris mirrored the behaviour of the other future parents, which allowed him to hide in the crowd from the teacher as if he was cheating in an exam. Still, I didn't let myself believe that just because he didn't like being watched and judged by strangers was evidence against him as a parent. I made sure to reassure him whenever he was doing something right, hoping that the more confidence he felt, the more enthusiastic he would be later.

I ignored the fact that he never even glanced into the room I had been preparing for our child for many weeks. Every time a new worry arose, I pushed it deep within myself.

After a few weeks, we reached the end of the course. The host gave us his card in case we needed his help in the future and then wished us good luck. I hoped I'd never have to call him. Chris smiled in relief as we left the building without turning back once.

Two days later, the director of the adoption agency called me. Hearing her voice through the receiver reminded me of my conversations with other future parents, who had said that she also checked candidates like in a final exam.

'Hello, Tom, how are you?'

'Good, thank you.'

'I hope I'm not bothering you.'

'Of course not. How can I help?'

‘I have a little problem. Together with some foster families, I organise painting workshops for children. One of the carers who was supposed to help has fallen ill, and I have no one to prepare the stations for the children and clean up after they finish. I thought maybe you’d be able to help us.’

My throat went dry.

‘I’d love to help.’ I tried to sound confident. ‘When and where?’

‘You are an angel. Would ten o’clock tomorrow be all right for you?’

‘No problem, I’ll be there.’

‘I’ll text you the address.’

The painting workshops were organised in a nursery in Workington, where foster families brought children to socialise and play. I was afraid that I would do something wrong and ruin our chance of adoption, but at the same time, I had never been so ready for a child before.

On the way, I noticed a flock of sheep stepping onto the road. I stopped and remembered how, at the airport, a small boy running past a group of tourists fell after bumping into the crowd. I ran up to him and knelt down to lift him up.

‘Are you OK?’ I held his hand. ‘Where are your parents?’

The little boy looked up in fear.

‘I don’t know...’

His eyes teared up.

‘Don’t worry, we’ll find them soon.’

We approached the information desk, where they announced the boy was missing, and a few moments later, a trembling woman was running towards us. She grabbed the boy and tucked him close to her chest. When she got up from her knees, she approached me, hugged me and whispered, ‘Thank you.’

When I arrived in Workington, I parked by the fence and headed towards the building. I pictured myself walking towards the nursery, hand in hand with my son. I opened the door and stepped inside. I spotted the director immediately, waiting for me in front of the entrance to the classroom.

'Thank you for coming.' She offered me her hand. 'It means a lot. Come in.' She opened the door and gestured for me to go in.

'The pleasure is all mine. What would you like me to do?'

'There are paints, cups, brushes and paper here.' Julie pointed at a cupboard. 'Prepare a set of painting supplies for each child. We have around twelve. The bathroom is through there. I have an urgent call right now, but I'll be back to check on you soon. You'll be great. Good luck.'

I watched her leave, then got straight to work. I walked between the tables, placing painting sets and paper towels on each of them. When I finished, I wanted to take a look at the final result, but the door opened with a loud bang and the children ran in, taking their places.

'What are we painting today, sir?' called a girl sitting to my right.

I was stunned. I was sure I'd leave before the class started. I looked around, hoping to spot a teacher, but I was the only adult in the room. I had to do something quickly.

'Children,' I improvised, holding my head up high to give myself confidence. 'Paint what you dream of. I would love to be able to see it in your work.'

'Cool!' a girl called from the back of the room.

'And then will our dreams come true?' asked a ginger boy.

'That's not for me to say, but who knows, miracles do happen.'

The children got on with their artwork. I expected shouting and little arguments, but they dipped their brushes into the paints and painted their dream presents. When the director appeared, I was passing between the tables, praising each child's progress.

She quickly walked over to me. 'Sorry, one of our teachers is sick. I had a phone call and didn't have time to warn you that the kids were coming.'

'They took me for a teacher,' I whispered in her ear.

She looked around the room.

'Then you did very well.' She winked at me. 'Stay until the end of the workshop if you want.'

'I'd love to.' I smiled.

Once the children finished their paintings, they lined up for me. They revealed their dreams: computers, phones, cars, cats. I praised each picture with equal enthusiasm, glancing at the director, who smiled at me every so often. When I had finished, the children sprang up like a frightened flock of birds and scurried towards the door, followed by the director, who could barely keep up. After a while, it became quiet. I looked at the tube of green paint on a table and thought, *What would my son paint?* Then I was snapped out of my musing by a rustling noise coming from the end of the room. I turned around, and again something rustled. It was coming from behind a cardboard box standing between two bookcases. I decided to move closer, and that's when I spotted a boy who, hidden behind the box in concentration, was still painting. I did not know what to do. I glanced at the door, then back at the boy.

'They're all gone.' I walked over to him. 'Do you want me to take you to the others?'

'I had to finish the drawing,' he mumbled.

'What are you painting?'

He lifted his head, looked at me uncertainly and slid the paper towards me. As I lowered my gaze, a shiver immediately ran down my spine. The drawing showed a man holding a little boy by the hand.

'Very nice drawing.' I tried to suppress my melting mood. 'Will you tell me what it is?'

'You asked us to paint what we would like to get for Christmas. I want a new dad.' There was longing in his eyes.

I felt a stab in my heart. Speechless, I looked at the drawing again. I was about to say something about how well he painted when I heard a tug on the doorknob and the director appeared in the doorway.

Even then, she must have noticed something. Something that my heart could not hide. Since that day, Harry and I saw each other every week. The headmistress brought him to the park, where we spent an hour.

Harry was abandoned right after he was born. His mother could not support herself and gave him to a foster family. Two other couples gave him up twice just before adoption. They feared he might have mental health problems because it was difficult for them to get through to him.

At first, he was cautious in Chris's and my presence. He was more observant, politely answering questions in short sentences. However, after just a few meetings, his answers became longer and more eloquent. He told us about Spider-Man, his favourite hero, new friendships with children and that he would like to learn how to rollerblade. He asked about our house, our garden and if we had pets. We brought him presents every time. He thanked me but was embarrassed. It was obvious he wasn't expecting anything. My heart swelled to see Chris take Harry on his lap, and, engrossed in the story of the cosmos, the boy stared at the sky, hypnotised. Chris showed him a passing plane at one meeting, and was explaining we would fly it to Warsaw one day when something moved in the grass. Harry jumped up, frightened, and Chris quickly took him in his arms.

'It's just a little frog; it's scared too.' He stroked him.

Harry looked Chris in the eye, then snuggled into him. I felt my heart beating fast and stopped worrying that Chris wouldn't make it. During one of the meetings, Harry asked if we would take him, and I was completely speechless for a moment.

'But then... you'd have two dads.' I wanted to make sure he knew.

'I would like that very much,' he replied softly, and my love rushed out to him, and I could no longer stop it.

I will always remember the day when the letter from the director arrived. I was afraid to open it and waited for Chris, who promised to return early from work after my call. As soon as he entered the house, we sat on the sofa and Chris opened the letter. He started reading it, pausing now and then to hug me because I couldn't hold back my tears. The letter said that Harry couldn't imagine any other parents but us and loved us very much, so she had no choice but to speed up the adoption process. And so a seven-year-old boy named Harry came to our house two months before Christmas.

The day we went to pick him up, I felt a mixture of excitement and anxiety. Harry had been placed with another foster family just two months before, and to spare him more stress, the director decided that we would pick him up from her office so he wouldn't feel like the families were passing him around like a thing.

We waited outside. I paced nervously, and Chris calmed me down.

'Tom, you have nothing to worry about. Everything is behind us. Harry is ours.'

'I know, but I'm still nervous. What if he changes his mind and doesn't want to stay with us?'

'He'll stay, you'll see.'

After some time, the headmistress appeared holding a small brown suitcase in one hand and Harry's hand in the other. I refrained from running up to them. I wanted Harry to see in me the peace he needed. My gaze met his blue, scared eyes. The headmistress took off his baseball cap and fixed his tousled blonde hair. Harry was silent, then looked down.

I spoke first. 'Hello.'

'Good morning,' he replied.

'Are you ready to go?' I pointed to the car and took the suitcase from the director.

After a moment, I noticed Harry squeeze her hand tighter as she led him towards our car. He was probably stressed, just as my hands were shaking. I couldn't decide which side to walk on, but I eventually decided to stay behind them. At one point, Harry turned around as if checking to see if I was still following them. I smiled broadly, and he smiled back. I couldn't wait to reach the car.

'Hello, Harry.' Chris was waiting for us.

'Good morning,' he replied, and lowered his head.

The director put him in the back and fastened his seat belt.

'Do you remember what we talked about?'

'Yes, Auntie.'

'I'll visit you soon, and you'll show me your room.'

'We'd love to have you over,' I said, shaking her hand. 'Thanks again for everything.'

I put his small suitcase in the boot. It was not heavy at all. I thought about how little life had given this boy.

'Chris?' the headmistress called.

He approached her.

'Congratulations.' She squeezed both of our hands. 'You've done a great job.'

'Thank you. It wouldn't have been possible without you.'

We exchanged goodbye hugs quickly. I couldn't stop thinking about Harry sitting in the back waiting for us. When we got in, Chris turned the key and started the engine. I still couldn't believe Harry was really ours.

On our way home, I watched him in the mirror. He leaned his head against the window, staring into the changing landscape just as I had when we first arrived in Cumbria.

'Are you hungry?' I turned to face him.

'A little,' he replied shyly.

'How about a burger and fries? Do you like burgers?'

'I like them a lot, but my foster mum wouldn't let me eat them. She said it was unhealthy.'

'You know, she was kind of right, but I guess we can make an exception today.' I winked at him. 'What do you think?'

He nodded.

'Then it's settled.' I smiled.

Chris parked outside MacDonald's in Workington, and we went inside. With his eyes, Harry followed the large electronic board, where

I ordered a Happy Meal for him and a Double Big Mac for Chris. I didn't choose anything for myself. I couldn't eat.

We sat down at a table, where Harry unwrapped the surprise toy. It was a tiny kitten, which he stroked and placed in front of him. He ate without taking his eyes off it, as if he was afraid that the kitten would jump off the table and run out of the restaurant at any moment. Chris took big bites of his Big Mac, and a small dollop of sauce dripped onto his tray. I handed him a napkin. *This is our first meal together*, I thought.

Once we'd parked outside our home, I helped Harry out of the car, but he stopped beside it and stared at the building for a long time.

'This is your new home,' I said without taking my eyes off him.

'Huge,' he whispered.

'It just seems that way.' I smiled.

I extended my hand towards him, but he ignored it. I couldn't tell if it was because he hadn't noticed it or if he was afraid or wasn't ready yet. I remembered the director's words. *Don't force him into anything. Give him time.*

'Shall we go in?'

'Yes.'

Initially, he was shy, spoke little and preferred to observe. We showed him around the rooms, but only I talked while Chris just smiled. After he had seen the whole of the first floor, we paused by the last door, the one to Harry's new room.

'This is yours.' I opened the door for him.

'Wow!' Delight jumped out of him, and curiosity quickly drew him inside.

'Do you like it? I know he's your favourite hero.'

Spider-Man jumped between the walls, and a hammock imitated a cobweb in the corner. Under the window, we had installed a desk with a computer. A red-and-blue duvet covered his new bed on the opposite side – Spider-Man's colours.

'It's just like I dreamed it,' he whispered, and sat on the bed.

'I'll help you unpack.' I placed his suitcase on the bed and was about to open it when he suddenly jumped and covered it with his body.

'I'll do it!'

'No problem.' Surprised, I moved back. 'I'll go to the kitchen to sort dinner while you unpack and make yourself comfortable. I'll come and get you when it's ready, OK?'

'OK,' he muttered.

I stopped in the hallway. I looked at Harry's little shoes next to ours and felt relief and warmth in my heart that spread throughout my body. Chris came over and hugged me.

'Everything will be fine now.' He stroked my back. 'But don't make me give him my iPad.' He grimaced pleadingly.

'We'll buy him a new one.'

As I laid the table a couple of hours later, I glanced at the empty seat where a real boy, no longer a figment of my imagination, was about to sit.

When Harry joined us, he was silent for a while. He must have been stressed about the new place and the circumstances he found himself in.

'Would you like some?' I turned to him.

'Yes, please,' he replied timidly.

'Is there anything you don't like?' I reached for his plate.

He shook his head.

During dinner, Harry kept glancing at Chris as if he saw something intriguing in him, something he wanted to work out. Chris exchanged looks with him but didn't do much more than that. I tried to initiate a conversation, but every time, the topic died shortly after it started. Eventually, I accepted that our dinner would be quieter than I had hoped. There was something in our shared silence, something I began to appreciate later.

Afterwards, we went for a walk to show Harry around. He liked the neighbours' sheep, which came very close to our fence. He gently reached out to stroke them, smiling carefree. Our return home was noticed by Judith, who ran out to meet us. Harry perked up and started talking even more.

Our first night peeked unexpectedly through our windows.

I asked Harry if he needed help with his bath, but he seemed ashamed and said he would wash himself. Afterwards, I brought him a new electric toothbrush. He was happy and asked if we could brush our teeth together. I went to get my toothbrush, and once we started brushing, I began to fool around in the mirror. That was the first time I heard his carefree laughter.

As I covered him with the duvet, I noticed he wasn't ready to sleep yet. He was scanning the room as if looking for something to play with.

'Shall I tell you a bedtime story?'

'No one has ever done that,' he said, surprised.

'There's a first time for everything.'

'Cool!' He shifted, making space for me. I sat down, took a deep breath and started to make up a story on the spot.

'Once upon a time, there was a little boy exactly your age. His name was Patrick. He had no parents and lived in a big old oak tree in the middle of a big forest. During the day, he picked blueberries and raspberries, which he gave to his forest friends. The animals were very fond of Patrick and came to see him daily. They played together, running around the forest, until one day, the boy ventured further than usual, deep into the trees. After walking for a long time, he spotted a spring. He felt thirsty, so he stepped closer, and just as he was about to take some water with his hand, a little fairy suddenly appeared in front of him. Startled, he took a few steps back.

'"Don't be afraid, Patrick," said the fairy. "I want to warn you. If you drink this water, you will never be able to leave the forest again and will stay here forever."

'Patrick thought about what he should do for a long time and finally decided it would be best to go home. He fell asleep in the great old oak when the night covered the forest. The tree guarded the entrance with its giant hands so no one could get inside...'

Listening to the story about the boy, Harry lay motionless, absorbing every word I said, but after a while his eyes began to close involuntarily.

I glanced at my watch. During the parenting course, they had told us about the importance of routine. Eight was the perfect time to sleep.

'We'll leave the rest for tomorrow,' I whispered. 'Time to go to sleep. Goodnight.' I leaned in and kissed his forehead. He slowly closed his eyes. I reached out to turn off the lamp.

'Can we not turn it off?'

'Sure, no problem.'

I went back to our bedroom. Chris was already in bed, playing a game on his iPad.

'How did it go?' he asked without looking up from the screen. 'Is he sleeping?'

'Yes.' I waited for him to put down the tablet, but he continued to play. I sighed softly and lay down next to him. Despite being tired, I couldn't fall asleep for a long time. I still couldn't believe Harry was sleeping in the next room.

Around three in the morning, a shrill scream woke me. I jumped out of bed and ran barefoot to Harry's room. When I opened the door, he was sitting up in bed, jittery.

'What happened?'

'Someone wanted to take me. He was tugging on my hand.' His breathing was quick and irregular.

'It's just a bad dream; you're safe here.' I took him in my arms and stroked his head. Harry closed his eyes. He cuddled up to me for the first time, and I felt like I could be a parent. I stayed with him until he calmed down, then returned to the bedroom and took out the dragon medallion from the drawer, the one Chris had given me when I went to Tracy for therapy.

'I'd like to give you something,' I said when I returned to Harry's room. I sat on the bed and showed him the medallion.

He stared at it for a long time, then took it hesitantly. Unable to take his eyes off the dragon, his mouth dropped open, and his eyes flashed in delight. I smiled to myself.

'Long ago, when fears visited me, your dad, Chris, gave me this. I wore it all the time, and the dragon within it protected me from all the terrible things, so now I would like to give it to you. He will protect you like he protected me.'

I unfastened the necklace and placed it around his neck. Harry squeezed it in his hand and cuddled up to me.

In the morning, I went straight to his room and knocked.

'Can I come in?'

'Yes,' I heard through the door.

He was sitting up. His blond hair stuck out in all directions, and he stared at me with sleepy blue eyes. I remembered pictures from my childhood, and even though we weren't related, we resembled each other so much.

As I got closer, I noticed the medallion around his neck. I smiled and sat down next to him.

'Would you like to go hiking today? I could show you some cool places.'

He didn't answer, just stared deeply into my eyes. I felt that he was looking for the answers to a lot of questions.

'We don't have to. We can go another time if you don't feel like it.' I instinctively reached out to stroke him, but he flinched. I quickly pulled back. He was silent, and I got up and headed for the door.

'I'd like to,' he whispered so softly I almost didn't hear him.

'Great! And after the walk, you can meet your grandmother if you want. For the time being via computer, but she will certainly visit us soon.'

His eyes shone with joy.

The sun looked at us shyly that day. I opened the front door, and a gust of wind swept away the withered leaves. At the gate, Harry stopped and lifted his head to meet my eyes. After a moment, he gently slipped his little hand into mine. My undisguised joy ran to him. I knelt to hug him. Even though he didn't return the hug, he didn't defend himself against me, which was a great improvement.

'Shall we go?'

'Yes.' The whisper was full of excitement.

We reached the forest, and after each of us had found a large stick resembling Gandalf's staff, we began to walk, slightly parting the ferns to make room for our steps. Harry marvelled at the nature, which he was unfamiliar with. The trails led us into the unknown, and I lost our time on them.

Back home, we sat down in front of the computer. I nervously clicked the Skype icon, but the app didn't launch immediately.

'Daddy, you have to click twice quickly, and then it will run.'

I froze. I wasn't sure if he was aware of what he had just said. My heart skipped a few pirouettes. I hugged him and kissed him.

'Thank you. Maybe you could try. I don't think your daddy can handle it.'

He clicked twice quickly, and Skype immediately launched, and then a call came from my mother.

'It's calling!' he exclaimed as her picture popped up on the screen.

'Pick up. Grandma is waiting for you.'

A blush covered his cheeks. At first, he was a little embarrassed, but he spoke more confidently as time passed. He told her about our walk, the sheep he petted and how much he liked his room. There was uninterrupted emotion on my mother's face. She promised to call every day right after our morning walk.

And so each morning began with us making breakfast together, followed by a morning wash, singing in front of the mirror while brushing our teeth, and then a walk in the woods, from which a conversation with my mother effectively pulled us.

After one of them, I decided to play a game with Harry that had been on my mind for some time. I wanted to get to know him better, but I was afraid that asking too direct questions would awaken memories he would rather not revisit yet.

That evening I sat next to him on the bed. He was waiting for another fairy tale but jumped up excitedly when I offered him a game.

'The game is called Secrets,' I explained. 'The one who can reveal the biggest hidden secret wins. What do you think?'

'I don't know this game. What are the rules?'

'There are only two. Players only tell the truth, and what they say stays between them.'

He considered.

'You can ask me first,' I said.

'About anything?' He shifted on the bed.

'Yes.'

I saw him searching for the right question.

'Have you ever done something that Dad doesn't know about?'

'Good question.' I straightened up. 'Yes. I ran a red light once.'

Fear covered Harry's face.

'Aunt Julie always says to look three times before we cross the street.'

'Nothing happened. Fortunately, there was no one there. I was lost in thought for a moment. I was careless. Then I was ashamed to admit it to your dad, but I needn't have been. I can always count on him, knowing he will understand. My turn. Is there anything Aunt Julie doesn't know about?'

Fear covered his face; he immediately looked away and fell silent.

'Harry?'

'No one will find out?'

'Those are the rules of the game.'

He fell silent again, then took a breath and let it out, getting the words out with difficulty. I was terrified of what I was about to hear.

'There was a family I didn't want to go to, but they wanted me very much.'

'Why didn't you want to?'

'I don't know...' He didn't look at me.

'Try to explain.' I stroked his head.

'I couldn't feel anything for them. I don't know why.'

'It happens sometimes. It's not a bad thing. What happened next?'

'They let me go, and I was relieved. Auntie asked what happened, but I didn't know... so I didn't know what to say.'

'I have a request.' I tried to meet his gaze.

'Yes?' He looked at me.

'If that happens to us, just tell me about it. OK?'

'It's not going to happen, Daddy.' He hugged me tightly.

Two weeks before Christmas, when Chris came home from work in the late afternoon, he barely said a word. After dinner, he got up from the table and went to the living room, taking his place on the sofa with the remote control.

'Wait for me here,' I whispered to Harry, and got up from the table.

‘What is it?’ I lowered my voice as I stood in front of Chris. ‘Why are you behaving like this? You’re scaring Harry.’

‘I’m not even allowed to breathe now?’ His gaze was cold.

‘Chris, can you hear what you’re saying?’

‘I’m not in the mood to talk.’

I waited, but he was hiding in his private world, not letting anyone in. I was alone with everything again. I went back to Harry, wondering if maybe his presence would change Chris’s mood.

‘What happened?’ asked Harry.

‘Dad is having a bad day; someone must have upset him at work. Maybe you’ll take him a cookie?’ I stroked his head. ‘He likes them a lot.’

Harry reached hesitantly for a cookie, then went into the living room, and I discreetly spied on him by peeking out from the kitchen. He sat down next to Chris.

‘This is for you, Dad.’ He handed him the biscuit.

‘Thank you. Shall we watch something together?’

‘A movie?’ Harry asked timidly.

‘Sure, if you want.’

‘I’d love to.’ Harry slid deeper on the sofa.

I stepped back and had just turned on the dishwasher when I heard the sound of breaking glass.

‘What have you done?’ Chris yelled. ‘What’s wrong with you!’

I ran out of the kitchen, and at the same time, Harry disappeared down the hall.

‘Are you crazy?’ I looked at Chris in disbelief. ‘What are you doing? He just wanted to be with you!’

'Can't you see what he did?' he roared, pointing to the broken crystal candlestick his mother had given him. 'I knew there would be trouble.'

'How dare you! It was an accident! How many times have I told you not to put it on the coffee table by the sofa.'

'Do you know how much it cost?' he snapped.

'Jesus! I'll buy you another one!'

I went to Harry's room, but the door was locked.

I knocked. 'Can I come in?'

He didn't answer, but I could hear his little legs pacing the room.

'Harry, I'm coming in,' I announced.

He still didn't answer. I opened the door, and the sight paralysed my body. There was an open suitcase on the bed, into which Harry was quickly stuffing his things. After a few seconds, he closed the lid and sat beside it.

'What are you doing?' I stared at him in horror.

'I'm waiting for Aunt Julie,' he said with his head down.

'But why? Why are you waiting for her?'

'He will come for me... I was naughty...'

Dazed, I crouched before him, trying to find his gaze.

'Harry, nothing you do or say will change our feelings for you. Chris was having a bad day, but he shouldn't have reacted like that. He loves you too. You are our son, and we would never give you back.'

He was silent, his eyes fixed on the carpet.

'I love you very much and don't want you to leave us. I would miss you terribly.'

He lifted his head, and then I saw his glazed eyes. He immediately snuggled into me, and I felt warm drops trickle down my neck, and I couldn't control my tears.

After a while, Chris entered the room.

'Can I have a hug too?'

Harry raised his head and looked at me expectantly. I nodded slightly, closing my eyes. He extended his hand to Chris, and he came over to us and hugged Harry, kissing him on the temple the same way he had kissed me when he peeked into my room a few years earlier, waiting for me to come out from it. From that moment on, I believed our little family grew stronger every day.

*

Christmas came. I woke up to Harry scrambling onto my bed in maroon pyjamas covered in reindeer.

'Daddy, wake up,' he whispered in my ear, stroking my cheek. 'Grandma will be here soon.'

'Honey, where's Dad?' I mumbled.

He jumped off the bed and ran to the window.

'Dad's on his way to pick up Grandma,' he exclaimed enthusiastically.

'What! He was supposed to wake me up.' I jumped to my feet. 'Quickly, let's brush our teeth and get ready for breakfast.'

All morning Harry would walk around the house and look out the windows, then snuggled up to me. I patted his head and assured him everything would be fine.

A few minutes before Chris and Grandma arrived, Harry and I were waiting in the living room. Even then, he could not sit still and went excitedly to the window every now and then, looking at the gate.

'Are you nervous?' I hugged him and kissed him on the cheek.

'A little bit.'

'Unnecessarily. Let me tell you a secret: Grandma loved you before you first spoke to her.'

'Really?'

'Yes, baby.' I hugged him tighter.

At the same moment, a loud ringing filled the house. Harry grabbed my hand tightly, and we walked to the door together. I unlocked it, Harry never taking his eyes off it, and turned the handle.

'Good morning, prince.' Mum smiled from ear to ear.

Harry blushed, and his eyes flashed with excitement.

'Hi, Mum.' I kissed her cheek.

I took a box wrapped in red ribbon from her, and she walked over to Harry and crouched beside him.

'Finally, we can see each other in person.' She adjusted his fringe.

Ashamed, he hung his head.

'Santa visited me yesterday, and when he found out that I was going to visit you, he asked me to bring you this.' She pointed to the box I was holding.

'Wow!' Harry's eyes fixed on the gift.

'Will you show me your room?' She extended her hand towards him, and he hesitantly offered her his.

Together we went to his bedroom. Harry glanced at his grandmother from time to time, and she smiled broadly at him. In the room, Harry took out all his toys; Mum complimented each one. Later they went out to the garden because he wanted to show Grandma the swing and the bicycle and pet the sheep behind the fence. I've never seen my mother as happy as that day. Enchanted in each other's company, they could not part even for five minutes.

I was loading the dishwasher when Chris showed up in the kitchen. He approached me, took the dishes from my hands and placed them on the counter. He moved closer and put his hands on my shoulders.

'What are you doing?'

'Finally, I have you all to myself.' He smiled, devilish sparkles in his eyes.

'I'm always here.'

'Yeah, but usually with Harry, like Mum now.' He kissed me.

'Chris, Mum and Harry are in the next room.'

'So I can't miss my husband anymore?' He made a sad face.

'Later,' I whispered. 'Now go to them because I have to finish this.' I kissed him.

After returning to the living room, I watched my mother, who sat with Harry in the armchair. Their mouths spewed thousands of words that seemed to wash over the room like a rushing waterfall. I glanced at Chris. He was focused on looking for something in the cupboard, and he must have found it because after a while he pulled out a large box containing a telescope.

'Harry?' He turned to his son. 'It's time.' There was a contagious excitement on his face, which quickly transferred to Harry's.

'I'm going to lie down now.' Mum got up from the armchair. 'I'm a bit tired.'

'Yes, get some rest. It's been a long day. Thank you for everything.' Chris walked up to his mum and hugged her tightly.

'But will you be here tomorrow?' Harry wanted to make sure he would see his grandmother in the morning.

'Of course, my darling. Where else would I be? I'll make you a delicious breakfast.'

Harry joyfully embraced his grandmother, and she kissed him on the cheek.

'Good night, Tom.' Mum came over and put her hand on my shoulder.

'Good night, Mum.' I stroked her hand.

After Mum left, I felt Harry's gaze on me, and when I found it, he decided to approach me.

'Daddy, are you angry?' he whispered, snuggling into me.

'Why should I be angry with you?'

'Because I love Grandma very much, but I love you and Daddy too.' He looked at me uncertainly.

'Sweetheart, your little heart can hold a lot of love for each of us. It's not bad; it's wonderful that you can love us all the same.'

'I love you.' He embraced me tighter.

'I love you a lot, too, my little spider.'

The next day, I got up first. Chris was still asleep because he had got Harry interested in his telescope last night, and they stayed up late stargazing together, looking for Santa's sleigh.

As my mother exited the bathroom, I was walking quietly up the stairs.

'Are you awake?' she asked.

'Shhh, you'll wake everyone up. Harry stayed up late last night with Chris,' I whispered.

'OK,' she said, lowering her voice. 'Let's go to the kitchen.'

Busy preparing breakfast, we didn't even hear Harry appear in the doorway, rubbing his sleepy eyes.

'Oh! There's our prince!' my mother called.

He came over and hugged his grandmother, who smoothed his messy hair, and then he cuddled up to me.

'Daddy, can we open the presents now?' He lifted his head and looked at me pleadingly.

'Honey, we'll open the presents together after breakfast, OK?'

'OK.' He quickly sat at the dining room table, and my mother and I exchanged smiles.

After a while, Chris came down. Eight in the morning was not his dream time, but the smell of breakfast and the thought of gifts were enough to drive him out of bed. He took a seat next to Harry.

'Where's breakfast?' Chris and Harry exclaimed while laughing and high-fiving each other.

'And what are these hungry people who came here? Patience!' Mum laughed.

A few minutes later, she placed plates of pancakes in front of us. Harry started devouring them like it was a race, getting his face mucky, and Chris tried to compete with him. I remembered the first time we had dinner together. Harry hadn't even dared to reach for his fork. His wide eyes searched for permission in our every move. Now, however, he would easily ask for more.

'Don't tease a baby,' Mum admonished.

Moments from our lives were arranged on the shelves of memories, which we eagerly reached for later. That Christmas, he joined the shelf named Harry.

Right after breakfast, my son jumped up from the table and ran to the Christmas tree, where we had left the presents. With Chris and Mum, I moved to the sofa, waiting for Harry's first reactions. He sat down by the tree and turned to us. His eyes shone excitedly, and he reached for the boxes. As a child, I never liked Christmas. It was a nightmare. My mother screamed all morning and made me scrub the floors, then the toilets, and put up the Christmas tree, which could never bring me joy again. Then I wrapped gifts I knew well – usually pants or socks. My grandfather often waited for us in the car in the evening because my mother could never get ready on time. There was almost always an argument. It wasn't until we were at Grandma's that I forgot all about it for a while, but the evening ended too soon, which meant going home. Now that, as a parent, I could give Harry the Christmas I never had, I felt fulfilled and happy.

'Daddy, can I open it now?'

'Yes, honey.'

A few seconds later, Harry tore into the paper greedily.

'Honey, slowly, no one will take it away from you.' I laughed, and a moment later, Mum and Chris joined me.

I took a sip of hot cocoa and watched red ribbons fall one by one onto the carpet, decorated with Harry's squeals of delight at each present he opened. Sitting between me and Chris, Mum put her hands on our shoulders and pulled our heads together, kissing us on the cheeks.

'I'm so glad,' she whispered, and I glanced at Chris, who had turned his head slightly to try to hide his glassy eyes.

*

After New Year's Eve, we drove my mother to the train station. I didn't want her to go home so soon, but she had some business at the borough council. We said goodbye, and Harry continued to wave long after the train started moving.

'So, what now? Shall we go home for cheesecake and hot chocolate?' I looked at him as the last carriage disappeared around the bend.

'Yes!' he called, and grabbed my hand.

On the way home, Harry played a game on his iPad in the back seat. The Eurythmics song 'There Must Be an Angel' was playing on the radio.

'Our first family Christmas. It was great, right?' I looked at Chris.

'Yes,' he muttered.

His face remained impassive, and his blank gaze fixed on the road. Had he argued with his mother before she left? I decided to come back to it later.

When we got home, Harry hurriedly took off his shoes in the hall and dashed to the computer. Chris disappeared into the living room, and I thought this was the right time to talk. I followed him and sat next to him on the sofa, trying to cuddle, but he didn't react, shifting his scowl to the window.

'What is wrong?'

'Nothing,' he replied coldly.

'What do you mean, nothing? I can see you're sulking.'

He grabbed the remote and turned on the TV. I took it from him and turned it off.

'Shall we talk?'

'About what?' He still didn't look at me.

'Chris, tell me, what's going on? I'm tired of guessing.'

'It's a bit uncool that I don't have a husband.' He turned to me and gave me a reproachful look.

'What are you talking about?'

'You spent the whole Christmas with Harry, forgetting about me.'

'You're not jealous, are you? We have a baby, remember?'

'And me? I'm no longer important?'

I didn't know how to answer.

'This is why I didn't want a child. I knew you would pour all your feelings into him and I would be left alone!'

'What are you talking about? How can you be so selfish?'

'I'm selfish?' He sprang up from the sofa. 'Who initiated the adoption?'

I stared at him dumbfounded. He turned and left, slamming the door. I froze on the sofa and stared at the door, trying to understand what had just happened.

3. Lucas

The night I found out you died, I was in the hospital. Together with the rain, I mourned your departure. It didn't stop until the morning, when Lieke came to take me home. Crossing the threshold, I stopped, covering my face with my hand. The sun's rays mercilessly attacked my eyes, pricking them with a thousand needles, and the intense sounds of cars and the hum of talking people swirled around me as if someone had turned up the radio all the way. For the first week, I practically didn't leave my bed, snuggling into the T-shirt that still carried your scent from our last night. I could smell our moments, which I craved like a junkie.

'Will you be up for breakfast?' Lieke entered my room and walked over to the window, cracking it open.

'I'm not hungry.' Even the words took a lot of effort.

'You need to eat something.' She sat beside me and ran her hand through my hair, just like my mother used to do.

'Go away, please.' My sore throat struggled to let out the words.

'Lucas, it's been a week. People from your job are calling, and I don't know what to tell them. I sit alone in my room and suffer because you suffer. I wish I could take this pain away from you, but I don't know how.' Her eyes filled with tears.

I was silent. I hoped she would leave soon, but she was still here.

'Lucas, say something...' She looked at me painfully and stroked my arm.

'It's so hard for me to believe he's gone.' I burst into tears, and they choked my throat. 'When I close my eyes, I can still see him. He comes out from the hall, smiles and walks over to me. He embraces me, and I feel his warmth, his voice ringing in my ears.'

'Lucas, I feel so sorry for you. I can't imagine how you are suffering, but I want to help you because I love you. Go to therapy. I made an appointment for tomorrow morning,' she whispered, stroking my head.

I don't remember how I ended up in the psychotherapist's office, but I regretted that decision, and all I could think about was running back to my room. Jumping into bed and disappearing under the covers, blocking out the light and sounds that annoyed me. I wanted to hide with you in memories that would help me forget for a while that I would never see you again.

'Lucas, how are you feeling?' The therapist's voice echoed around the room.

'Dead.' I struggled to get the words out, my eyes roaming the wall.

She was silent for a moment. I didn't know if she was horrified by what I had said or was waiting for something more. After a while, however, she continued.

'I understand that something happened in your life that took away your strength to move on.'

I shifted my gaze to her. I studied her face, wondering if she had a husband or boyfriend she returned to after her sessions with patients. They'd eat dinner together, then cuddle up, watch a movie and start making love.

'Lucas?' Her voice broke my thoughts and dragged the words to my lips.

'He... he died. I didn't make it...' I cried. I couldn't catch my breath for a long time. The therapist handed me tissues and waited for me to calm down.

'The grieving process has many stages, and everyone goes through it differently. It's your job to be able to say goodbye to the person you've lost.'

'I can't. It hurts so much.' I turned towards the door.

Lucas, I know you are suffering, and I can't even imagine how much, but I am here to help you.

We will do it together. It will be a long process, but I promise you, you're exactly where you need to be. You may feel like you'll never get out of this right now, but the mere fact that you're here with me proves that you'll soon feel differently.'

I didn't have the strength to reply. I didn't care.

'Your sister mentioned that you have lost the meaning of life and you don't get out of bed. I will prescribe medications that will support our therapy. Remember that they will not solve the problem but only calm the emotions.'

She prescribed me pills to numb the pain. At first, nothing changed; I still felt the same. Three weeks later, she gave me an assignment. In the moments when I couldn't suppress the pain, I was supposed to write you letters. This conversation with you was supposed to help me get through the day and strengthen me for the next one.

The first letter was the worst. I kept crying, and the ink smeared on the sheet of paper, but pulled by some magnetic force, I reached for another piece and started over.

After a while, the medication made your absence less painful, and the intensity of your memories waned. I decided to go back to work, which helped keep my mind occupied, slipping away to you less and less.

My co-workers and my boss organised a welcome party for me. The hall was decorated with balloons and a large banner: *WELCOME BACK*. A lot of people came from different departments, but I only knew half of them. Everyone exchanged hugs and a few words with me. It was nice.

The boss clearly spared me for the first month because I didn't get any big orders. Instead, he involved me in helping the apprentices. Initially, I found myself in this role, but after a while, I began to feel redundant. One day I waited until everyone had left and went to his office.

I opened the glass door. 'Do you have a minute?'

'Sure, sit down.' He gestured to the chair by his desk. 'What's up?' He looked friendly, but I felt he was keeping me at work out of pity.

'Tim, don't get me wrong, I'm grateful to you for everything you do for me. For the chance to get back to work and your friendship. However, I get the feeling that you've been lenient on me for quite some time, and I don't want that.' I looked deep into his eyes. 'I would really like to return to work to give my best. Like before.'

Silence fell, adding to the seriousness in his face.

'Lucas. You know I think of you as a friend. You've been through a lot. I can't even imagine how much. Are you sure—'

'Yes,' I said. 'I'm absolutely sure.'

'Then I will assign you a project in Germany. Gert is not yet independent and is afraid of this assignment. I don't think he will find a better teacher.'

'Thank you, Tim. It means a lot.'

We got up simultaneously, and he hugged me when I shook his hand.

'OK, end of the tenderness,' he said after a moment. 'Let's get to work! We're late.' He laughed.

'Yes, boss!' I said, saluting.

My therapist was proud of me, and I couldn't believe I was doing so well. I felt like I was running a marathon, taking the lead, and you were up there cheering me on.

Only Emma was worried about me. She asked me several times if I could do it, but I told myself that Tom would want that for me after all.

My co-workers organised a small party for me to celebrate the new assignment in Germany. They joked that I would forget my mother tongue by the time I returned.

The job helped me get back on my feet. Frequent trips and falling asleep in the office while working on projects distanced me from my memories step by step, although I never forgot about you. I was learning to live again, in a completely new world.

On the weekends I usually hung out with Emma and Sven, who filled my time exactly as they had done after my divorce. Their first question about you came after a year. We were playing a board game. We took a little break, and Emma walked over to the desk where our picture was and picked it up, smiling.

'I've always been curious about what happened that night after we left.'

'Emma, only the moon knows that.' I winked at her.

'Just curious.' She put the photo down.

'If you're asking if we spent that night together, the answer is yes.'

'I knew it!' she exclaimed. 'How did that happen?' She smiled flirtatiously.

'You're very curious,' Sven laughed.

'I'm not asking what they did; I'm asking how it happened. I am romantic.'

'It was an accident. I set up Tom in my bedroom and went to the sofa in the living room. We both couldn't sleep, and Tom went into the kitchen in the dark to get something to drink. We exchanged a few words, and I asked if we could talk if we were both awake.

'Oh! How sneaky,' Emma giggled.

'Please, it wasn't like that at all... OK, maybe a little.' I laughed along with her.

'I knew it!'

'Tom tripped over a table in the dark and would have fallen if I hadn't caught him. We fell on the sofa, and that's all you need to know.'

'Was it nice?'

'It was wonderful... like never in my life.' I froze with a dreamy expression on my face.

Returning to the game on the floor, I couldn't help but glance at the sofa several times, recalling that evening.

*

On the anniversary of the explosion, I asked Emma and Sven to come with me to the airport. I was under a lot of stress that day. I was afraid of the memories that waited for me there. I couldn't finish my breakfast, and while I was washing my face in the bathroom, I heard the sound of water running down the pipes. I turned to the cubicle. For a moment, I was sure I saw you there taking a shower. My heart sped up. I reached into my cupboard to get something to calm down.

I waited on the sofa, ready, and after a while, I heard a car horn outside the window. I reached for my phone on the desk, and my eyes landed on our photo beside it. The moment we captured came back to me. Your smile and awkwardness as I brought my face closer and our cheeks touched. The warmth of your hand as it started to rain and I grabbed it to run with you.

'Everything all right?' Emma asked as I got into the car.

'Yes, let's go.'

I leaned my head against the window and, driving through the streets where we used to walk, I couldn't shake off the images of our wandering. In the distance, I saw the market where you bought a cap that day.

'Sven, can we stop for a moment?'

'What's up, Lucas?' Emma turned to me.

'It's all good. I want to buy some flowers.'

'Sven, park here.' Emma gestured to a space. 'Want me to go with you?'

'No, thanks. It will only take a moment. Be right back.'

I entered the market. I couldn't resist the temptation and found the cap stand. I picked up one similar to the one you bought back then.

'Are you looking for something for yourself or a gift?' The saleswoman who had taken our picture stood in front of me.

'I'm just looking.' I quickly put down the cap and walked away without looking at her.

There was a flower stand nearby where I bought a rose, the reddest they had.

At the airport, I felt sad, but it was different than before. Some peace. Nostalgia. Emma held my arm, and Sven walked beside us. We passed shops. Memories quickly brought back images of the day you chose my clothes for our date you had no idea about. In the sounds of the bustling airport, I heard your voice. I missed you so much. We reached the pillar. I looked at the corridor door and felt that you would appear at any moment. I was bending down to put a rose by the pillar when an older woman dressed in black approached me.

'My son died right over there,' she said. 'Who did you lose?'

I raised my head. 'My love.' Tears filled my eyes.

She came over and hugged me like we were family. I looked down the corridor, hiding images of the explosions. A rumble, a crumbling floor, screams of people and dust that entered the lungs, and then the wall covering you.

I sat in the last row when Emma and Sven escorted me to our gate. You seemed to be sitting there and greeted me with a smile, and then we read the same book together.

'Everything OK, Lucas?' Emma touched my arm.

'Let's go.' I wiped my cheek with my hand.

At Café Chocolate, I felt calm. We each ordered a croissant, and when the waiter placed the plate in front of me, I asked for a knife. Emma and Sven looked at me intently but said nothing. They watched me cut the croissant in half and leave one piece for you. They didn't ask. They knew. At the same moment, I heard a door opening and the wheels of a suitcase being pushed. I looked up from my plate, and my heart sank. A man in a dark navy suit entered the coffee shop, and I almost jumped up to run to him, but Emma touched my knee. I glanced at her, and she smiled warmly. I looked back at the man, and only then did I notice his stern and travel-weary face, nothing like yours.

This visit filled with memories soothed my heart, and though I missed you so much, a sense of peace surrounded me as if you were hugging me with your presence and telling me that I must live on.

After visiting the airport, Emma and Sven took me to their place. Emma cooked dinner, and then we played cards and watched old movies, during which we parodied familiar dialogues, laughing until we cried.

Two months before Christmas, I arranged to meet up with Emma, which she insisted on. I thought it was about the wedding they had postponed because of me many months before.

We decided to meet at my place after work, but Emma called a few minutes before the agreed time.

'Lucas, I've got Braam with me, an old friend I ran into. Could I bring him?'

I was surprised because I thought she only wanted to talk to me, but when they came, her eyes couldn't hide the lie, and I immediately knew it was a dating ambush.

'You could have warned me,' I hissed through my teeth as we went to the kitchen to fetch wine.

'I'm sorry,' she whispered. 'I knew you'd say no.'

'And you pushed me anyway, knowing I'm not ready.'

'Come on.' She waved her hand at the door. 'He's a nice guy; give him a chance.'

I didn't know what to think. It wasn't the right time, although I wondered if the right time would ever come.

Braam was energetic and reminded me of when I first met you – handsome, a year younger than me, with gelled blonde hair. There was something about his smile that spread across his face, revealing snow-white teeth, but when my mind tried hard to find some part of you in it, I was terrified. I thought I would always look for you in someone, remaining locked in a world I missed.

We opened the wine. Emma began to recall how she met Braam when he accidentally ran into her at a party, spilling the entire contents of a glass of red wine on her. Almost in tears, she ran to the bathroom, trying to wipe the stain off her dress. Braam kept apologising to her. Later, when they started complaining about the guys together, that was how their friendship began, which had survived to this day. They also talked about travelling together and how Sven was jealous of Braam when he didn't yet know he was gay.

'It's time for me to go.' Emma stopped my hand as I reached for her glass. I looked up. I was sure they'd leave together, but when I looked over to Braam, he was pouring wine into his glass before returning to the sofa.

'Be good,' Emma whispered jokingly at the door.

'Stop it,' I said, my voice low.

After she left, I opened another bottle of wine.

'So, are we complaining about our exes?' Braam grinned widely. 'I'll go first.'

He could talk non-stop. He had so much energy that he expelled it strongly by gesticulating with his hands. He told me about his failed relationships, his family, who loved him very much, and the love he was still looking for.

'It's your turn now. But before that, let's drink to our health.' He clinked his glass with mine.

At first, I didn't want to say anything, but the expectant silence pressed so hard that I decided to tell him about the divorce, deliberately omitting you. I don't know why, but this topic was still too precious for me to share.

When I finished, Braam got up and walked over to the desk, where there was a picture of me with you. He picked it up and turned to me.

'And who is that?' He froze with the frame in his hand.

Enchanted in silence, I fixed my gaze on our photo.

'Tom died a year and a half ago,' I said, but didn't want to say more.

'I'm so sorry.' He put the photo back in its place and returned to the sofa.

He never asked about you again, although I was sure Emma must have told him something. He quickly changed the subject and told me funny stories about his life. I heard myself laugh for the first time in a long time. That evening took away my sense of time, and when Braam got up to say goodbye, I realised it was almost two in the morning.

The next day, he called during lunch.

'Hey, how are you feeling today? I think we overdid it with the wine yesterday.'

'It's true, I'm having a bit of a hard time focusing,' I laughed.

'Listen, as a thank you for the nice evening, I'd like to take you to the cinema. Would you like to go tonight?'

His invitation made me realise that it had been ages since I had been to the cinema. I had almost forgotten that there was a life besides work – a life that was leaking through my fingers. You were gone, but I should live on. You'd probably want that for me.

'Why not? I haven't been in a long time.'

'Seven o'clock at the Cinecenter?'

'Sure.'

That day, a grumpy customer kept me at work, and I glanced nervously at my watch from time to time. When we were done, I grabbed my jacket and ran out as fast as I could. I barely made it. Braam laughed when I couldn't catch my breath or say a word.

'I see that the cinema is very important to you.' He winked and opened the door for me.

Shortly after the session began, Braam put his hand on the armrest, and a moment later, I felt the warmth of his skin. I glanced at him, but he was watching the movie. I thought it was an accident, but after a while he gently dragged his slightly trembling finger over my hand. It was nice to feel it.

After the screening, we walked for a long time, unable to decide where to stop for food. In the end, we chose pizza. The topics raised in the film opened the door to a long conversation. I got lost in time listening to his childhood stories, which often resembled mine. It was getting late, so I offered to walk him to the station. While waiting for the train, Braam reached for my hand.

'Thank you for a nice evening.'

'It's me who should thank you. I haven't been out for a long time.'

'Then I hope we can do it again.' He looked at me questioningly.

'I'd love to.' I smiled.

After that, we started seeing each other more often. City trips, to the cinema, a walk or visiting friends together, where we were always asked about the nature of our relationship. Braam was usually silent, but his face shone with joy when I replied that we were together.

One day he called me.

'Hey, do you have time after work today? I bought a new bed and need help putting it together.'

'Sure. No problem. Send me the address.'

'You are amazing! Thank you.'

I went straight after work. Before I could ring the bell, the door was already open.

'Hi, thanks for coming.' He hugged me and kissed me on the lips.

In the centre of the living room were four large boxes and a big bag of metal parts, just brought in. I took off my jacket, and a few minutes later, following the instructions, we were building a new piece of furniture step by step, which turned out to be quite difficult. Sometimes we managed to skilfully mix up parts or screws, creating an artistic mess. We burst out laughing, which was difficult to curb, slowing down our creativity.

'Let's take a break. You didn't eat after work, and I put you to work. Rest while I prepare dinner.'

I was putting a piece of lasagne in my mouth when Braam stopped eating and looked at me.

'Lucas, what do we have in common?'

Surprised by the question, I also stopped eating, looking at his serious expression.

'Don't you feel anything for me?' he went on.

'No, it's not like that,' I replied immediately.

'Like how? We're just friends who hang out together?' He put down the cutlery.

'Braam, I don't want to spoil anything. I love the moments I spend with you, but I need more time.' I felt my face burning.

'I'm glad you said that. I have a clearer picture of the situation.'

'Have I disappointed you?'

'In a way, I'm relieved. I was afraid to hear that I couldn't count on anything more. And now I can think about how to shorten this time that you need.' There was a little devil in his smile.

The evening resulted in more wine. We lay down on the mattress for the new bed. I stared at the ceiling silently, trying to collect my thoughts after our earlier conversation. What did he lack? What would it take to make me feel for him what I felt for you? As I turned to Braam, he unexpectedly leaned in and kissed me. I kissed him back and was lost in lust. However, half an hour later, we were lying beside each other, covered with a blanket, and I realised something was missing. Something that was still undefined.

After that day, we alternately stayed at each other's for the night, and I didn't even notice when he put your picture in a drawer.

One Saturday, I woke up, and for some reason, looking at his sleeping face as we lay side by side, images of my last evening with you began to come back to me. I held your hand and felt you move it at some point, checking if I was still there. My heart beat faster, and the smile never left my face. I cuddled up to you and fell asleep.

The memory was interrupted by the sound of an incoming call. Braam jerked out of his sleep and picked it up immediately, probably thinking it was his phone.

'Hello?' he said in a sleepy voice, then turned to me. 'It's Emma.' He handed me the phone and turned to the side.

'Sorry, I didn't think you were asleep still,' she said.

'Don't worry. We went to bed late. So, what's up?' I got up and walked to the living room.

'Can you come over today? I'll cook something, and we'll enjoy some wine. What do you think?'

I agreed, but somehow without conviction. We ended the conversation, and I went to the kitchen for breakfast. I poured the egg yolks into a pan and instinctively put the tea into the espresso machine. Moments later, the kitchen was filled with the smell of strawberries. I looked at the espresso machine and froze, as if you were giving me a sign that you didn't blame me.

'What is that smell?' Braam stood in the doorway, snapping me out of my stupor.

'I got the teas wrong, sorry. I'll change it now.' I grabbed the jug.

'Leave it.' He came over to me and held my hand. 'We can try something new.'

He reached for the pot and poured it into the cups on the table. I put scrambled eggs on the plates and took my seat. I watched as he took his first sip.

'Ugh.' He shuddered, his mouth twitching. 'Sour. I prefer a black one.'

I didn't answer. The image of our breakfast flashed back to me as we ate in a hurry and you looked the other way while you drank tea. I didn't want you to go then...

'Lucas?'

'Yes?' I shifted my gaze to him.

'What's going on? You seem absent.'

'I don't know. I don't think I'm feeling well,' I lied.

'Then go back to bed, and I'll take care of everything.'

That day, Braam relieved me of my household chores. I wanted so much for you to hang around the house with me. I pushed those thoughts away so they wouldn't take me down again. I wanted to speed up the process somehow, to feel something for Braam. I forced myself to love him, but my heart still searched for you in him.

On the way to Emma and Sven's, we passed the cheese museum, where I put a piece of cheese in your mouth and you blushed. I kept my eyes on the building. Your smile and the embarrassment of saying goodbye when I touched your ear with my lips, not by chance. You closed your eyes then.

'Here we are!' Braam tapped me on the shoulder. We got out of the taxi, although it took me a few seconds to realise where we were.

'At last!' Emma called from the doorway.

'We had a hangover.' Braam winked at her.

'Come in.' She stepped aside to make room for us.

During dinner, busy talking, they did not notice my absence. Occasionally, I heard scraps of conversation about going away together. I glanced at their smiling faces then, but I didn't have the strength to join the conversation. At some point, my phone rang. I apologised to everyone and went to the kitchen.

'Lucas.' I heard my boss's voice. 'I'm calling you because we got a new contract and I would like you to lead it. You already know the city from a previous assignment.'

'Where?'

'Warsaw.'

Hearing that word made me shiver.

'Lucas, are you there?'

'Yes, I'll take it.' I don't know why I said that.

'Thank you very much...' He said something else, but I wasn't listening anymore. My mind had started wandering the streets of Warsaw.

When I returned to the living room, Emma, Sven and Braam stared at me.

'What happened?' Emma asked.

'Nothing. My boss called. He's starting a new contract and is sending me to Warsaw.'

Emmie's fork slipped out of her hand and landed on the plate, about to bounce off it and land on the tablecloth, but she quickly caught it. Sven exchanged a glance with her.

'What's going on?' Braam looked from me to Emma.

'Nothing, sorry, that was clumsy of me,' Emma answered for me.

'Lucas?' Braam wasn't letting it go.

'Like I said, I have a new assignment, and they're sending me to Poland.'

'For a long time...?' His voice trailed off on the last word.

'I don't know yet... maybe a month.'

Braam froze, then sank back against the soft back of the sofa. Emma and Sven looked at each other.

'Lucas, are you sure that's a good idea?' Emma asked.

'The boss asked me; I couldn't say no.'

Emma looked at Sven again as if expecting him to back her up.

'Honey, work is work,' Sven said, and Emma shook her head.

'Let's have dessert.' She jumped up from the chair.

'Yes, please,' Sven said.

'Me too,' I said to Emma.

'Who wants wine?' Sven looked around our faces as Emma left the living room.

'I'd love some.' Braam pushed his glass closer to Sven.

Emma returned with ice cream and set it out in front of us. For the next few minutes, the sound of spoons tapping on ceramic bowls echoed around the room.

'Are we going somewhere on vacation together?' Emma broke the silence and looked at Braam, who quickly turned his head away.

'Lucas?' She looked at me.

'Maybe Spain?' Braam once mentioned that he had never been there and wanted to go. I turned to him, but his mind was wandering somewhere.

'That's a great idea.' Emma reached for her bag and took out her phone. 'I have a friend in Spain; maybe we can stay with her? I will write to her.'

‘Great, I’ll arrange the car so we don’t have to rely on buses.’

Despite repeated attempts to get him to talk, Braam, with whom it was usually impossible to get a word in, had paled and seemed to only answer the questions put to him.

‘Maybe we’ve had enough?’ I asked as Braam filled I don’t know which glass with wine.

He didn’t respond, so I decided to leave him alone. Emma and Sven exchanged helpless glances, unsure how to liven up our evening.

Braam leaned over to me. ‘Can we go home?’

‘Sure, let’s go.’

He remained silent in the taxi. I glanced at him several times, but his gaze was fixed on the glass.

Back at the apartment, he immediately started cleaning the kitchen, although there was nothing to clean. The message was clear: don’t come near me.

Later, as I turned off the lamp and our breathing filled the silence, Braam turned to me.

‘Why did you leave me out of it?’

‘What are you talking about?’

‘About your leaving.’

‘I was supposed to tell my boss I had to ask you for permission? That’s what you expected?’ I turned to him.

‘You could have said you’d think about it.’

‘And would it change anything?’

Braam fell silent.

‘Good night,’ he said coldly, facing the wall.

'Can you explain what's going on? Silence isn't going to solve the problem.'

'I'm tired. Good night.'

I felt ruefully conscience-stricken. I knew I had to say goodbye to you, and I could only do that in Warsaw. Otherwise, trapped in my memories, I'd never feel for Braam what he felt for me. I had to leave you. But before I could do that, I wanted to see you one last time through the places we had been to together.

Emma called the next day as I was finishing work and collecting my things.

'We need to talk.' I could hear the sadness in her voice. 'I left you some messages, but you didn't answer.'

'Sorry, I was going to message you, but it completely slipped my mind. I can be with you in half an hour?'

'Yes, I'll be waiting.'

When I got to her apartment, Sven opened the door.

'Honey, Lucas has arrived!' he shouted. 'I'm going out.' He grabbed his jacket and gave me a friendly smile. 'Emma is waiting for you in the living room,' he announced as he passed me.

I took off my coat and walked hesitantly towards the living room. Emma was standing by the window, watching the street.

'What's going on?' I said, sitting on the sofa.

She turned in my direction.

'Lucas, you know I love you like a brother, so I'll say it straight. Don't go. Cancel it. Let someone else take the job. It took you so long to pull yourself together after Tom. This trip will ruin everything.' She froze with pleading eyes, waiting for my answer, which I was afraid to give. She came over and grabbed my hand.

'Say something.' She squeezed tighter.

'Emma, I can't explain it, but I have to go.'

'Lucas...' Her voice shook, tears glistening in her eyes. 'He's not there anymore.'

I hugged her tightly, and after a while, I felt her warm tears touching my skin.

'We cancelled the wedding for you.' She quickly freed herself from my arms, wiping her cheeks with the sleeve of her sweater. 'Doesn't that mean anything to you?'

'Don't say that. You know I know how much I owe you, and how I love you like family, but...'

'But you'll go anyway, won't you?' Her gaze froze on me.

'It's just a job.' I stroked her hand.

I had never seen such terror in her eyes before. Like she was afraid she'd never see me again.

*

Braam tried to start a conversation several times but kept backing out. Finally, as I turned off the bedside lamp one night, I heard his hesitant voice.

'Shall I wait for you here or return to my flat?'

'You can wait. You have the keys.'

For some time, I lay staring at the dark ceiling. A few passing cars lit up the bedroom for a second, and each time it got brighter, Braam took a deep breath as if he wanted to add something else but didn't. We stayed in silence until we fell asleep.

Everything went wrong the day I left. I woke up two hours early and desperately tried to get some more sleep, in vain. I tossed and turned in bed, and to not wake Braam, I switched off the alarm. I finally got up and went to the bathroom. I must have been squeezing the tube too hard while applying toothpaste to the brush because it shot straight into the mirror. I tried to wipe it off, but it only made it worse. I caught the paste that had fallen on the floor with my sleeve. I took a deep breath and let it out.

Later, I ran around the apartment looking for something that turned out to have been packed long ago. Braam silently watched me from the sofa. He got up a few times to pace the living room nervously, then returned to the sofa. I thought I'd make it up to him when I got back. Emma, Sven and I would go somewhere and talk it over.

He came up to me in the corridor.

'Have a good trip and call me when you arrive.' He hugged me and kissed me.

'Sure.' I kissed him on the lips and left the apartment, heading for a taxi that was already waiting outside the building.

My emotions fought an internal battle within me. On the one hand, I was afraid of those places that might make it difficult for me to return to my everyday life, and at the same time, I kept telling myself that without this trip, I would not be able to start a new life. The mere thought of all the places we visited together made me more and more excited. I imagined you picking me up at the airport and getting into a taxi together. It took me a while to realise you wouldn't be there. So much time had passed, and I still couldn't get over your absence.

At the airport, I sat in the last row at our gate, and images of shared moments began to wake in my mind – your smile, our conversations and never-ending goodbyes when boarding was announced.

I went to Café Chocolate, where I ordered our croissants, and the memory of me wiping the chocolate off your face with a napkin flashed instantly. I didn't think I'd remember every detail with such accuracy.

On the plane, I remembered our first meeting. You stood in the aisle, surprised someone had taken your seat. When I looked at you, I died. I had to meet you. You don't know this, but I followed you and watched you look around for food after you got off the plane. I quickly realised that you were looking for a meatless sandwich because they were hard to find, and when you opened the display case to grab the last one, I was right behind you. It was the best idea I ever had. You got so sweetly mad that I could barely hold back my laughter. A week later, I was waiting for you at the pillar, and you didn't show up; I was devastated. I couldn't forgive myself for not asking for your phone number. Every Saturday, I checked for morning flights and waited there, hoping you'd show up. It took a month for me to accept the thought that I would never see you again. And one day, so elegant, you walked into the conference room. You said hello to Pierre, and I breathed out of happiness, and my heart jumped in a pirouette...

After I landed at Chopin Airport, Warsaw greeted me with sunshine, but it wasn't as hot as that day when you took me for a walk around the Old Town. I asked the taxi driver to take me there and drop me off at the escalator. Through the window, I watched people walking in the streets. I couldn't stop my imagination from picturing us walking together. I felt no pain, only longing for someone who made me wake up in the morning and run happily to the airport. It was different with Braam. No exhilaration that gave me energy.

After getting out of the taxi, I looked around, and although the place was bustling with life, I felt alone in it. I followed our trail to the stairs and Plac Zamkowy, where daters meet under Sigmund's Column.

I walked through the market and found the ice cream window. I asked for the biggest one and barely ate it before it melted. I passed a restaurant with dumplings, and after a while, I crossed the gate into the Krasińskich Garden, finding the bench where we rested. I sat on it and for a long time watched the pigeons walking in the grass, couples with children running around, and an old lady on the next bench reading a book. Birds sang in the background, and the trees moved in the wind as if they were clapping their hands. Only now I could feel this place, see it through your eyes. People look for a connection like ours all their lives and never find it, and I was lucky for a little while, and if I could get the same time today, I wouldn't change a thing about it.

I arrived at the hotel at dusk and saw several missed calls from Braam when I looked at my phone.

'Lucas? God, what's going on? I haven't heard from you all day; I was worried.'

'I'm sorry, I got caught up in a series of business meetings.'

'Where are you now?'

Not wanting to hurt him, I chose the simplest solution.

'I just got to the hotel, but I'm exhausted, so I'm going to bed now.'

'Get some rest. We'll talk tomorrow.'

I went to bed but could not fall asleep for a long time. Refreshed memories flooded my mind, taking me to archives I couldn't stop looking at.

Every day I waited impatiently to leave work and ran to the Krasińskich Garden. I took my place on our bench, staying until the gate closed. On weekends we walked around the Old Town, visiting Sigmund's Column. We greedily ate ice cream that froze our brains, and every time I heard the Polish conversations of passers-by, I saw your smiling face. Deeply buried in the echoes of our moments, I fed my longing with memories that hugged me like you used to.

Emma sent me countless text messages. I told her that I was working a lot and everything was fine, but I wasn't sure if that reassured her.

One weekend, Pierre invited me to a business dinner, which investors and board members attended. We sat around a large table, dividing our time between eating, talking and forced laughter at dirty jokes that weren't funny at all. I'd been running away from this dinner with my thoughts on you. I just wanted to spend this time with you.

'And how are you, Lucas?' asked Vincent, a member of a prestigious Italian company.

'I'm sorry, what was that?'

'I'm curious what dating is like now. We are already much older, and there was no such tolerance for everything in our time. How is it now? You are in love?'

I fell silent, and Braam's face flashed before my eyes.

'I haven't found the right person yet.' I looked away.

'Lucky!' someone called. 'My wife is always controlling me, and we fight all the time.'

Everyone burst out laughing, and I took the opportunity to run to you again.

The last day of my stay in Warsaw came. I wanted to stay longer and never leave. This trip had made me realise that my heart would always belong to you, Tom. I knew I had to talk to Braam and explain everything to him. It didn't make sense anymore. We were both getting tired, and I didn't want to hurt him. He deserved to be happy.

When I arrived home, I gently slipped the key into the lock, hoping Braam wouldn't hear. I left my suitcase in the hallway, kicked off my shoes and walked into the living room. He wasn't there, where he usually read a book wrapped in a blanket on the sofa. I went to the kitchen, but that was silent too.

'Braam?' I called, but the sound of my voice quickly faded away.

I peeked into the bathroom and immediately noticed that his toiletries were missing. I ran to the closet and opened the door. The shelves were empty. I went back to the living room, and then I saw the letter on the desk. It was folded in half. I picked it up.

We need to talk when you get back. Braam.

He had disappeared before I could explain everything. Before I could apologise. He didn't pick up when I grabbed the phone and called him. I sat on the sofa and turned on the TV but couldn't focus on any programme.

The next day I went to see him after work. Standing in front of his door, I hesitated before knocking.

'Hey,' Braam said as he opened the door. 'Come in.'

I couldn't read any emotion on his face. Before I entered, he headed towards the kitchen without glancing in my direction. I paused for a moment, unsure if I should keep going. Braam had never been so cold to me, even when I wasn't paying him attention.

'I'm making myself dinner,' he called from the kitchen. 'Are you hungry?'

'If it's not a problem for you?'

The hall smelled of tomatoes. I wanted to go into the kitchen and help him, but instead, I made my way to the living room, glancing at Braam, who was standing next to the fridge, staring at his phone.

I sat on the sofa, re-editing my speech in my mind. *I love your company, I wish I could stay in it, but that would be unfair to...*

However, when Braam appeared in the doorway with plates full of food, the mounting stage fright took away all my words. He poured wine into glasses and took his seat.

'Bon appetit,' he said casually, and began to eat.

He glanced at me now and then, but his gaze was cold. I hoped he would speak first, but even more, I hoped he never would. Because was there anything he could say that we didn't already know? He was no longer fighting, his face filled with resignation and disappointment. I looked back at the plate.

'Lucas, this couldn't have worked,' he said after a moment, putting down the cutlery.

'I'm sorry,' I whispered, unable to meet his eyes.

'Do you know how many times I've wished you would love me the way you still love him?'

He reached for his glass of wine and drank it all at once. Tormented by remorse, I turned away.

'It wasn't our time,' Braam said after a moment. 'You weren't ready.'

I looked at him. I was grateful for his calmness in this situation.

'Sorry. I'd like to explain.'

'You don't have to explain anything to me.'

'I know how much I've hurt you. I did not want to.'

'At first, it was difficult to understand what was happening, but then I found the letters you wrote to him. Sorry, I couldn't help myself and read them all. Then I realised that even though he is no longer here, your heart still misses him. I can't fight this feeling, so I'm backing off. Maybe if you had told me about it, we could have worked it out together somehow. It's too late for that now.' His gaze froze. 'I'm going to my parents',' he said. 'I need to get some distance.'

I couldn't get a word out. I got up from the table and hugged him tight. Braam cried. We have had no contact since then, and I fled into my work, which became my hiding place.

4. Therapy

The wind blew through the streets in a curtain of rain, and I stared at my reflection in the mirror, practising a new role I found difficult to play in front of Chris. By choosing the intensity of the smile, I checked its naturalness. After a while, I took a deep breath and walked down the stairs to the hall. Harry was waiting by the door. He had to know. He was the only one who could see deep inside me. A longer look during our farewell was like a silent conversation: *Daddy, I understand.*

I got in the car, and when I saw them smiling at me from the window, I waved at them. I started the engine, and as soon as I was on the main road, I felt relief, as if the air had been expelled from me and the hood had come off.

Half an hour later, I parked outside Tracy's house. The wind was pushing hard against my umbrella, and fighting it, I quickened my pace to reach the door.

'You're finally here.' She got up from her chair. 'I was worried about you.'

'It's raining terribly.' I sat on the sofa, greeted with the memory of the time I once spent here; I felt at home. 'I'm sorry, I couldn't talk on the phone. Chris was standing next to me the whole time... I have to be careful.'

'I'm still having a hard time understanding all of this.' Tracy reached for the coffee pot from the espresso machine and poured me a mug of hot tea, the scent of which instantly wafted around the room, just as it had years ago.

I smiled in thanks.

'Will you tell me what happened?'

*

After arriving at Lucas's apartment, we talked a lot. I told him about the period after the accident, Harry and my marriage. He listened carefully without missing a word and then told me how he was doing. Before we knew it, an uninvited evening peeked into our windows, and embarrassment drew itself over us. The time that had passed had made us relearn our closeness.

When Lucas returned from the bathroom, he slipped under the cover, and the rustle of sheets immediately filled the silence. My heart sped up, and our eyes met. Lucas turned off the lamp and moved his hot body to me. I was still unsure of the moment's reality, and when he put his arm around me, I shivered. I felt him breathing slowly, as if he wanted to calm his strongly beating heart.

The moonlight showed our faces in the darkness, and for a long time, our eyes met in silence. Now I could see how difficult that period had been for him. His eyes were filled with fatigue, counting hundreds of sleepless nights, and silver strands glistened in his hair, telling a difficult story. I don't remember when we fell asleep.

In the morning, I felt the warm touch of lips on mine. I opened my eyes, and Lucas sat beside me with a tray full of food. When he smiled, I could see the sparkle in his eyes again, the same sparkle I had seen on our last evening.

'Would you like some breakfast?'

'With such a handsome man? Always.'

I couldn't concentrate during breakfast. Did Chris already know? My thoughts circled around this question, and my heart beat faster, like the drums of an impending cataclysm.

Afterwards, we sat on the sofa in the living room.

'Remember, take it easy, don't get distracted. I'm here.' Lucas took my hand as I dialled Chris's number and put the phone on speaker.

'Tom?' Chris sounded surprised.

I pictured him in the kitchen preparing breakfast for Harry. Lucas squeezed my hand tighter, and I looked at him.

You'll be fine, he mouthed.

'Yes, it's me. I wanted to tell you that I'm better now, and I'm coming home tomorrow.' I tried to speak casually, though I was afraid Chris would recognise some trace of panic in my voice or hear my heartbeat, which grew stronger with each word.

'That's great!' he said happily. 'Tom, was Tracy there?'

The question sounded as if he had sent her to me himself. What did he expect from this meeting?

'Yes, we talked, and I will have to go back to therapy again.'

'Tom, you know... The man at the airport... He was similar – it happens sometimes.'

Lucas and I looked at each other, and I wanted to shout into the phone that this similar man was sitting next to me right now, you liar!

'Tracy helped me understand that my mind was playing tricks on me,' I said, continuing my act of calmness.

'Daddy, Daddy!' I heard Harry call.

I immediately sprang up from the sofa, letting go of Lucas's hand.

'Honey! I'm coming home to you tomorrow.'

'Daddy, are you OK now? All good?'

'Yes, my love.' I went to the window.

'I've missed you so much!'

'I've missed you so much too.'

'Grandma made an apple pie, and we went to the fair to see the chickens. They were so huge!' He spoke so fast, as if he was afraid he wouldn't get it all out in time.

'Darling, you can tell me everything tomorrow; I can't wait. Can you put Dad back on now?'

'OK, Daddy.'

'Tom?' Chris's voice again. 'Harry and I will pick you up from the airport. What time is your flight?'

I looked at Lucas, who closed his eyes and nodded to indicate that he was OK.

'I should be there at eleven in the morning.'

'Then I'll see you tomorrow. I'm happy.'

'See you tomorrow.' I hung up.

'So maybe he doesn't know.' Lucas's gaze was lost for a moment in his absence.

'That's better; I'll have more time.'

Lucas got up and went to the window. He folded his arms across his chest and fell silent.

'What's going on?'

'I don't want you to go back to him.'

I got up from the sofa and walked over to him.

'I'm not going back to Chris. I'm going back for Harry. You know that. I won't leave him there alone.'

He turned to me.

'Every time you leave, I'm afraid I won't see you again. If anything happened this time, it would be too much for me, you understand?'

'I will be back.' I held his head with both hands. 'I promise.'

Lucas was trying to anticipate all possible scenarios. The first one was where Chris knew everything and was about to make a fuss. The second was where he also knew everything but pretended nothing had happened. The possibility that he didn't know seemed unlikely. Lucas was afraid to let me go alone and called the flight attendant friend through whom he had once given me a note.

At first, when she heard about me, her voice went a little hesitant, as if she thought Lucas was fantasising. Then he put the phone on speaker.

'It's me, Tom,' I said.

There was a silence during which she couldn't utter a word, and then she sighed with relief. She promised to switch flights with a friend so she could accompany me.

No sooner had we hung up than another call came in. We looked at the display. Emma. They'd known about me for a few days now, but they had no idea I was sitting next to Lucas right now.

They came almost immediately. Emma approached me with wide eyes and hugged me, and after a while, Sven joined us. They didn't let me out of their arms for a long time.

'Well, that's enough. Let him go, or I'll get jealous.' Lucas walked over and took my hand.

I talked with them for a few hours, revealing scraps of my lost time. When I got to Harry, Emma asked me for a picture. I showed her a photo on my phone, and her eyes immediately flashed with unconscious desire.

'This is one of our hikes. We have a common passion.' I displayed a photo that Chris had immortalised. We were sitting on a rock, tilting our heads in the same direction, staring into the distance.

'How wonderful!' exclaimed Emma. 'You even sit the same.' She giggled. 'And who took this photo?' She looked up from the phone.

'Chris,' I replied quietly, looking over at Lucas, who smiled broadly.

'How did you feel that first day Harry entered your house?'

'At first, I was terrified. I was afraid I wouldn't be able to cope and wouldn't be accepted by him as a parent, but his affection embraced me so quickly. I couldn't be given a better gift.'

'And Chris?'

'Chris turned it off as soon as he had proposed adoption. Mum helped me a lot. It would be hard without her.'

I wondered if Harry woke up screaming at night, looking for me, and if Mum was with him to calm him down.

'Doesn't that put Harry at a distance from Chris?'

'He loves him, only in a different way. You know, I spoil him and Chris scolds him.' I laughed nervously. 'What's new with you? How was the wedding?' I wanted to divert attention from myself.

There was silence for a moment, and everyone looked down.

'You know... when Lucas thought you were dead, his world collapsed.' Emma broke the silence. 'No one could reach him, not even his sister, Lieke. We decided to postpone the wedding until he got himself together.'

I looked at Lucas. The guilt he carried was imprinted on his face in sadness.

'Then somehow time flew by...' Emma added, and fell silent, looking away.

'So what's your plan, guys?' Sven quickly filled the silence, turning to Lucas.

I glanced at Lucas; our gazes couldn't get enough of each other.

'I'm going to divorce Chris,' I said, and it wasn't until my voice wavered that I realised how hard it was for me to say the words. Lucas took my hand and started stroking my back with his other.

'Tom is returning for Harry,' he continued for me. 'We'll live together. I'll find a bigger apartment because Harry needs a room and a good school. On weekends we'll stay in bed until noon watching Spider-Man movies with Harry, and for Christmas, we'll invite Tom's mother-in-law and my sister. Then, if Tom agrees to my proposal, we'll get married and be damn happy for the rest of our lives.'

I watched as the words flying out sparkled with the morning dew rippling on the cobwebs stretched between the blades of grass. My eyes glazed over, and he whispered: 'I love you.'

'Oh my!' cried Emma, wiping her cheek. 'I'm sorry, I got emotional. I can't wait to meet Harry.'

'He's a little copy of Tom,' Lucas laughed.

'It's not true. Lucas is joking.' But it made me feel good.

'I know what I'm saying. Anyway, you'll see for yourself.'

In the evening, when we were alone, Lucas lit a candle in the living room and covered us with a blanket. We lay on the sofa watching an old movie. At some point, the candle let out a last sputter and the flame went out. I wanted to get up, but Lucas stopped me.

'Stay,' he whispered, then brought his face close and kissed me.

That evening, under the cover of darkness, barely illuminated by the TV, our love, holding hands, ran along the illuminated avenue of stars.

In the morning, a cruel alarm clock woke us, and a few moments later, we were getting ready to leave for the airport. When the taxi pulled up to the house, Lucas cuddled up to me and put his head on my shoulder. Neither of us said a single word. We just exchanged longing glances.

At the airport, we sat at our gate. I felt a warm blanket of memories around my back that reminded me of the times I had spent here, and at the same moment, a familiar sound reached my ears. Our song. Someone was playing it in a nearby convenience store.

'As per order.' Lucas's eyes brightened.

'As if we were meeting here again, for the first time. The only thing missing is a sandwich,' I sighed.

'I can have one here in a moment.' He straightened his back, getting ready to stand up.

'No need. We had a delicious breakfast.' I held his hand.

When we heard the boarding announcement, we got up from our seats and headed towards the gate. We stood there for a while longer, holding hands and staring into each other's eyes, then simultaneously turned on the locators on our phones, and I switched off the sound for incoming messages.

'I'm scared,' Lucas whispered.

'Me too.'

It had been a long time since I felt as happy and safe as when he hugged and kissed me goodbye. It gave me strength.

'How do we explain this to Harry?'

‘We’ll tell him the truth.’ The words came confidently out of Lucas’s mouth.

I lifted my head and found his eyes filled with happiness. My heart immediately beat faster, and at that moment, I realised that Chris would never use the word *we* in this situation; he would rather ask, *What will you do now?*

‘Thank you for the “we”.’

‘We’re in this together, remember?’ He pulled me closer, and I could feel his heartbeat, which had escaped me.

‘I’ll start looking for a bigger apartment.’

‘Won’t you wait for us?’

‘Sorry, you’re right; we’ll do it together.’

As I let go of his hand, I already missed him. I turned around before entering the corridor, and Lucas was watching me longingly. We exchanged a silent *I love you*, and I headed for the plane filled with love.

Lia was waiting at the entrance, greeting passengers as they entered with a broad smile.

‘Hello.’ I stood in front of her.

‘Tom, my God!’ She hugged me. ‘I can’t now, but I’ll come to you later, and we’ll talk. Take your seat.’

Throughout the flight, I felt uneasy, tormented by the prospect of talking to Harry. How was I supposed to tell him that his room would no longer be his room and that his school and home would change to something new? The parent he loved would disappear and a new one would take his place. He’d been through so much, and I wanted to take it away from him when his life was at peace. I’d have to ask for Tracy’s support. I couldn’t do it myself.

'Tom, I'm so glad to see you.' Lia approached me. 'Rumour has it that you have a son.' She smiled warmly. 'Lucas and I texted before we took off.'

'Yes, it's true. And yes, he is fascinated by planes and dreams of meeting a flight attendant. Would you like to say hello to him?'

'It would be a great honour for me.' She put her hand on my shoulder.

After landing, my hands trembling as I waited to disembark, I clutched the strap of my shoulder bag tightly, but moments later, I followed the column of passengers towards the exit. Although I tried to walk slowly, my breathing quickened with each step. I stopped at the exit where Lia stood, saying goodbye to the passengers.

'See you in a moment?'

'Yes, wait for me in the arrivals hall.'

'Sure, thank you.'

I followed the passengers and turned on my phone. After a while, a message came through.

You must have landed already, and my heart is dying of longing. Lucas.

I replied immediately.

I'm going to check in. I miss you more. Tom.

After passport control, I went to the arrivals hall, and before I entered, I stopped, closed my eyes, took a breath and put on a smiling mask. I let out my breath and moved on. When the door slid open, I saw a crowd besieging the barrier, and after a while, I heard a call.

'Daddy, Daddy!' Harry ran towards me, ignoring the people standing around.

I grabbed him, hugging him tight and kissing him. I could barely hold back my tears as he jumped for joy like a little puppy.

'Daddy, you're finally here!' He looked deep into my eyes.

'Yes, son. I am.'

Chris followed right behind him.

'Let Daddy catch his breath; he's tired from the trip.'

Harry stood next to me but didn't let go of my hand. Chris leaned in to kiss me. Pretending not to notice, I quickly hugged him. He was confused but tried not to show it.

'So, shall we go home?' he asked.

'Just a minute, I have a surprise.' I smiled at Harry.

In the distance, I saw Lia walking towards us.

'There's someone who would like to meet you.'

'Me?' Harry's eyes opened wider.

Lia crouched beside Harry, and he lowered his head in embarrassment, though he couldn't stop glancing at her.

'My name is Lia, and I'm a flight attendant for KLM. Your dad told me that you like aeroplanes a lot.'

'Oh!' He blushed delightedly.

'I have something for you.' She handed him a miniature aeroplane.

'Wow!' Harry jumped. 'Thank you.' He snuggled into her.

'Does the pilot have someone to help him fly?' He lifted his head and looked at Lia.

'Of course. There is always a co-pilot with him.'

'And the fuel? What if you run out?'

'Everything is calculated so that it can't.'

'And how long does it take to practise flying to become a pilot?'

'Harry, that's enough,' I admonished him.

'I hope to meet you on board soon, and I'll tell you more then.' She winked at him.

'I don't think it will be soon,' Chris said arrogantly. 'We've had enough of hard times already.'

Lia stood up, adjusting her uniform, but ignored Chris.

'It's time for me to go,' she said with a smile. 'Nice to meet you, Harry.' She shook his hand and left.

'What was that? She didn't even say hello to me,' Chris said indignantly.

'Maybe you should have been nicer.'

'And how do you know this stewardess?' He stared at me.

'It's not the first time I've flown this airline,' I grumbled. 'Are we going to interrogate each other like this, or are we going home?'

'Let's go. Mum can't wait to see you,' Chris announced.

'Daddy, did you see what I got?' Harry proudly held out his aeroplane. After a moment, he lifted it upwards as if it were taking off.

'Yes, darling, it's very nice.'

'Thank you, Daddy!' He raised his hands in the air.

I stopped and crouched beside him, hugging him tightly.

'I was very worried,' he whispered.

‘I know. I’m so sorry our trip didn’t work out.’

‘Daddy, it’s OK. We’ll go another time.’

‘Yes... it won’t be long now.’ The words ran out so fast that I didn’t realise what I was saying until it was too late. I looked away.

‘Are you coming?’ shouted Chris, who had stopped at the door.

‘We’re coming!’

I remained silent the whole way back, glancing in the mirror repeatedly. Harry must have felt when I did this because he quickly found my gaze as if we were talking without words. After a few unsuccessful attempts to strike up a conversation, Chris let it go and concentrated on the road. I hid in the silence, filled with thoughts of Lucas.

When we got to the house, my mother immediately ran out of it and threw herself into my arms. For a long time, she couldn’t stop alternately kissing my cheeks.

‘Mum, you’re going to strangle me,’ I said, laughing nervously.

‘God, I was so worried! But the most important thing is that you’re here; now we’ll take care of you.’

‘I’ll take care of you too!’ exclaimed Harry, shaking my hand.

‘Harry, do you know you have to clean your room?’ Mum rebuked him with her eyes. ‘We’re going to have Aunt Julie visit this afternoon. You don’t want her to see this mess, do you?’

‘All right, Grandma.’ He hung his head.

‘Are we having visitors today, Mum?’

‘Yes, your arrival came so suddenly, so we didn’t have time to cancel this meeting.’

‘That’s fine, I can help.’ I took her hand.

She looked into my eyes with a hidden weariness that I understood perfectly. She had more than just Harry to look after. I had begun to think that she would be able to rest when I left and took Harry away, but wouldn't she suffer for it? Miss her family being gone? And Harry? How would he bear it? Would he understand? Or would he hate me for taking him away from his father?

'Are you just going to stand outside like that?' Chris called, looking out from the house.

'Let's go inside. I've baked an apple pie. Or are you not hungry?'

'I'm not hungry, Mum; I just need to rest.'

When we entered the house, I immediately went to the bedroom and hurried into the bathroom, locking the door. I took out my phone and wrote a message to Lucas.

I'm home now; we're about to have a follow-up visit from the adoption agency.

Is everything OK?

Yes, I'll get back to you when I can, love.

Me more.

Suddenly someone grabbed the door handle. I twitched, and the phone fell out of my hand.

'Tom, have you locked the door?' Chris's voice.

'I'm sorry.' I looked at the phone. The display was covered with a crack right across the screen. I quickly picked it up and put it in my pocket.

'Are you going to open it?'

I walked over to the door and turned the lock.

'What's going on?' Chris asked.

'My fears have come back.' I shifted my eyes away and walked past him. I sat down on the bed. Chris came over and sat down next to me.

'You are safe here, you know. I will take care of you.' When he embraced me, I felt disgusted for the first time. I closed my eyes and stiffened, imagining I was not there.

'I came up because Julie has arrived. She's earlier than we agreed. Will you come down to join us?' He stroked my arm, raising a shiver all along it.

'Give me five minutes.'

'Sure, we'll be in the living room.'

In the bathroom, I washed my face, changed my clothes and, fixing my hair, looked in the mirror. *You can do it. It's only a short moment.*

I went down the stairs and into the living room, where Mum and Chris were already sitting on the sofa, holding Harry's hand. Next to him, in an armchair, was Julie. Harry broke away from Chris and ran up to me.

'Daddy, we were waiting for you.' He took my hand and led me to the sofa. I sat down next to Chris, and Harry snuggled into his grandmother.

'Harry and I will go out, so you can talk freely.' Sue stood up and took Harry's hand. 'Come on; let's not disturb your aunt.' She led him out of the living room.

Julie turned to me as soon as Mum closed the door. 'Tom, I heard about the accident. I'm very sorry. What a relief that no one was hurt.'

'It was just a little fainting from exhaustion.' I avoided her gaze.

'I was concerned to hear that Harry was left alone, unattended, in a foreign country. Surely you understand the gravity of the situation.'

'I understand, but accidents cannot be predicted.'

‘If it hadn’t been for Chris’s quick reactions, who knows what might have happened.’

I looked at Chris, who was smiling proudly.

‘I guess if it wasn’t for the quick reactions of the police—’ The words popped spontaneously out of my mouth.

‘I’m a bit disappointed. I put you in charge, Tom.’

‘Julie, what are you trying to say?’ I could barely contain my irritation.

‘Tom, Chris asked you not to go, and yet you went and put Harry in danger.’

I had to gain control of the anger that was trying to get out of me. I took a deep breath, calming my thoughts.

‘Julie, I don’t know what version of events Chris told you, but why didn’t he come with us if he was so worried about us? Does that mean his lack of responsibility has disappointed you too?’ I looked her in the eye.

‘This is not the best time to talk,’ Chris interrupted immediately. ‘Tom has just returned from the hospital and is still weak.’

‘You’re right.’ Julie nodded at him.

‘As you can see, everything is under control. Mum is helping us, and Tom is recovering.’ He smiled at her in a friendly way.

‘You have reassured me, Chris.’ She shifted in her chair.

Chris took my hand, which didn’t escape Julie’s notice.

‘I just wanted to point out that it’s too early to change the environment Harry is still getting used to. He goes to therapy, doesn’t he?’

‘Every Wednesday,’ Chris was quick to respond.

‘From what I remember’ – she looked at her notes – ‘I think the psychologist’s initial recommendation was a year?’ She looked questioningly at Chris.

'Six months to go,' he replied without thinking.

I watched, amazed at how easily he played the role of a good and loving father.

'I am delighted that Harry has found such a caring and loving home. How you try to provide everything for him is fully appreciated. After adoption, not all parents want to cooperate. They often think they already know everything better. Complications start forming, forcing me to report to the adoption agency. There has been one case of adoption reversal in the past, so we are now particularly sensitive, but I see that I have nothing to worry about. Keep me updated on the progress of the therapy so that I can write only positive reports.'

'We all want Harry to be happy,' Chris declared, stroking my arm.

It occurred to me that I wouldn't be able to leave with Harry until at least the therapy was complete. My hopes vanished into thin air like a plane taking off and hurtling into space.

'Great. It's time for me to go.' Julie stood up, and I immediately slipped my hand out of Chris's.

'I'll walk you out,' I offered as I stood up.

As Julie got into the car, I stopped her.

'Julie, I know the situation with the trip didn't go well, but I just wanted to say that I didn't have any bad intentions. Harry wanted to see Amsterdam badly, and I couldn't say no.'

'Tom, I know you already, and I understand your intentions. However, it would be best to remember that you are now his parent, not his friend.'

'You're right,' I sighed.

She kissed me goodbye and got into the car. We waved goodbye to each other, and she drove off. I glanced over my shoulder, ensuring no one was watching, and set off towards the forest. When the trees surrounded me, I took my phone out of my pocket and called Lucas.

'Tom, is something wrong?' I could hear the anxiety in his voice.

'There's a problem. The director from the adoption board was here. Harry can't leave therapy, or she'll report it to the board, and they can take my son away from me. Chris presented the situation at the airport to the director in a way that was unfavourable to me, so it came out that I was to blame for the whole mess.'

'Fuck!' It was the first time I had heard Lucas swear.

'I won't be able to take him; I don't know what to do.' My voice wavered.

'Where are you now?'

'On a walk in the woods near our house. No one can hear me.'

'Go back to them. I'll think of something. I love you.'

After we ended the conversation, I immediately deleted the call log and then, as if I had just been out walking, headed towards the house.

At the door, Harry ran up to me and hugged me tightly.

'I missed you!'

'I've only been gone a short while.' I laughed, but it immediately dawned on me how scared Harry was that he would lose me. 'Come, will you show me what's new at school?' I took him by the hand.

Walking through the hall, we passed Chris as if he wasn't there. Out of the corner of my eye, I noticed his confusion.

While Harry was showing me notebooks and drawings, I couldn't concentrate. Thoughts of running away were receding somewhere far away, and I couldn't see any solution.

'Darling, did Dad explain the situation at the airport to you?'

He hesitated for a moment, which worried me. Maybe Chris had forbidden him to say anything?

'Yes... that I was the reason you were in the hospital, and it was my fault because I wanted to go there.'

'What?'

'He said that some evil monster wants to take you away from us. He takes different forms, sometimes even a wolf, and kidnaps people. I'm scared of him.' He looked at me with frightened eyes.

'Darling, Dad was probably joking.' I hugged him tighter.

'He wasn't joking.' He looked into my eyes. 'He said he's tried to kidnap you before, and I need to keep an eye on you. Daddy, when did the monster try to kidnap you?'

I fell silent. What the hell was Chris doing? He was dragging his innocent child into this mess, and now he might have anxiety and wake up at night. I hugged Harry tighter and stroked his head.

'Darling, I don't know why Dad wanted to scare you, but there are no evil monsters.'

'Then Auntie Julie arrived,' Harry continued. 'I explained to her that I really wanted to see the boats, but Dad didn't want to come with us.'

'What did she say?'

'She just listened.'

'And when was Aunt Julie here?' I sat with him on his bed.

'She came to see me when we got home from the policemen.'

‘I’m sorry, sweetheart.’ I hugged him tightly again. ‘You must have been scared.’

‘No, Daddy. The gentleman from heaven was with me.’

‘The gentleman from heaven?’ I tilted my head and looked at him thoughtfully.

‘The one you told me about, an angel took him away. Daddy, he came back to you.’

‘Harry, we need to talk.’ I took his hand. ‘Do you remember when we met at the painting workshop?’

‘Yes.’ His face lit up.

‘At that time, I was very down. I thought I had lost my friend forever.’

‘The one the angel took to heaven?’

‘Yes, that’s the one. I saw him when I fell at the airport. He was whole and healthy. He was the one who gave you the cake.’

‘I know, Daddy! I spoke to him when the ambulance took you away.’

‘Did you?’

‘He told me that he is your friend, and now that he has found you, he will never leave you again. He also asked me not to tell my dad about it. I didn’t.’ He looked deep into my eyes.

‘Thank you, my little spider.’ I hugged him.

‘Is that the evil monster who takes on different forms?’

‘No, dear. I already told you there are no evil monsters. Dad was trying to scare you.’

*

Tracy remained silent. I reached for the tea and took a big gulp, which moistened my throat, dried out by the story. I set the cup down and looked at her.

‘Lucas will come to England every Wednesday when I bring Harry to you. He’ll be staying at the Washington Central Hotel in Workington, and I’ll do whatever it takes to get there.’

5. Washington Central Hotel

Every Wednesday at seven forty I drove with Harry to Tracy's therapy in Whitehaven, carefully guarding every minute that Julie could include in the report. I led him to the door, kissing him goodbye and praising him for his courage. Harry hugged me tightly, whispering, 'I love you, Daddy.' A few minutes later, I was on my way to the centre of Workington. Harry's therapy lasted fifty minutes, and getting back to Workington took me twelve. Every traffic jam, long red light or conversation with a stranger stole time I desperately protected.

I rolled down my window in a multi-storey car park on Central Way and pressed the button on the metal pole. The machine made a metallic screech, spitting out the ticket, then lifted the barrier. I drove inside and immediately headed to the second level, where there were always empty spaces. Moments later, I was walking towards the hotel's main entrance. I went inside like a regular guest, which in effect I was.

A girl at reception wearing a freshly ironed uniform smiled in greeting, and I smiled back. In the elevator I chose the third floor, waiting excitedly for what would happen next. I quietly entered the room, although no one could see us there. I set the alarm on my phone to avoid losing track of time, which flowed through our fingers like water.

I opened the window and the crisp air and the busy city's bustle immediately rushed in. I undressed, leaving my clothes on the bed, and went into the bathroom to shower. I turned on the water, closing my eyes to keep it from getting in, and the stream immediately began to warm my chilled body. After a moment, I jumped, feeling a cold hand on my stomach and a body pressed against my back.

'Sorry I'm late,' Lucas whispered. 'I went out to get our croissants.'

The longing was immediately saturated with our presence, and the bouquet of passionate kisses was flooded with streams of water, shedding the petals of time.

A moment later, sitting on the bed, white bathrobes barely covering our bodies, we were eating croissants. Lucas cut them open, and we exchanged halves. At one point, amused, he removed the excess chocolate accumulated in the corner of my mouth with his finger.

'Have you ever wondered what our life together will be like when all this is over?' His eyes were dreamy.

'What exactly do you mean?'

'The day we'll be together.' He perked up and smiled at me. 'You know... when I lie in bed at night, I imagine us with Harry. In the morning, he comes running to our bedroom, climbing onto the huge bed.'

'Why huge?' He'd made me laugh.

'Huge enough for us to get lost in,' he said. 'I pretend to be asleep, and as Harry crawls closer to me on all fours, I grab him and start tickling him, and he laughs out loud, then he cuddles up to us, and we all fall asleep for a while.'

'A wonderful picture.' I studied his dreamy face. 'But we'll have to wait,' I sighed.

The simultaneous sound of alarms on our phones made us ruthlessly aware of the end of our time. Over the last five months, we had worked out every meticulous detail of the intricately arranged plan, woven into life, which was only a game of appearances and waiting for the end of the spectacle.

'It's time.' Lucas leaned in and kissed me, leaving some chocolate on my lips. I wiped it with my tongue.

As we dressed, we glanced at each other, drawing our vivid portraits in memory, which we could recreate in the longing of the day and night, awaiting the next Wednesday.

I left first. As I walked out of the hotel, I exchanged smiles with the receptionist. A few minutes later, as I started the engine, I could still smell the scent of Lucas's spiced eau de toilette on my clothes.

It was only these meetings where we completely lost ourselves in each other that strengthened me for the next seven days.

I parked in front of Tracy's house, and she appeared in the doorway holding Harry's hand. I'd made it on time.

'How did it go today?' I asked as I approached them.

Harry immediately held his hands up, and when I picked him up, he snuggled into me, burying his face. I felt his warm, heavy breath on my neck. Suddenly, he raised his head and narrowed his eyes slightly, piercing me with his stare as if he was trying to find something in his memory. Something he already knew.

'I know that smell, Daddy.' His gaze lingered on me.

'Yes?' I froze.

The words coming out of his mouth made me shiver. After a while, he cuddled into me again, and I felt him draw the air gently through his nose.

'Today we touched on difficult topics, but Harry and his daddy are very brave.' Tracy winked at me.

'Thank you.' I smiled.

In the car, Harry was silent. I glanced in the mirror, watching his gaze fixed on the glass. It's amazing how similar he was to me.

When we got to his school, I crouched next to him.

'Everything OK?'

'Yes.' He hugged me.

'There are only two meetings left, and then you won't have to go there anymore.'

'I know, Daddy.'

'Run inside now. Your dad will pick you up today.'

Doubts attacked me every day. I didn't mean to hurt him by taking him away so soon. But the thought of staying in that house was unbearable.

'How did he do today?' Mum asked when I got home.

'Tracy said it was pretty good. There are still two appointments left, and I hope this is the end of his therapy. He seemed very tired today.'

'They'll leave us alone soon.' Mum's voice gave me the confidence I needed.

'Do you think they'll let go?' I took off my jacket and hung it on the hanger.

'I hope so. They're probably scared after that last adoption reversal and don't want it to happen again.'

Mum's phone rang. She answered the call, but as I turned towards the door, she motioned for me to stay and follow her into the living room. I sat next to her, listening to the conversation. I studied her face, which took on a thoughtful expression, as if she were searching for the right words, and then all I heard was that she needed to think about something.

'What's happened?'

'It was the town council. There are some issues with the new park they're making a playground for. They want me to come, but I can't leave you.' She got up and walked over to the table.

'Mum,' I laughed as she adjusted the flowers in the vase. 'I admire you for that energy. Come, sit here next to me.'

She moved the vase slightly and looked around the living room as if to see if anything else needed to be adjusted.

'Come on.' I waved my hand. She sat next to me. 'You've already helped us a lot; without you, it will be difficult, but now others need you, and you should go. I know you need it.'

'But Harry...'

'We'll manage. After all, you will visit us many more times.'

'Yeah, but I'd feel bad leaving you with all this.' She took my hand.

'Unnecessarily. Everything is going according to plan.' The words flew inattentively out of my mouth.

'According to plan?' she repeated in surprise, staring at me.

'Well, yes...' I immediately looked away. 'We don't want the director to write in her report that Harry missed or was late for therapy. Then they'd start looking at us more.'

'You're right.' She hugged me.

I always wondered why she never asked what exactly happened at the airport. I felt she was afraid to broach the subject. After my return from the hospital, I caught her long, searching looks several times, but she never said anything. I often wanted to tell her the truth, but fear held me back. Not because I didn't trust her but because I was afraid of her condemnation. I was married to Chris. We rebuilt our marriage, we adopted a child, and I wanted to run away.

‘When do you want to go, Mum?’

‘I shouldn’t stay too much longer.’

‘Don’t worry. I’ll drive you to the station, but now I have to get back to work. I have outstanding reports, and if I don’t finish them, they won’t let me work remotely anymore.’

‘Of course. Off you go.’ She pecked my cheek. ‘I’ll take care of dinner.’

I went to my office and, filled with joy that everything was going as planned, threw myself into work. As I finished another report, I glanced at my watch and dialled Chris’s number.

‘Is something wrong, Tom?’

‘No, I just wanted to make sure you remembered to pick Harry up from school today?’

‘Yes. I’m leaving right now.’ The office hum was audible through the handset.

‘I need you to do his homework with him today because I have to finish some urgent reports.’

‘Today? Can’t you put it off until tomorrow?’

At that, I stopped drawing a heart on a piece of paper, which I was shading with a pen.

‘I’ve been putting it off for a week. What do you have to do that’s more important?’

‘*Supernatural* is on tonight.’

‘You can record it and watch it when Harry goes to sleep. Spend some time with your son.’

Dissatisfied with giving up what he liked, he suppressed himself with silence. I knew it was boiling inside him, but he couldn’t say anything because that would mean admitting that he never wanted a baby. I hoped Harry never felt this. It would be a hard blow for him to know that someone didn't want him again.

Upon returning home, Harry immediately ran over to greet me. Chris appeared right behind him.

'Let Daddy do his work.' He came over and pecked my cheek.

Then I remembered Harry's words: *this monster takes various forms, sometimes even a wolf, and kidnaps people*. If only he knew that this monster existed and lived with us.

Harry kissed me once more on the cheek and left with Chris, and I got lost in my work. I didn't notice when the curtain of night covered the windows. It was after ten when Chris checked in on me.

'Aren't you coming to bed?' He came over and put his hand on my shoulder.

'I have to finish this. Management are waiting for the reports. If I screw up, they won't agree to remote work anymore.'

'You always have something that needs to be finished,' he hissed under his breath.

'It's important; I'm sorry.' I stared at the screen, my heart racing like a scared rabbit.

'I miss you.' He leaned over me.

I flinched as the air from his mouth brushed my ear.

'You have to be patient. We have a lot of responsibilities.'

If only he knew how much our lives had changed. The tension I had been living under for the last few months, guarding gestures and words. All so that he wouldn't notice. Was he as scared when he was dating Brian?

Did they have a plan? Was it just fun? My excuses were running out. I could no longer hide behind work or tiredness or fall asleep while telling Harry fairy tales.

Chris straightened up.

'I'm being sent to Glasgow for a few days in two weeks,' he said grimly. 'Can you manage on your own?'

'Sure.' I turned to him.

'I'm asking because Mum said she talked to you and wants to go home. I'll talk to my boss and reschedule this trip if necessary.'

'Don't worry about it; I'll be fine, you know that.'

'Don't stay up too long.' He didn't kiss me again before leaving.

As he shut the door, I closed my eyes and let out a relieved breath. His news was the best gift he could give me. I opened the calendar on my computer and meticulously counted the weeks. His departure was on a Friday, right after Harry's last session. In my head, the escape plan fought with the guilt of taking Harry home.

The following Wednesday, Chris started work later than usual. There was a staff meeting in the morning. I was finishing my morning wash when he came to the bathroom door.

'Something important?' he asked without taking his eyes off the bottle I was putting on the shelf.

'I don't understand.' I turned to him.

'You only use that cologne on special occasions.' He waited for my reaction.

'You're right, but they've been there so long that I decided to use them before they get stale.'

'I love them on you.' He stepped closer and inhaled the scent, touching his nose to my neck. 'They make me want to keep you here right now.' He looked deep into my eyes.

'You know Harry can't be late. They'll put it on the report.'

'I don't have the strength for this anymore,' he said irritably.

'What are you talking about?'

'Since you came back from the hospital, all I get from you is coldness. You keep avoiding me and won't let me get close to you.'

'Daddy, are we going?' Harry appeared behind Chris as if he had sensed exactly when he should come.

'Yes, honey.' I took his hand, and we walked towards the door.

'Hey, wait, where's the goodbye kiss for Dad?' Chris called after us. He walked over to Harry, leaned over him and gave him a quick peck on the cheek.

'Have a nice day, Dad.'

'And you, my son.'

Raising his head, he looked at me.

'Can't I get one from my husband?' He leaned in, waiting.

I looked at Harry. There was a question in his eyes. *What's going on, Daddy?* Quickly finding a smile, I went over to Chris and placed a kiss on his cheek.

'Have a nice day,' I whispered.

'Have a nice one too, honey. Take care of yourself.' He looked at us.

At that moment, Harry must have seen something he didn't understand yet. As we got into the car, he gave me a furtive glance. How would I explain to him what was going on? What should I say and when? I wasn't ready for that conversation yet.

I drove him to Tracy's and went to the hotel. On the way, I imagined our life together. Mornings, breakfasts and Harry, who loved Lucas like a dad.

I knocked on the door to the room this time. I heard the lock release mechanism, and soon I was greeted by Lucas's smile.

'Delivery for you, sir,' I announced with the seriousness of a courier.

'I was just waiting for it.' He opened the door wider and pulled me inside by the hand, pinning me against the wall. 'You probably need a signature.' He stared at me with hungry eyes.

'I can't leave a parcel without a signature.' I could barely hold back a laugh.

'Naturally.' He moved his lips to mine, and our feelings ran across the illuminated glade, touched by the sun's warm rays.

*

Seagulls chirped through the open window. I got out of bed to close it, but Lucas grabbed my hand.

'Stay, let them cry.'

I put my head on his shoulder.

'Lucas, we need to talk.'

'Always.' He pecked my cheek.

'Mum's going home tomorrow, and then Chris is going on a business trip to Glasgow. It's time, if you haven't changed your mind.' I looked at him uncertainly.

'You know I don't want anything else.'

I kissed him.

'I'll buy the tickets as soon as Chris leaves and email them to you so you'll know when to pick us up at the airport.'

'And Chris? He won't let you go.'

'I can handle it, but I'd rather be far away.'

The alarms on our phones rang simultaneously. The sheets were getting cold. Lucas lay on the bed in a white hotel bathrobe that slightly exposed his torso, and I glanced at him as I dressed. He smiled as he looked at me.

We exchanged hungry kisses at the door.

'Two more weeks, and we're out of here forever, right?' he asked.

'Yes.' I opened the door, and as I stepped into the corridor, I felt uncertainty mixed with excitement.

*

Dreaming the memories of only moments ago, I was doing up the last button of my shirt when there was a loud knock at the door. I was sure Tom had forgotten something and immediately ran over, gripping the doorknob vigorously.

A man I didn't recognise was standing in the corridor. He jumped as the door opened. Fear mingled with anger in his eyes.

'Lucas Espen?' he asked, narrowing his eyes slightly and tilting his head.

'Yes... and you are...?'

'Chris Anderson, Tom's husband.'

The words caught my breath, and my heart nearly leapt out of my throat. Time seemed to freeze for a moment.

'Can I come in? I'd like to talk with you,' he said calmly.

'Please.' I nervously stepped aside to make room for him. He slowly crossed the threshold, looking around. He glanced at the bed.

'Shall we sit?' I suggested, ending his insistent examination of the room.

He unbuttoned his jacket and sat down. He was silent for a moment, looking straight ahead as if the sight of me caused him pain.

'How did you meet my husband?'

'That's not what you came here for, is it?'

'You're right.' He looked around as if searching for something. 'So this is where…' he began after a moment. 'Now I understand. Those constant excuses. Falling asleep in Harry's room.'

'What exactly did you come for?'

'Do you know we've been married for almost eight years and have a son?'

'This is coming from a man who cheated on his husband right after they got married and then lied to him that I died.' I couldn't contain my anger.

'That was the easiest way to get rid of you.' His icy stare made me shiver.

'For whom? Because it's definitely not right for Tom. How can you sleep at night knowing what you've done? You watched him suffer daily, then drove him to therapy, knowing it was needed because of you. That's what you call love?'

I noticed a vein throbbing in his neck. He turned toward the window, and there was more silence as he tried to catch his breath. Once he had mastered it, he looked back at me.

'I'll tell you what we'll do. Tom will never know about our conversation, and you will disappear from our lives, but this time, forever.'

'You don't get to decide that.'

'Listen, you're still young, you can find someone quickly, but Tom has a husband and a son. Next week, you'll see Tom one last time to tell him you're leaving. How you do it, I leave to you.'

'You have to be kidding.' I shook my head.

'This is not a request. If you don't and Tom leaves me, I'll take Harry away from him, which won't be that hard considering his medical history. Do you think he will break again? And who will watch him suffer this time?'

'You are a fucking asshole!'

Chris stood up and walked over to me, bringing his face close to mine. I instinctively moved back.

'I believe you'll do it for Tom's sake.' He sneered. 'Have a nice trip home.' He turned and headed for the door.

I watched him silently. I twitched at the sound of the door slamming. I realised what a dangerous situation Tom and Harry were in. I grabbed my phone, dialling, but Tom's was turned off. He must not have made it home yet.

*

I had barely sat down at my computer to catch up on overdue reports when I heard a car in the driveway. I looked out the window. A shiver of fear ran down my spine when Chris got out. As I walked down the stairs, my fear grew. Had he found out? Or was he following me? I immediately tried to wipe the terror off my face by dressing it in friendliness.

'What's happened? Why aren't you at work?' I hid my trembling hand by grabbing the railing.

'There wasn't much to do today, so I decided to come home early.' He kissed me on the cheek. 'I'd like to take you to a certain place for lunch today.'

'For lunch?' I looked at him as if he had lost his mind.

I was surprised by his behaviour. He never initiated spending time together. I was always responsible for the planning. At first, I enjoyed it, but I gradually relieved myself of the duty. Why was it so important to him now? Maybe he had found something on my phone? No, that wasn't possible. I deleted everything. What was he up to?

'There's some sunshine today, and you've always wanted to go there.' He smiled mysteriously.

'There?'

'It's a surprise. I thought we could spend some time together. We have so little now since Harry came along. Where's Mum?' He looked into the living room.

'She went to say goodbye to Judith. She's leaving tomorrow.'

'Great, we have a moment to ourselves.' He extended his hand.

'So where are we going?' I gathered the last remnants of myself to give him my hand.

'You'll see.'

'I don't know if that's a good idea. Mum will be worried.'

'You're right; I'll call her and tell her we're leaving.'

'And Harry?' I swallowed hard.

'Harry's finishing a little later today; they have some sort of competition at school. We'll pick him up together. He will be happy.'

'I'll get changed.'

I walked up the stairs towards the bedroom. I left the door ajar so I could hear Chris if he came up. He called Mum and said we were going out to eat, and then there was silence. I wanted to text Lucas, but I saw that I hadn't turned on my phone.

'Honey, are you ready? Shall we go?'

'I'm coming!' I called.

I walked down the stairs slowly, feeling uneasy. I glanced at him, and he looked back at me. I was afraid he suspected something. I thought that if he asked directly, I would deny everything. That would be safest.

In the car, he turned on our favourite station, Heart.

'Remember when we first came here and dreamed of going on a picnic in the Lake District someday?'

'It was so long ago... Anyway, we're not prepared for that.' I looked at him indifferently.

'We are. I have everything,' he replied happily.

'Chris, a mid-week picnic? That's a little wild for you. What is this really about?'

'Tom, we've grown apart recently. We've been busy with work and responsibilities, and I'd like things to return to how they used to be.' He stroked my knee.

His touch irritated me, and I was tired of pretending. The easiest thing would be to tell him I was leaving, but I was afraid for Harry. I had to improvise.

'We have Harry now, and he fills our time.'

'Yes, but if two people love each other, they will always find a moment for each other.'

Well there you go, you can do it after all, and I have been begging for a moment's attention for so many years.

'Chris, did I forget something? Have I missed a special occasion, a date?' I looked ahead.

'No, you didn't miss anything. You don't need an occasion to be able to spend time with your husband.'

'This is not the best time to run away from our responsibilities. We should go back.' I saw him take a deep breath and let it out. 'Chris, I can see what's going on. Will you just tell me?'

'Tom, in a marriage, you should solve problems together and be able to forgive each other. I forgive you.' He swallowed hard.

'You? Forgive me?' I turned to him. 'What do you forgive me for?'

'Let's not argue.' He didn't take his eyes off the road.

'I would like to know.'

'Tom, this is not the right time for this conversation. Let's not spoil things.'

'Chris, what's the matter? Just tell me.'

He fell silent for a moment. I felt he was holding back from saying something.

'Tom, we both know you're meeting that man from the airport.'

His tone cut deep into me like a knife to my throat.

'How can I be meeting up with someone who's dead?' I tried to keep my cool.

'Stop!' he yelled.

His face pulsed with anger. He took several deep breaths.

'I'm sorry, I got carried away. Tom, I know it's my fault, so I'm trying not to get mad, but it's very tough.'

I turned my head towards the window.

'We can forgive each other and forget about it. That's what happens in a marriage. You did it for me. Now I'm ready to do the same for you.'

'Excuse me? You built my return to you on another lie. Do you realise what you've done? You tricked me again, and now you're talking about forgiveness? How could you do this to me? Stop the car immediately! We're not going anywhere!'

'I did it for us!' he screamed, fury burning in his eyes.

'For us? What us? We are long gone!'

'We are not!' he shouted, staring at me.

Nervously, I looked back at the road and saw a tractor pulling out of the woods, completely oblivious to us.

'Chris, stop!' I shouted.

Chris hit the brakes, struggling with the steering wheel, but it was too late. Time slowed as we hit the tractor. The metallic sound of crushing sheet metal surrounded us tightly. I squeezed my eyes shut as the windshield shattered into thousands of tiny pieces that slid over me, slicing through my skin like blades. Then there was just the tug of the hands of darkness and silence. Blissfully soothing, cradling me in her arms. I surrendered to her as she hummed her song to me.

6. Loss

Tom had been in a coma for a month, and I couldn't properly answer Harry's constant questions. When will Daddy wake up? When will he come home? I was overwhelmed by everyday life, and even though my mother helped me, I still felt tired. How did Tom manage it? I would fall onto the bed after a whole, full day, and even then, I couldn't rest because Harry wanted me to read him a bedtime story.

Twice a week, we went to the hospital together. He watched out for those days and never missed one. He would wait ready in the hall on a chair, and when I came in, he would look up at me the way Tom used to.

'Shall we go?' I asked one day. 'And what is that?' I pointed to the book he was holding.

'I'm going to read to Daddy. Maybe when he hears me, he'll wake up.'

'Surely.' I hugged him.

He was silent in the car. Leaning his head against the window, he stared dully at the streets and houses we passed.

'What's on your mind?'

'Hope,' he sighed.

'Hope?'

'Daddy taught me that whenever bad things happen, I must never lose hope.'

'He was right, my son.'

‘But it’s so hard when he doesn’t move.’ His eyes glazed over, and he quickly turned towards the window.

‘I know, but Daddy will come back to us soon, you’ll see, and it will be just like before.’

Harry would run to the bed in the hospital room, kiss Tom on the cheek and cuddle up to his hand. Then he would stare at his face for a long moment, hoping for movement. I often watched with him, but Tom never so much as twitched.

‘Won’t you say hello?’ He looked at me in surprise as I sat down in the chair. I felt stupid to be reminded of this and got back up. Tom’s pale face was lightly illuminated by the rays of the sun coming through the window, and the beeping of the machine monitoring his vital processes indicated that he was still breathing. I kissed him gently on the lips. They were warm but completely lifeless. I stroked his hair and went back to the chair. Harry took out the book and moved closer to Tom. He grabbed his daddy’s hand with one hand and opened the book with the other.

This was how our hours passed every Tuesday and Thursday. My mother joined us on the weekends. It was hard for her. She couldn’t control her tears every time she entered the room.

‘Don’t cry, Grandma.’ Harry hugged her. ‘Daddy is just resting and will wake up soon.’

Each visit, Harry enthusiastically told his daddy about school, his friends and the trips he was about to go on. Mum would wipe Tom’s face with a damp handkerchief, telling him about Judith and people from work asking her about his health. At the end, I went to Tom. I would hold his hand, trying desperately to shake off the guilt. Nothing bad would have happened if it wasn’t for that conversation in the car.

The nurse told me that Tracy was visiting Tom. However, she preferred to do it alone, never with us. Maybe she was talking to him about things they only discussed in therapy.

We would return when the light started to fade and Harry, exhausted, fell asleep beside Daddy. I took him in my arms and, kissing Tom goodbye, we left.

At home, Harry would be sad that he had failed to wake up his daddy yet again and would shut himself in his room. I would go to him, but he wouldn't answer when I knocked. I would slowly open the door and see him standing motionless by the window, staring at the tree.

'I've often wondered what Daddy sees in that tree,' I said one day as I stood beside him. 'Now that you're looking at it too, I feel like I'm losing you.' Harry slipped his hand into mine, looking up.

'Dad, I'm here; the branches calm me down. I feel my daddy hugging me.'

'I only see a tree, nothing else.'

'It's nothing, Dad.' He hugged me, and we stayed like that for a while longer.

The following weekend, Harry went on a school trip. At first, he didn't want to, but I promised to call him immediately if Daddy woke up. Mum and I drove him to the bus. He was so excited about this trip that he kept waving long after the bus had started up. Mum blew kisses with her hand, and I didn't stop waving back. When he disappeared around the corner, we drove to Tom. The doctor entered the room shortly after we sat down at his bedside.

'I have good news,' he announced softly from the doorway.

'Yes?' We got up and went to him.

'The test results are perfect. The nurse said she saw Tom move his hand yesterday evening while she was on duty.'

Mum covered her mouth with her hand.

'That's great news.' I shook his hand.

*

I was not aware of the images haunting me. My mind created them, distracting me from my limp body. As the doors of consciousness began to let light through and intense sounds vied to enter my head, the pain gripping my hands began to tighten them. There was someone in the room, but I could barely hear the hushed conversations in another language filtering through to me.

I tried to lift my eyelids, which seemed to weigh kilos. The image was blurry. I squeezed my eyes shut and opened them again, and then the surroundings began to come into focus. I clumsily moved my hand, and pain spread through my body as if someone had touched me with electricity. After a while, the indistinct spots began to take on clearer shapes. I was lying in a bed, next to which stood some people talking in low voices. I recognised the language but couldn't remember a word of English when I opened my mouth.

'Where am I?' I stammered in Polish.

They flinched and looked in my direction, but the doctor stopped them from moving towards me with his outstretched hand. Fear mingled with joy in their faces.

'My goodness!' the woman screamed, and burst into tears, and the man standing next to her began gasping for air in nervous, short intervals like a fish.

The doctor approached me.

‘Tom, you’re in the hospital; you had an accident. Do you understand what I’m saying?’

‘Yes...’

‘How do you feel now?’

English words hugged Polish ones, replacing them.

‘I don’t know...’ Through the dryness in my throat, I could barely draw the words.

The doctor reached for a small plastic bottle on the bedside table and poured water into a glass. He brought it to my lips, holding my head lightly, and the water moistened my throat.

‘How long have I been here?’

‘You’ve been with us for almost a month.’

‘What?’ I felt like I had drunk too much the night before and couldn’t remember what had happened. I’d lost a month? Horror lifted the hairs on my arms, and a cold breath swept down my back.

‘You just slept through it. Your body needed it.’

The doctor examined me. He took my temperature and blood pressure, meticulously recording everything on my hospital card. I ran my gaze over the room, and the woman holding the hand of a man with blond hair, his terrified blue eyes fixed on me.

‘He might be a little confused.’ The doctor turned to the woman. ‘Please give him some time. Don’t flood him with information. Slowly.’

‘I was so scared.’ The man walked over, placing his hand on mine. Feeling pain, I drew it back immediately.

‘I’m sorry, I’m so sorry, it’s my fault,’ he added in a shaky voice.

I stared blankly at his mouth as it flooded me with words. 'Did you cause the accident?'

The man glanced nervously at the woman, who immediately opened her mouth wide but only sucked in air. They stared at me in confusion.

'What's going on?' I looked at the doctor.

'Honey...' The woman came over. 'This is Chris, your husband.' She smiled as if I had made some not-very-witty joke.

'Husband? And who are you?'

I almost expected her to burst out laughing and say she was having me on, but there was fear building in her eyes.

'I'm Chris's mother, your mother-in-law. You remember me, right?'

I held my left hand up to see if I had a ring. There wasn't one.

'You're not wearing it,' the man said quickly. 'You keep it in the nightstand drawer with a picture of our son, Harry.'

His words began to echo in my head. What the hell was he talking about? Why were they doing this to me? What son! I frantically searched my mind for images that would confirm the existence of a husband and child, but instead, I came across a black patch that completely covered everything. Why were they trying to tell me a different reality?

After a moment, the woman strode briskly out of the room.

The pale man turned to the doctor. 'You said the tests were excellent.'

'Tom had a head injury and was in a coma, which can sometimes cause disorientation and memory loss. It is a natural defence of the body.'

'Natural? He...'

The doctor approached me.

'Tom, I know you might feel strange right now, but that should subside soon. Do you remember anything about the accident?'

'I remember… a bang… and… I don't know…'

'Do you remember this lady?' He pointed to the woman, who had just returned, crying.

'I don't know her,' I whispered in panic, avoiding her gaze.

The doctor took a pen-sized flashlight from his pocket and turned it on.

'Don't be afraid. I'm just going to test your reactions to stimuli.'

He held my eyelid with two fingers, then did the same with the other. The harsh light stung me with thousands of tiny needles. I couldn't help but blink.

'The reactions are correct.' The doctor turned to them. 'Tom needs to rest now. I'd like you to come to my office.'

The man took a step towards me but immediately stopped. The woman was so terrified she couldn't utter a word. That was weird. They looked at me as if they knew me, but they were strangers.

After they left, I closed my eyes, hoping that when I opened them again, the dream that had trapped me would release me. It did not work. I was still there. I looked around the room. There was a phone on the dresser. I reached for it, but my hand trembled, and I had to wait a moment before trying again. Once I had it in my hand, I found the folder with photos, and in the first one, I saw a child cuddling up to me. It was impossible; it must be some kind of photomontage. However, the boy appeared in almost all the photos, including ones with this strange woman. She held his hand, but none of the pictures showed her son, who the woman said was my husband. If he was, why wasn't he in the photos? Were they tricking me?

After a while, the doctor came back.

'How are you feeling, Tom? Do you need anything?'

'Doctor.' I grabbed his arm tightly. 'There's something wrong with me. I don't know who I am. I remember only the sound of the impact and nothing else. Please help me. I don't know what's going on.'

'Tom, take it easy.' The doctor freed his hand. 'You've just come back to us. Sometimes the mind hides memories from us to protect them. I hope it's temporary and your memory will start to come back soon. Until then, we'll keep you here.'

'I don't think I would know where to go anyway. I don't even know where I live.' I felt tears welling up in my eyes.

'Tom, do you remember your therapist, Tracy?' The doctor kept his eyes on me.

'I don't think so.'

'You went to her for therapy. She's going to visit you tomorrow. When you talk with her, maybe you'll remember something.' He sat down in the chair next to me.

'And these people? This woman and this man? They caused the accident, right?'

'Tom, I understand this may be difficult for you, but that was your husband and mother-in-law. They're worried about you.'

'I'm so afraid. Please help me.'

'I will do everything in my power.' He got up from the chair and moved to the edge of the bed. 'That's why I'd like you to talk to your therapist tomorrow. After that, we will decide what to do next.'

That night and the nights after I had the same dream. A man with a blurred face was calling my name. He held out his hand, which I couldn't grab. I ran to him, but he was walking away, very fast. I woke up, gasping for air, and fell asleep again.

A knock woke me up that first morning. I moved higher on the pillow. The door opened slowly, and a woman in a navy-blue dress and flat shoes stepped in. It was hard to judge her age, but her warm smile seemed to ease any hardships that might have befallen her. She looked around the room calmly, then turned back to me.

I felt my whole body relax. She was no more than fifty years old. But then, filled with tension again, I ran my eyes over her, to no avail. There was nothing familiar about her.

'Good morning, Tom.'

'Good morning.' I looked at her uncertainly, trying to remember.

'Do you remember me?' She sat down in the chair next to me.

Then I noticed her necklace – a silver pendant with green eyes. I felt pressure in my head, as if someone had stuck a pin in it. I grabbed on to it, and images, like a jigsaw puzzle, immediately began rushing into place. The room where the clock kept the time. The chocolate sofa I was sitting on and the big window that overlooked the street...

'Tom? What's going on?' She got up. 'I'm going to call the doctor.'

'Tracy, wait.'

She froze.

'I remember you.'

'What do you remember?' She moved her chair closer to me.

'We met in your office. I remember every detail exactly. The study with the big window overlooking the street, the chocolate sofa and the clock that kept the time.'

'That's a lot.' She smiled. 'And do you remember why we met?'

'I don't think so.'

'It doesn't matter. Everything in its own time.'

'Tracy, I'm scared. I have a husband, a mother-in-law and a son. A family I don't remember. I don't even know who I am. I feel so powerless.'

'Let your mind decide when it will show you more memories. Don't fight it, and it will open up for you.'

'I feel like there is something else everyone is deliberately avoiding.' I watched her face.

'Tom, not all at once. Small steps. I would like the first one to be a conversation with your mother-in-law. You two were very close. Maybe that will be a good start, and you will remember something?'

Sue arrived the next morning. She opened the door, and I saw her hair was as white as milk. Without taking her eyes off me, she entered the room, carrying a bag from which a sizeable photo album protruded.

'Good morning, Tom.' She walked over uncertainly. 'How are you feeling?'

'Terrible. It's like I've taken someone else's place, and everyone around me expects me to be like the previous person.'

'I brought pictures. Tracy said it might help. Shall we look at them together?'

'Yes, let's try.'

She moved her chair closer and opened the album to the first page, watching me intently.

Flipping through the pages, she told me about the highlights of our life together, how she met me, our secrets, Harry and my work and the people who called her asking about my health. In truth, I couldn't keep up with her words. I found it hard to comprehend how those moments recorded in her album could belong to me.

'Were we happily married?' I looked at her from the corner of my eye as she showed me a wedding photo.

'You had your ups and downs, as is often the case in marriages, but after the incident in Amsterdam, a lot has changed.' She lowered her gaze.

'Amsterdam?'

'You went with Harry because he wanted to ride a boat through the canals. Chris didn't want you to go, and you argued. You only went with Harry.'

'Why didn't he want to go?'

'He was afraid for you.' She lowered her eyes again.

'Why was he afraid?'

'I'm worried about Harry,' she began after a moment. 'He loves you very much and misses you. Every day he watches out the window, waiting for a car to pull up, looking for you in it. I'm afraid of how he'll react when he finds out you don't remember him. We're keeping it from him.'

She stooped down to her bag and took out a handkerchief, in which she collected her tears.

'I'm sorry. There's so much to take in; I feel overwhelmed. I'm letting everyone down. I wish I could remember all these things, but they are... sort of not mine.'

'Tom, maybe this is too much for today. You probably need some time alone to collect your thoughts. I'll go now.'

At that moment, there was a knock on the door.

Tracy looked in. 'Am I disturbing you?'

'No, come in.' Sue nodded. 'I was just getting ready to leave.'

They exchanged hugs, then my mother-in-law came closer to me.

'Can I give you a hug goodbye?'

'Of course.'

She held the hug for a long moment. I smelled her lily perfume. I seemed to know the smell. Sue straightened up and quickly wiped a tear from her cheek. She grabbed her photo album and bag and left the room. Tracy gave me a friendly smile and grabbed a chair.

'How did that go?' She slung her bag over the backrest.

'She showed me the photos. It was strange to see myself in them.'

'I understand. This is where you need time or some stimulus to trigger your mind to find the memories. Maybe next time it will work.'

'Tracy?'

'Yes?'

'How did the accident occur? What happened?'

'You and Chris went to lunch. Some guy drove out of the woods unexpectedly and you collided with him.'

'What happened to him?'

'He only had minor injuries.'

From then on, Tracy came every day. We had conversations about my life, marriage and Harry. I felt lost, as if I was being prepared for a new role I had to play.

A few days later, Sue returned. She came with Tracy. She was very tense. She said hello and immediately sat in the chair, hiding her trembling hands behind the purse on her lap. Tracy tried to distract me by asking how

I was and if I needed anything. It sounded like Sue was taking an exam. Her additions to the conversation were short, single sentences or simple nods. At some point, a nurse entered the room carrying a tray with a small cup of medicine and a glass of water. Sue and Tracy exchanged a knowing glance, and then Sue walked over to the nurse, who handed her the medication. She came back to me and held out the cup of pills. Her hands were shaking again. The cup slipped, and the tablets rolled over the sheets. Images like puzzles took their place in my memory. I saw a room, a glass of water and Sue coming in. The pills in my hand... She took them out slowly, and they fell to the carpet. She then said, Have you thought about me? I need you. She cried, and I cried with her.

'Mum...' My voice shook, and tears began to distort the image.

She grabbed me in her arms, and we cried together, just like when she came to save me.

'You remember me, don't you?' She held my head in her hands. 'Do you remember?' She kept hugging me.

'I remember you, Mum.' I buried my head in her arms.

'And Chris and Harry?'

'Sue, take it slow,' Tracy said. 'Not all at once.'

I lifted my head and looked into her eyes.

'I remember you have a son, but I don't remember my relationship with him. I can't find any memories of the baby either.'

'The important thing is that you already remember something,' Tracy said. 'It's a big step.'

*

Our daily therapy revealed a forgotten world that had pushed me out of myself. I didn't recognise anything but wanted to remember as much as possible. We talked a lot about Chris, and I felt we were getting closer to his visit.

The day he arrived, the rain played a tune on the windowsill, and its drops danced on the glass. I pushed myself up in bed as Chris entered the room, soaking wet but smiling.

'How do you feel?'

'Aside from the lack of memory, pretty good.' I laughed, and Chris joined me after a moment, although with some hesitation. He looked at me with a nervous smile.

'I have some questions, if you don't mind.' I kept my eyes on him.

'Sure.' He squeezed his hands tighter.

'Will you tell me how we met?' I corrected my position on the pillow.

'I wrote to you on the portal. After a few days of silence, I was convinced you wouldn't write back, but then I found your message and I was so happy. I felt special. You used to live in Poland.'

'In Warsaw, right?'

'Do you remember that?' An apprehensive hope opened his eyes wider.

'Yes. Some memories came back yesterday. And what happened next?'

'We started talking every day, and after half a year, you came to me. Then we drove to each other, taking turns, and I proposed to you. We married, and you came to live with me in England.'

'Was our marriage happy?'

He was silent and looked at the floor.

'We had difficult moments... but we survived it and were happy. We adopted Harry, which brought us even closer together. Then the accident happened, and I thought I had lost you forever. Tracy explained your situation to us, and I know there's a lot you don't understand right now, but I'm going to help you. I love you so much.'

He cried and moved closer, resting his head on my legs. I sat motionless, and then for some unknown reason, I stroked his hair, and he closed his eyes.

The next day, in therapy, Tracy asked about our meeting. I told her what we had discussed, and she said it was a good start.

'How do you feel about all this information?'

'How am I feeling? It's like someone has pushed me into someone else's life, and everyone around me expects me to be an exact copy of that person. I'm afraid I might not be like that.'

'Take your time. Don't force anything. You can't fool the mind.'

*

A month passed. The nights visited earlier, and the birds, unaccustomed to the darkness, sang in it for a long time. However, they fell asleep in the morning because dawn woke up a little later.

On one of those grey mornings, a doctor came to see me. He sat on the edge of the bed and smiled warmly.

'Tom, we have performed a series of tests and we don't see any brain damage. Your vitals are as they should be. We have no reason to keep you here any longer. You should go home and get back to a normal life, and hopefully, your memory will return.'

'Is there anything I should do?'

'What do you mean?'

'Anything that will bring back my memories.'

'When you get home, the stimuli can come very quickly. Some of them will not evoke any emotions in you, while others will help you remember things. Browse through old photos, videos, but don't try to watch everything at once. Small portions. Don't avoid meeting people you've had contact with before. Interacting with them can be helpful and can get you back into a routine. The same shop, the same saleswoman, the bank, the post office can help you a lot. You should try to live a normal life, if I may call it that. You will find my recommendations in the documents.'

The day my mum and Chris came to pick me up, I watched the wind-blown tree in front of my window, and questions jostled through my head. Where would I live? Would I have a separate room? Would Chris insist that I live with him? What about Harry? What would I tell him? How should I behave? Pretend not to notice? Questions jostled through my mind, making me uneasy.

'Hello, darling.' Mum came into the room, followed by Chris pushing a wheelchair. 'Ready?' She kissed me. 'Chris, help Tom.' She motioned with her hand.

He offered his arm so I could grab it and transfer myself to the wheelchair.

'Thank you.' I heard the nervousness rising in my voice.

In the hall, we were stopped by a nurse who gave Chris some papers to sign. He scribbled a few signatures, and we headed to the parking lot. When he opened the car door, I could barely breathe.

'Wait!' I called out.

'What's going on?' Chris looked at me intently.

'Can we wait?'

'Sure.' He exchanged glances with his mother.

'Honey, what's going on?' Mum crouched down by the wheelchair.

'I can hear the sound of breaking glass in my head, and this horrible banging.'

'Tom, you're safe; nothing bad will happen.' She took my hand. 'Wait a minute,' she said to Chris.

'Maybe we should go back for the doctor?' Chris stepped back.

'Let's wait.' Mum's voice was warm and gentle.

I remembered what Tracy said about breathing in stressful situations. I closed my eyes and took a deep breath, letting it out slowly. I repeated it several times, then got into the car.

Our drive home was in silence. Out of the corner of my eye, I saw Chris and Mum glancing at me in the mirror now and then. I leaned my head against the glass and scanned the passing landscapes. What if my memory didn't return and I was trapped with people in a world I didn't know? With a child I could feel nothing for? I pushed those thoughts away with all my might.

'Mum? Do I have any clothes at home?'

She turned to me. 'Of course, honey. What do you need?'

'I'd like to take a shower and change.'

'All right.' She stroked my hand.

Chris helped me out of the car when we got to the house. A seagull flew above us, making a loud squawk. I shuddered and lifted my head.

'Seagull... This has happened before...' I whispered.

'Yes, it was the day we saw this house for the first time. Do you remember?' Chris looked at me as if he expected images from the past to creep into place immediately.

'I don't remember the house, but I remember that I got out in front of this gate, and then there was that sound.'

'Tom, that means your memory is starting to come back.' Mum hugged me tight.

'Careful. You'll knock him over.' Chris laughed.

He took my arm and, with great care, helped me back into the wheelchair, then steered it towards the main entrance. I looked around as we went. Everything was alien, and it scared me that I would be stuck here forever, not knowing who I was.

A woman was standing in the neighbouring garden, observing us. Mum noticed her, too, and exchanged a wave.

'Who is that?' I asked.

'That's Judith. Your neighbour,' my mother replied. 'I asked her to leave us alone for now. Otherwise, it would tire you out.'

I nodded. There must have been many people in my life whose faces I couldn't even imagine. *Slowly*, I told myself. I closed my eyes and took another breath.

Mum had decided I would use the guest-room until the cast was removed and rehabilitation was completed. She was right. I couldn't climb those narrow stairs with a cast on my leg.

Chris stopped the wheelchair in front of the bedroom door, and when he opened it, the light from the window fell directly on my face. I felt a sudden stabbing in my head. I closed my eyes, grimacing, and more images began to appear before my eyes.

'I've lived in this room before.' I looked around. 'But it was different.'

Chris glanced nervously at his mother.

'Yes, darling,' Mum replied quickly. 'You were very sick then.'

'Sick?'

'You were depressed, but that was so long ago that it's not worth going back to.'

I saw in their eyes that they were hiding something from me.

'We'll leave you. Rest.' Mum put her hand on my shoulder.

After they left, I sat on the bed and scanned every inch of the room. The wall straight ahead conjured up memories of a chest of drawers that wasn't there now. There was a dried flower on it. By the door were stacks of newspapers that had once blocked my way. Why did I remember such details but not the house or the child? I didn't remember my own family. What kind of disgusting person must I be that my mind had repressed that? What did this child do to me that I was punishing him like this?

A knock on the door distracted my thoughts.

'Tom?' Mum stood there. 'I'll ask Chris to help you in the bathroom.'

'Mum, that's a bit embarrassing.' I winced. 'I'll do it myself.'

'I understand.'

'I'll let you know if I need anything.'

'All right.'

'Where is Harry?'

'Harry is sleeping at Judith's tonight. Tracy asked for your meeting to be held a little later. There's so much going on that we shouldn't rush things. But he's ready. He knows you don't remember him.'

'How did he take it?'

'He cried all night. This is very tough for him.'

I hugged her, and we were silent. I could feel her restless breath on my shoulder. I looked at the mirror on the wall and saw my reflection. I was being stared at by a terrified man who did not know his husband or son, and the house where he lived was a stranger to him.

Mum kissed me on the cheek and headed for the door. I watched her go. I looked at the man in the mirror again, trying to find something in him that would rekindle hope.

That night, I had the same dream that had haunted me since the accident. A man with a blurred face reached out to me and called my name. I ran to him, but his voice faded away with every step he took.

I woke up in a cold sweat. I sat awkwardly on the bed, barely moving my leg in the cast. Just then, I heard the rustle of gravel outside the window. I twitched. Someone was walking under my window. I wanted to get up and walk as fast as I could to chase away the intruder, but the plaster made it difficult. I slid off the bed and limped to the window, discreetly drawing back the curtain. In the light of the lantern, I saw the little boy from the pictures I had looked at on my phone. He was shivering from the cold. He had a jacket thrown over his pyjamas and was trying to peer through my window. I hid for a while. Filled with fear, I tried to force my mind to find some memories. Yet it was still empty. I leaned out further from behind the curtain, and when the boy saw me, he jumped away in fright. In his eyes, I saw a painful longing. I opened the window.

'What are you doing out there at this hour?' I looked around to see if anyone was with him.

'I wanted to see you, Daddy,' he cried.

His words touched me with remorse. I began to feed on the hope that I would remember something and discover hidden images in my head, but nothing changed.

'Don't cry. Come on, jump in before you get sick.' I extended my hand to him.

He walked timidly to the window and held out his cold little hand, and I gripped it tightly and helped him into the room. Questions jostled in my head. Who was taking care of this child if he could wander alone at night? Was Chris really capable of being a good parent?

'Daddy, what about your leg?' Harry pointed at it.

'It's just broken; it'll heal soon.'

'Does it hurt?' He touched the plaster carefully.

'A little bit. You must have been cold. Who walks around the garden at night in pyjamas and a jacket? Take it off, get in bed, and I'll make you some hot cocoa. You like cocoa, don't you?'

His face was filled with undisguised surprise.

'You always make it for me when I feel bad,' he whispered.

'Really?' The words he had so confidently uttered touched me. 'I'll get some for you now.'

I went to the kitchen without turning on the lights. I thought about how much courage he must have had to sneak out at night regardless of the danger. He must have loved me very much. What a father I was. What kind of relationship had we built with Harry, and what role did Chris play in that? I wanted so badly to feel like a parent if only to see a smile on that boy's tear-stained face. Harry, Harry, Harry, Harry. Repeating his name in my mind, I hoped it would awaken something in me, but my heart didn't even flinch.

I walked on the carpet barefoot, awkwardly dragging the one in a plaster cast behind the first. I entered the living room. A vase with artificial flowers stood in the corner. I paused momentarily, and my mind began to recognise these flowers. I picked them up at Dunelm. I couldn't find the right colour and chose these white lilies. I was here. I'd been here before.

In the kitchen, I turned on the light and was opening the cabinets one by one in search of a cup when, out of the corner of my eye, I saw my mother standing in the doorway.

'Do you need something?' she asked in a sleepy voice.

'A mug. I wanted hot cocoa.'

'Cocoa?' She was surprised. 'You used to make it for Harry.'

'I just feel like it.' I looked away.

'I'll help you.' She walked over to the middle cupboard and confidently took out a mug. Then she reached for a small saucepan, put it on the gas stove and poured milk into it. When it was hot, she measured two tablespoons of cocoa into the mug, poured the milk in and stirred it.

'Are you hungry?' She looked at me as she handed me the drink.

'No, that's quite enough. Let's go to bed; it's very late.'

I waited in the hall until Mum had disappeared up the stairs, then limped to my room.

'We almost got caught,' I whispered, handing Harry the cocoa.

He smiled slightly, as if enjoying the secret. He greedily drank the cocoa, a trail of brown liquid drawing a crescent above his upper lip.

'Slower. It's hot,' I laughed.

When he was done, he put the mug on the cabinet and moved very close, never taking his eyes off me.

'My daddy is in there somewhere,' he said, as if he saw him in me.

I felt a shiver. What had they said to him? Was it the truth or only part of it? Or maybe something more?

'I've got something for you, Daddy.' He reached under his pyjamas and clumsily pulled out a slightly crumpled piece of paper, folded in four. He offered it to me.

I carefully unfolded the paper and saw a drawing of a boy holding a man's hand. Suddenly, I felt a twinge in my head, and several bright lights flashed. Harry handing me this drawing in an empty room. I clutched my head as if I was afraid that all the images would fall out of it.

'Daddy, do you feel bad?'

I felt his warmth as he clung to me, our hearts beating like scared rabbits.

After a while, everything stopped. I could look at the memories stacked on the shelves, though some were still empty. The hope of regaining my lost life had just knocked on my door, followed by the thought that Chris really was my husband. I looked at Harry.

'Who put you in those disgusting pyjamas? Where's Spider-Man?' A smile spread across my face.

'Daddy! I knew you were there.' He threw himself into my arms, and I couldn't stop hugging and kissing him.

*

Three months later, I was leaving the garage and heading towards the gate when I saw Chris running after me in the mirror. He was calling something, but I couldn't hear him over the radio. I stopped and rolled down the window.

'What's happened?'

'Honey, you left your wallet in the hall. How are you going to shop?' He leaned in and pecked me on the lips.

'Thank you.'

'Maybe I should go with you?'

'Help Harry with the herbarium. You know all these weeds better than I do, and I'll get Harry some new trousers and a T-shirt. He grows out of everything so quickly. Unless you'd like to pick something up for him?' I tilted my head in a half-smile.

'I'll take care of the herbarium.' He leaned in and kissed me again. 'Drive carefully and call me when you get there.'

'Sure.'

Chris opened the gate, and I drove out onto the road. I smiled as I saw him waving at me in the mirror, his figure shrinking and disappearing around the corner.

My memories of Chris hadn't returned, so I was learning to get to know him again. At home, I would find small pieces of paper that he attached to various things, writing on them the dates and circumstances in which a given object ended up in our house. Once when I reached for my pyjamas, a note fell out: *I bought them for you because you were always cold. I love you, your Chris*. I pressed my pyjamas to my face to smell them and hoped that I might remember something, but I didn't.

On reaching Workington, I parked on the garage's second level and headed towards Debenhams. I called Chris, who answered right away.

'I've arrived. Now I'm entering the land of childish madness.'

Chris laughed.

'If you want me to come...'

‘Kiss Harry for me. See you in an hour!’ I ended the call.

I went from rack to rack, looking for something Harry would like. I had just picked up a blue sailboat T-shirt and was imagining what Harry would look like in it when out of the corner of my eye, I saw a man watching me in the distance. At first, I thought it was just me, but when I caught his eye again, I was sure he was staring at me. I hung up the T-shirt and looked in that direction again, but he was gone. Half an hour later, I finished shopping and headed to the exit with my bags. I opened the trunk in the parking lot and put the groceries inside.

‘Tom?’ I jumped when I heard my name behind me and turned around. There was a man with jet-black hair. He had fear in his large auburn eyes.

‘Excuse me, do we know each other?’ I took a step back.

‘Yes.’

‘You were the one at the store.’ I put my hand in my coat pocket and grabbed my car keys. I looked around for cameras.

‘We need to talk. Tom, your husband is hiding the truth about that day you had an accident.’

‘I know who you are.’ I nodded.

‘Yes?’ His eyebrows rose in surprise.

‘My husband warned me about you. You caused this accident. You were drunk.’

‘Did he tell you that?’ His eyes widened. ‘I’m not surprised at all. It’s his style.’

‘What do you want from me?’

‘Tom, it’s me, Lucas. You had an accident and lost your memory. I know everything. I’d just like to talk, but… this is not the best place.’

‘You are scaring me.’

‘No, wait. You don’t have to be afraid of me. Let me show you something.’ He took out his wallet and slid out a photo. ‘This is us when you came to Amsterdam. You must have the same one.’

I couldn’t stop looking at it. The strange man in it was pressing his face to mine.

‘Tom, I don’t want to hurt you. Your husband has taken care to erase me from your life, but I will prove I am telling the truth. It would be best if you found the letters I wrote to you. You hid them from him. Find them, and you will understand that I am telling the truth. Here’s my number.’ He handed me a piece of paper. ‘If you’d like to talk, I’m staying at the Washington Central Hotel.’

He looked around nervously and left. I stood staring at the white sheet of paper for a long time. I was trying to understand what had just happened.

On the way back, his words kept ringing in my head: *Your husband is hiding the truth… It was us when you came to Amsterdam… The letters… You hid them from him.*

When I entered the house, Chris appeared in the hall, immediately followed by Harry.

‘Daddy, what did you buy me?’ Harry threw himself at the bags.

‘Patience, darling.’ I leaned in and kissed his cheek.

‘Everything all right? You’re kind of pale.’ Chris took my coat.

‘I’m a bit tired. You know how hard it is to find anything.’

‘I know.’ He hugged me. ‘Thank you.’

‘Unpack the shopping together, and I’ll lie down for a while.’

‘Go upstairs, rest, and we’ll take care of everything here.’

I started up the stairs towards the bedroom, Lucas's words still ringing in my head: *letters, you hid them from him*. I opened the door to the bedroom and looked around. Where could I have hidden them? I opened the wardrobe and ran my hand along its walls. I looked deep into the shelves, but my search was fruitless. I went to bed with some relief. Could this be the madman Chris had talked about after all? At the same time, some strong feeling kept me thinking about today's meeting. There was something in the man's face and his voice...

When Chris left for work the next day, I began to search the other rooms. I opened shelves and wardrobes, looked in the utility room and checked the garage. There were no letters anywhere. I sat in the office.

I glanced at our bookcase, and my attention was caught by an inconspicuous book, slightly protruding compared to the others. I reached for it. A guide to England that I had bought as soon as I got here. I started to turn the pages, but I noticed nothing special besides pictures and descriptions of famous places. I was looking at the maps at the back when I saw a large red dot drawn with a felt-tip pen by the Washington Central Hotel, Workington. My heart sped up, and I felt weak. I sat on the bed. I put off calling the number Lucas had left me for a long time, but questions about my life before the accident haunted me.

'Tom?' I heard the surprise in his voice.

'I haven't found the letters, but I found something else. Meet me. I will come to the hotel.'

I went into the hall and nervously grabbed my jacket and car keys.

'Are you leaving?' I heard my mother's voice behind me.

'Yes. I forgot to visit the ophthalmologist. I feel like my eyesight has deteriorated recently. Maybe it's just overwork, but I'd rather get it checked out.'

'Sure. You are absolutely right. It needs to be checked out.'

Escaping my mother's gaze, I kissed her on the cheek and hurried out of the house.

On the way to the hotel, I felt very stressed and made several U-turns. However, the desire to learn about my past was so strong that I always ended up back on course.

'Welcome back, Mr Anderson,' the receptionist said, greeting me as if I was a regular guest. I hesitantly approached her.

'Good morning. I have an appointment with Lucas Espen,' I said, lowering my voice. The girl was initially confused, but after a while, she looked at the computer and gave me the floor number.

'Excuse me, which way to the elevator?'

She looked at me cautiously and tentatively reached out to point me in the right direction.

I went up to the third floor. I looked at the room numbers as I walked down the hall. At thirty, I stopped. I raised my hand to knock but hesitated. *What am I doing here? This is madness.* I'd just started putting my life back together. Who was this man anyway? Why would he know more about me than Chris or Mum? I was about to leave, but then the door opened.

'You have come. Come in.' He stepped back, allowing me to enter. Hesitantly, I stepped inside and headed for the armchair at the window. Passing the bed, I noticed an open suitcase that was almost packed.

'Are you leaving?' I kept my gaze on it.

‘I have to get back to work. They need me. Will you sit down?’ He pointed to the chair. ‘You don’t have to worry about me.’ He sat on the bed.

‘That’s what murderers usually say to their victims.’ I laughed nervously and took a seat.

‘I’m not a murderer, Tom.’ His tone was serious.

‘Then who?’ Our eyes met. ‘How do you know me?’

‘We met at the airport… actually, on the plane. I took your seat.’ He smiled. ‘You were coming back from Warsaw, from work…’

As he told me about our meeting, his face took on many shades of joy, and the hope in his eyes, waving at me like a child in the street, terrified me. He knew so much about me. From where? Where could he find this information?

‘Your husband knew, Tom.’

‘What did he know?’

‘Chris showed up here that day, after you left. He threatened to take Harry away from you if we didn’t break up. I called you, but you didn’t answer, and after a few days of silence, I knew something was up. I hired a detective to find you.’

‘Chris knew we were together?’

‘Yes, Tom. On the same day you had an accident.’

‘Where did we meet?’

‘Here.’ He gestured around us. ‘In this room.’

I looked him over slowly, but everything was alien.

‘I didn’t find the letters, but I found this.’ I took the guidebook out of my jacket and handed it to him. ‘This hotel is marked with a felt-tip pen.’

'You didn't have time to give it to me,' he laughed. 'I beat you and got here first.' His face radiated pure joy. 'Tom, I think you must have hidden the letters in a place Chris can't get to them.' Anxiety greeted him suddenly and planted a kiss on his face. 'They could tell you a lot about us.' He looked pained.

'What was in those letters?'

'After the bombing at the airport, I went to therapy—'

'After the bombing?' I wasn't sure if I heard correctly.

'Yes. There was an explosion at the airport. I couldn't get to you, and a collapsing wall separated us. I called you constantly afterwards. On one of the calls, your husband picked up and said you died.'

'Chris said that? Why?'

'As he said during our conversation, it was the best way to get rid of me. When I got here, I wanted to scream with helplessness because I'd lost you once again.' He took a deep breath; his face was red, as if he had a fever. 'I had to do something. I used to go to the pool and dive to the bottom. I sat there with my mouth open and pushed the pain out as hard as I could. The water tried to penetrate me, but I ignored it. It's the second time, Tom, but crueller this time.'

He buried his face in his hands and cried. I couldn't move. I couldn't believe I was part of this story.

'I miss you, Tom. So terribly,' he added after a moment, looking up. 'I wish I could hug you, but I'm afraid of your indifference.' He sniffed and wiped the tears from his cheeks.

I was silent. I didn't know how to answer him.

When he said goodbye, he asked if he could contact me and stated that he would not stop trying to find a way to make me remember him.

7. Warsaw

Summer rushed across the borders of Cumbria, although around here, it can hardly be called that – it's more like autumn forgot to pack its bags.

My memory was opening more hidden images to me every day. Sometimes they appeared as individual puzzles, filling in fragments of the past, and sometimes there was nothing. Once, when I was picking apples from our tree and putting them in a basket, I smelled their sweet scent. Immediately an image of the apples I would collect for my mum's apple pies filled my head. I froze, allowing myself to savour the moment. A memory that reassured me that my previous life, which I still had no access to, was happy.

Another time, when we were going for a walk, Harry, right at the gate, gave me his hand, and with that touch came back all the memories of our wanderings together. Tears welled up in my eyes as Harry bent down to adjust his poorly tied shoelace. I knelt next to him and quickly tied his shoes and, in my head, repeated his name. *Harry.* The son I almost lost.

Every day I felt more confident, although I still couldn't put all the memories together in a logical whole. Was I a good father? Husband? Son? Everything around me assured me that I had nothing to fear, but deep in my heart, something warned me to be careful.

More than once, I accidentally witnessed conversations between my mother and Chris in the living room. I would go to the door and listen. The topic was usually the same. Mum would ask Chris to give me more time. She promised him that eventually, I would remember everything, and we would be a wonderful couple again. I returned to the picture drawer and desperately tried to resurrect the memories of my feelings for him.

I had not found the letters, even though every day when Chris left for work and Mum fell asleep in the garden, I searched the corners of the house. I couldn't remember where I would have hidden them, which made me doubt their existence.

One Saturday morning, Harry was feeding the birds in the garden. On my way out to him, I bumped into my mother, who was walking down the hall carrying laundry in a basket to hang out.

'Wait, I'll do it.' I took the basket from her. 'Get some rest.'

Her face softened. We went out to the garden. She sat in the gazebo by the tree with Harry's swing while I reached into the basket for a towel. Then Chris came over and started handing me more items from the basket.

'Do you remember when we moved in, and the first thing you wanted was that gazebo? We spent a lot of time in it during the renovation, when you got mad at the workers because you had had enough of them. And there...' He pointed to the grass. 'You immediately wanted to remove this bush, which was taking up a large piece of our lawn.'

I looked where he pointed. I covered my oblivion with a smile. After meeting Lucas, I wasn't sure if Chris's stories were true, but I couldn't answer all the questions that had lined up without the letters.

'And do you remember when the electricians carved out the sockets on the right side of the wall, and we wanted them in the middle? Then the company's owner came, and you gave him an earful. He never showed up after that—'

'Chris.' I cut him off. 'Sorry, I'm tired. Finish hanging up, and I'll lie down for a while.'

'Sure. Go and rest.'

Chris repeatedly tried to recall moments from our lives, but it felt like he was telling me someone else's story. I was silent, feeling his suppressed helplessness and impatience. He wanted so badly to get back someone he missed. On Tuesdays, Chris drove me to Tracy's for therapy. He kept an eye on these visits more than I did. I felt like he was controlling me because I could have gone by myself. Each time he waited in the car, making sure I walked through Tracy's door. Later, he came to pick me up, as if he was collecting a small child from school.

'Hello, Tom.' Tracy smiled when I entered her office.

'Hi.' I sat down on the sofa. Strawberry tea was cooling on the table in front of me.

'How was your week?'

Tracy opened her notebook and assumed a pose, ready to write.

'My memory is coming back more every day. What more can I wish for?'

'How do you feel about that?'

'More confident. There isn't so much emptiness anymore.'

'And Chris?'

'That's what I want to talk about today. I have a problem.'

'Problem?'

I slid deeper into the sofa and took a deep breath.

'Chris controls me. He brings me here, but I could come alone. That's not all,' I added, seeing the look on her face. 'I'd like to go back to work. Pierre, my boss, called. We talked for a long time. This conversation reminded me of what I used to do. He suggested I should come back to the company, but how am I supposed to if Chris gets the shivers just from the word “airport”?’

‘Have you told him about it?’

‘Not yet. I’m afraid of his reaction.’

‘All right. Let’s try to rehearse your conversation as it might play out. I’ll be Chris. Where does he usually spend his time at home?’

‘In the living room on the sofa,’ I sighed.

‘OK. You walk into the living room, sit next to Chris and try to talk to him.’ Tracy assumed the position of a pensive Chris, looking off into the distance.

‘Chris?’ I fell silent. It wasn’t fear, but some kind of resistance, something that was blocking me.’

‘Go ahead, keep talking.’ Tracy filled the silence.

‘Chris, can we talk?’

‘What’s up?’ she mumbled casually.

I fell silent again, and the words seemed to cling to the frame of my mouth, trying not to leave. I shifted on the sofa and took a deep breath.

‘Pierre called today. He wants me to go back to work.’

‘What for?’ she grunted.

Her grunt was so similar to Chris’s that it left me speechless again. I sighed and slid deeper onto the sofa.

‘Tom, try a little trick. Say it as if you were asking him for help.’ Tracy reached for her notebook and jotted something down. ‘Let’s try again.’ She shifted in the chair. ‘Imagine it’s breakfast. This is a time when we are usually still sleepy. Maybe then Chris will take it better?’

I took a breath to throw it all out in one exhale.

‘Chris?’

‘Yes, honey? Will you pass me some bread?’ Tracy reached out for an imaginary tray of bread.

‘You know... Pierre called yesterday and asked if I would return to work.’

‘What? You’ve barely started regaining your memory,’ she grumbled.

‘During our conversation, more memories came back. I thought that by going back to work, I could get more of them.’

‘I’m not sure... I don’t know whether it’s too early. It’s a big step.’ Tracy feigned thought.

‘I need my life back. I would like to feel that I am doing something relevant again, that I am needed. You know what it’s like because you like your job. But to achieve this, I need your support. I know it won’t be easy, but if you help me, it might work. Will you help me, Chris?’

‘How?’

‘Come over there with me. I’ll feel safer knowing you’re by my side.’

‘Tom, great! What more can I say? That was it. That’s how you talk to him.’

‘Really?’

‘Sometimes fear turns the simplest things into something incredibly difficult, but you’ve done it. It’ll be fine, you’ll see.’ She gave me a smile.

The next morning, the mingled smell of damp trees and wet grass wafted into the bedroom through the half-open window. I sat up in bed. Chris was no longer there. I got up and walked over to the window, opening the curtains. The grumpy sky was a cover of downy quilts, from under which the sun’s unruly rays popped out occasionally. I was watching the bushes bending under the wind when I heard the sound of running feet.

'Good morning, Daddy.' Harry burst into the bedroom with his hair comically tousled. 'Are you awake?' His eyes smiled at me.

'Good morning, spider. I just got up. Where's Dad?'

He ran over to me, and I grabbed him and lifted him. He hugged me like we hadn't seen each other in a week.

'I saw him talking to Judith by the fence through the window.'

'You won't miss anything.' I laughed. 'Come.' I took his hand. 'Let's find Grandma. She must have already made breakfast.'

We headed towards the kitchen, from which emanated the smell of toast, eggs and tea.

'Good morning!' Mum turned as we entered.

'Good morning, Grandma. We've come for breakfast,' said Harry.

'Good morning, Mum.' I kissed her cheek.

'Sit down, please. Breakfast is ready.'

We took our seats at the table, and Mum put scrambled eggs on our plates along with crispy, still-warm toast that had just popped out of the toaster. Harry and I murmured in satisfaction as we inhaled the scent.

I tilted my head back, and that's when I saw Chris standing in the doorway.

'Good morning, family.' His smile filled half his face. 'Sorry I'm late, but Judith stopped me.'

He walked over to the table and kissed Harry and then me. Mum served him some scrambled eggs, and after a while, the only sounds were the chewing of toast and the sipping of tea. I looked at Chris. Now or never!

'Chris, since I'm feeling much better now and so much of my memory has come back, I'd like to return to work.' I kept my gaze on him. 'Pierre called and invited us to Warsaw.'

Chris immediately stopped eating, his cheeks taut with clenched teeth. After a moment, he looked at his mother, as if he was asking her for help.

'I think it's an excellent idea,' she said without meeting his eyes. 'You should go and see what happens.' She reached for the toast, smiling at me.

'I don't know if that's a good idea after what Tom's been through.' Chris didn't even glance at me.

'You won't know if you don't go. It seems that Pierre must have high hopes for Tom if he's called him. He must value him very much, and that's wonderful to hear.' Mum patted my shoulder.

Chris swallowed a bite of egg with difficulty.

'Do you really want to go back there?'

'I would like to try. And then, maybe they'd let me work remotely?'

'That would be good,' he said seriously. 'When do you want to go?'

'I don't have a specific date.'

Chris's eyes wandered for a moment. I waited anxiously for his final verdict. Mum added more egg to Harry's plate. He was tense despite not understanding the conversation. I put my hand on his shoulder and felt his body relax instantly.

'Since it's so important to you, I'll take some time off, and we'll go to Warsaw.'

'Thank you.' I put my hand on Chris's, and a small smile emerged.

A week later, Mum showed up at our door right after Chris had gone to the garage to get his car.

'Can I?' she asked uncertainly.

'Come in. I'm just finishing up.' I zipped up my suitcase and moved it to the floor, making room for Mum.

‘I’m so glad you’re going together.’ She sat next to me. ‘I’ll take care of Harry. Don’t worry about anything.’

‘Thank you for your support, Mum. It wouldn’t have been possible without you.’ I hugged her, and just then, I heard the car horn.

Harry couldn’t let go of me for a long time. I assured him it was only a few days, and we would be back home with him in no time. Mum gave me a tight hug and then walked over to Chris. She whispered something in his ear, and he nodded. A few minutes later, we were on the road. Mum and Harry waved until we disappeared around the corner.

At Liverpool Airport, Chris found a seat right by the departures board. I looked around. People were hurrying in all directions, and the noise overwhelmed me so much that I got dizzy. I hid it from Chris because I was afraid he’d make us turn back.

‘I’m going to the shop.’ I stroked his shoulder. ‘Do you need anything?’

‘Just something to drink.’

I kept picking up different snacks, looking at them and returning them. I couldn’t remember what Chris liked. Finally, I grabbed a packet of McCoy’s and two bottles of water and queued up at the checkout. Would it be like this forever? Would I never remember my husband and be stuck in this empty part of my life, depending on others?

‘It’s your turn!’ a woman called from behind me.

‘Sorry.’ I looked at her distractedly and headed to the cash register.

When I returned, I handed Chris a bag of crisps and a bottle.

‘You remembered.’

‘Of course,’ I lied, and looked away.

‘Thanks, babe.’

I was relieved when he didn't say anything else, and sat next to him.

When we landed in Warsaw, we went to the taxi stand. I felt a pleasant warmth in my heart, and I smiled as we passed familiar streets, houses and shops. Out of the corner of my eye, I saw Chris watching me surreptitiously, but that wasn't important now. The joy of coming home flowed through me as if I had returned from a long journey.

I was opening up the apartment when the neighbourhood watch system was activated. Across the hall, a grey-haired woman poked her pointed nose out the door. Dressed in a pink housecoat, she walked halfway down the hall, keeping a sharp eye on us. The rosary she held told us coldly that our appearance had interrupted her prayer.

'Oh! You have come!' Her intrusive gaze scanned Chris. 'I haven't seen you in a long time.' She looked at me.

'Short visit. You have to keep an eye on things these days.'

I hastily opened the door and gave Chris a little push so he could hide from her monitoring eyes.

'The Lord knows. And who is that?' She nodded her head at Chris disappearing through the door.

'Brother,' I replied without hesitation. 'It was nice to see you in good health.'

I crossed the apartment threshold, and before she could answer, I closed the door.

'What did she want?' Chris asked.

'In Poland, the thirst for information is like a hunger that needs to be fed quickly.'

We left our suitcases at the entrance and I opened the windows, the air immediately filling the apartment with freshness. Chris, meanwhile, began to remove the canvas covers from the furniture.

'Are you OK?' he asked.

'Yes. Are you hungry?'

'A little bit.'

'Let's eat the sandwiches from the airport before they spoil.'

I made tea, and we sat down at the table. Chris joked that the sandwiches turned out well, and I added that I had been making them all night. We laughed, and Chris kissed me.

'What time is your meeting in the morning?'

'Ten o'clock. We can go to bed early to rest after the journey.'

'Good idea.'

Chris helped me make the bed and took my hand when we were done.

'Shall we take a shower together? Like we used to?' He smiled invitingly.

'Sorry, I'm not ready for it yet.' I looked down.

'I'm sorry.' He stroked my hand. 'I shouldn't push you.'

In the bathroom, I stopped in front of the mirror. Why couldn't I get close to him? What was wrong with me? I couldn't find the answers to these questions.

In the morning, we were awakened by the barking of dogs as if someone had set them fighting. Instead of going with their pets to the square or the park, the animal lovers would stand on the lawn right under the windows near the entrance to the building. The pooches would settle their physiological needs right there. It used to annoy me, but now it made me feel sentimental about this place.

The loud screams of neighbours followed the animal fights, the pounding of pork chops so hard the ceiling might collapse at any moment, and then the horrendous noise of the garbage truck outside the window collecting glass waste. This wasn't Cumbria, where the rustle of leaves lulled us to sleep and the rain played lullabies on the roof.

'How could you live here?' Chris mumbled sleepily.

'You get used to it over time and don't hear it anymore.'

'Good thing we live in England,' he muttered, turning to me.

'We have to get up now. It's time to get ready for the meeting.'

In the taxi, Chris's head fell against the window. He hadn't had enough sleep. I smiled as he breathed louder. When we got there, I tapped him lightly on the shoulder.

'We've arrived.'

'OK,' he said nervously, rubbing his face with his hands.

As I entered the building, I was touched by memories of walking down this corridor and greeting the employees. Now it was the rustles of the past that welcomed me, and I smiled back at them. We took the elevator to the twentieth floor and went to Pierre's office. I knocked.

'You're finally here.' He got up from his desk and came over to shake my hand.

'Let me introduce my husband, Chris Anderson.'

'Nice to meet you.' Pierre and Chris exchanged handshakes. 'Sit down, please.' Pierre gestured to the chairs before his desk.

'Tom, how are you feeling?' he asked as we sat.

‘I’m surprised by this, but OK. My memory is coming back, especially when it comes to work.’ I laughed nervously.

‘Tom, I don’t want to throw you in at the deep end. You’ve been through a lot, and I care about your health first. I have a therapist in the family, and I did some research, and it was suggested to me that you come over for a few days and see how you feel about it. Then you can decide if you want to continue working with me. Of course, if you don’t feel comfortable here, I’ll understand, and we’ll start looking for someone to replace you. What do you think?’

I turned my head to Chris, waiting for his approval. He was silent for a moment, staring straight ahead.

‘Yeah... I think that’s a good idea,’ he stammered.

‘So it’s settled.’ Pierre rubbed his hands joyfully, and Chris’s phone rang simultaneously. At first, he rejected the call, but as the beeps continued, I realised it must be something important.

‘Sorry, it’s from work. I have to answer.’ He stood up and walked out into the hallway.

‘I don’t think your husband is happy that you want to come back.’ Pierre lowered his voice and glanced at Chris, who was leaning with his back against a glass wall in the corridor.

‘The accident took a lot out of him. He’s worried about me and has become nervous and overprotective. You have to understand him.’

‘Sure. Tom, maybe that’s enough for today. Come tomorrow when you want, and we’ll see what’s next. What do you think?’

‘All right. Pierre, I wanted to thank you for your support and for waiting so long for me, even though my return was a big unknown.’

‘We’ve all been waiting. There is no one else who can hold everything together like you do,’ he laughed.

‘Is that what you think of me?’ I said.

‘We need you badly, Tom. I hope you will stay with us.’

Chris looked into the office. He was trying to keep his face calm, but the vein throbbing in his neck betrayed his nervousness.

‘I’m sorry, I’m back. Where did we end up?’ He sat down without taking his eyes off Pierre.

‘Tom and I had a little chat, and I suggested he come by tomorrow, just off the clock. If he decides he’s up to it, we’d love to have him back.’

‘Could he work remotely?’ Chris shifted in his chair and wiped his trousers with his hands. ‘We have a high-speed connection and a camera. I’d feel safer if he didn’t have to travel.’

‘I understand. I think anything is possible, but first, Tom has to decide if he wants to work with us.’

‘Of course.’

We went home in silence. I glanced at Chris in the taxi, but his gaze drifted dully across the streets. Back in the apartment, he sat in the living room, and I could tell something was bothering him. I sat next to him.

‘Has something happened? You aren’t saying anything. Are you mad at me?’

‘I have to go back tomorrow – the system is down and nothing is working. I’m afraid to leave you alone.’ He took my hand.

‘Chris, I’m safe here. You shouldn’t be so bothered.’

‘I’d rather be here with you.’ He stroked my cheek.

‘I can handle it. You have to help them; after all, you forced them to leave, and now they need you.’

Chris spent the afternoon scrolling through the carriers' offers, every now and then letting out a small grunt of dissatisfaction at the ticket prices. I made dinner, and we sat at the table.

'Did you find anything?' I asked, pausing before I ate.

'Yes, I fly at nine tomorrow morning, but the ticket prices are terribly high.'

'That's because you've bought them at the last minute. I'll drive you to the airport and then go to Pierre.' I picked up the cutlery.

'Ask him to work remotely. That would solve a lot.'

'OK.'

In the morning, I drove Chris to the airport after breakfast. He held my hand for a long time as we said goodbye. He asked me to come back soon. When he disappeared at check-in, I went to the taxi stand and drove to the office.

The sun smiled at me, touching the warmth of its rays to my face. I felt the joy of reclaiming my life.

The driver dropped me off near the entrance. I lifted my head and looked at the very top of the skyscraper. Its glass walls reflected the sun's rays exactly as they had when I first came here. My heart raced as I realised how much I remembered. A few seconds later, I was boarding the elevator with an excitement unusual for employees of any company. Entering the twentieth floor, I looked around like a child. In the corridors I passed people who greeted me with nods. Each time I slowed down for a moment. Should I start a conversation? Some I remembered well, others I had my doubts about. I wasn't sure if they were new or if their faces were still in the darkness of my memory.

Pierre's office was easy to find. As I entered, I wanted to brag about all this to him, but I held back. I didn't want him to have any doubts about my abilities.

'Come in.' He waved his hand.

'Hi.' I stopped by the door.

'I'm glad you came. Here's the key to your office.' He handed it to me.

When I got to the office, I found the interior hadn't changed. I went to the window and looked out onto the street, bustling with life. I felt like I had gone back in time. I was sitting at my desk looking at the piles of papers spilling sideways when my phone rang. Lucas.

'Hello?'

'Hi, Tom. We haven't talked for a long time. Sorry, I've been a bit busy. We have a new order in Spain. Lots of work. What about you?'

'I'm in Warsaw. In my old office.'

'Are you going back to work?' There was surprise in his voice.

'Yes. My memory is returning, and I'm regaining my lost life.'

'And...' He paused. 'I'm sorry, I shouldn't.'

'I know what you wanted to ask. I searched the house and found no letters. God only knows how much I've been looking for them. After a month, I gave up, and I think it has to stay that way, and I'm not meant to learn everything. I feel terrible because I know you're waiting for my memory to return, and it's painful for you. Sorry.'

'You don't have to apologise; it's not your fault.'

'Lucas, the doctor said my memory might not return completely, and some of it might stay blank forever. And I want you to be happy and not waste your life waiting for something that may never happen. You should forget about me and start your life over.'

He fell silent; all I could hear was his rapid breathing, which masked his crying.

'You know...' he began after a moment. 'It's hard to explain to yourself that it's time to leave the man you love.' He sobbed.

'I'm sorry; I didn't mean to upset you.'

'It's nothing.' He quickly mastered his emotions. 'Still friends, right?'

'Sure,' I whispered excitedly.

'Cool. We'll be in touch. I'll call you soon.'

I put the phone down and stared at the piles of invoices and contracts scattered on my desk. They were like some of my memories, not in their assigned places. I reached for the first document and started to organise them. This process consumed me completely, and only when Pierre appeared in the doorway did I glance at the clock, which showed three o'clock.

'Tom, why don't you take a break? You haven't come out of here since this morning.'

'I wanted to finish this mess today.' I slid the last binder onto the shelf.

'No!' cried Pierre. 'Here, on the desk somewhere' – he pointed – 'were the documents from the investor.' His face paled.

I went to my closet and pulled out a blue binder.

'Here, it's all here.' I gave it to him.

He opened it hesitantly, glanced at the first document and smiled.

'It's good to have you back.' He touched my shoulder.

'But you know it's supposed to come back to me in its entirety?'

‘I was waiting for you to say that.’ He burst out laughing.

‘I’ll check the balance tomorrow. I can see someone has tried to do it several times, clumsily.’

‘Yes, the wife of one of the CEOs wanted to help us, but when she saw this mess, she quickly gave up.’

‘I’m not surprised.’ I shook my head.

Going back to work gave me more confidence. Slowly, I began to remember what role I played in life. What I did here, I did well. I was praised for my speed and meticulousness. I jotted down these traits in my head as if I were creating a character from scratch. When I got home, I called Chris. He answered immediately, as if he had been waiting by the phone. I asked to stay a few more days. He wasn’t thrilled. Harry took the phone.

‘Daddy, when are you coming back?’

‘Soon, honey. A few more days.’

‘Come back quickly, love you.’

‘Love you too, honey.’

In the evening, I went through the wardrobe in my apartment and threw out some things I didn’t need. Then I remembered I had a briefcase somewhere for work. I grabbed the ladder and started searching the top shelves. A few minutes later, I had it in my hand. It was slightly dusty and lay on top of a cardboard shoebox. I wiped it with a damp cloth and looked inside. It contained a notebook, a pen and even a small box of mints. I grabbed the shoebox and went to throw it away, but it was heavier than I expected. I opened the lid, and it took my breath away. Letters!

I climbed down the ladder and sat with the box in the living room. My hands trembled slightly as I took out the first letter. I opened it and started reading.

Dearest,

Your echo still echoes in me. You left behind a huge void that pierces me with thousands of needles daily. I don't have the strength to get up and start the day. I constantly run away to our moments together, but then I see this awful place. A collapsing wall that takes you away from me. Sorry. Forgive me for not making it...

For a moment, I felt the taste of plaster in my mouth. It was like spying on someone else's story trying to stick in me. My mind didn't want to accept it, although, on the other hand, I realised that everything Lucas had written about had to have happened. I greedily grabbed another letter, the secrets of my life opening up with each sentence. When I was done, I called Lucas.

'Tom?' He couldn't hide his surprise.

'I found the letters. They were in my apartment. I've read them, and we need to meet. I have so many questions.'

'Of course.'

'I'm returning to England at the weekend, but I'll fly via Amsterdam. I'll send you the time and flight number. Will you come?'

'You don't have to ask. I will.'

As I dialled Chris's number, I hesitated, wondering what I would say to him.

'Tom?' I was silent for a moment when his voice rang out. 'Tom, are you there?'

'Yes, I wanted to tell you I'm coming back via Amsterdam on Saturday.'

There was a moment of silence, and I wasn't sure if the connection had been broken.

He lowered his voice. 'You know you shouldn't.'

'I have to face my past, or I will always be running from it.'

'Can I come and get you?'

'Just pick me up at the airport.'

I read all the letters several times that evening. I hoped they would provoke images from the past, but the stories written in them remained alien to me. Even so, I couldn't stop fervently reading them again and again.

On Saturday morning, I boarded a plane at Chopin Airport. My questions for Lucas swirled around in my head, and I couldn't put them together. This rush of thoughts tired me out, and I finally fell asleep.

When we landed and the pilot turned off the engines, people ran wildly to the compartments for their luggage. More images flashed through my mind, reminding me that this was usually the case. I waited for the crowd to pour out of the plane, grabbed my suitcase and left. I was nearing the exit from the corridor when I felt a dryness in my throat. I swallowed and crossed the threshold.

In the distance, Lucas was waiting by the pillar. He smiled at me and waved his hand. The corners of my mouth lifted slightly, and, taking the first step, I felt the airport suddenly expanding rapidly and the vortex of air sucking me in, making it impossible to breathe. I grabbed the wall, and my mind immediately began to open library catalogues from which thousands of rustling images spilt out. They immediately filled the empty spaces on the shelves of my memory.

Lucas ran over to me.

'Tom? What's going on? Are you OK?' He held my hand.

His voice stretched like rubber, and I could barely hear his muffled questions. The sounds mixed together, and then everything stopped. I looked at a terrified Lucas, who froze for a moment staring at me, but a second later, he took my arm and led me to the gate. I sat down. Lucas didn't take his eyes off me.

'Tom, are you OK?'

I looked at his face, drawn with fear. I reached out and stroked his cheek, and his lost eyes showed longing.

'I remember you,' I whispered. 'I remember everything.'

His body shuddered, and his eyes filled with tears. He hugged me, and I could feel his warmth again, his love that he wasn't ashamed to show.

'Do you remember how we met?' He leaned back to meet my gaze.

'Yes, you took my plane seat, then stole my sandwich.'

'That's not true,' he laughed through his tears. 'I shared it with you. Tom, it's really you.'

'Were you expecting someone else?'

'Now I'm sure.' Lucas, closing his eyes, pressed my hand to his face, and I couldn't stop staring at him.'

*

I landed on time. Chris was waiting for me in the arrivals hall. I approached him, forcing my face to smile.

'You're finally here.'

I felt hatred that I could hardly contain, then anger. I planned to tell him everything at home, in my mother's presence, keeping my composure, although I felt I might fail.

'How's work?' Chris's voice pulled me out of my thoughts.

'OK,' I replied, looking ahead.

‘Will you be able to work remotely?’ He took my suitcase.

‘Yeah,’ I mumbled.

I was silent in the car. Chris turned on the radio, and I leaned my head against the window, wondering what to say to Harry. I feared he wouldn’t want to go to Amsterdam with me and would choose Chris. And what would Mum say? But it was too late; the milk had spilt.

When we got home, Harry ran over to me and hugged me.

‘I missed you,’ he whispered in my ear, as if he didn’t want anyone to hear.

‘Me too. Very much.’ I kissed his little head. ‘Honey, I have a request. Please wait for me in your room. I’ll come to you right away. I need to talk to Dad.’

‘OK, Daddy.’ He ran straight into his room.

‘Good morning, Mum.’ I kissed her cheek. ‘Let’s all go to the living room; I’d like to talk to you.’

Mum exchanged a quick glance with Chris, then followed me without saying a word. We sat down at the table. They shifted in their chairs in expectant silence, placing their hands on the table.

‘My memory is back.’ My words seemed to bounce off the walls and return to me. ‘I remember everything now,’ I said without looking at Chris.

‘Tom, that’s wonderful.’ Mum got up and hugged me.

I waited for her to sit down again and looked at Chris.

‘I’m leaving you and taking Harry. If you try to take him from me, I will report everything you did to me and Lucas to the police.’

Mum’s face turned pale, and she looked at her son in fear.

‘Tom, let’s talk.’ Chris tried to touch my hand, but I took it away. ‘I’ll explain everything. You don’t understand.’

'I understand, Chris. More than you can comprehend. That's why—'

'Tom, wait.'

'Chris, listen to Tom,' Mum cut in.

'Not now!' he yelled. 'I'm trying to talk to my husband!'

Mum took a deep breath and fell silent, and I watched quietly as a mixture of emotions moved over Chris's face. Panic came first, his eyes frightened, followed by despair and fear.

'Tom, we'll fix everything. It will be like before. You'll see,' he said, trembling.

Despite everything he had done to me, I realised how sorry I felt for him. He was clinging to me like a child about to have a toy taken away.

'Say something.'

I looked at him silently, with sympathy.

'Please don't leave me.' His eyes filled with tears.

'It's over, Chris.' I was surprised I could say it so calmly.

8. Gate D5

The dancing sounds of the kitchen wafted into the bedroom, tickling my ears. I woke up, and when I opened my eyes, Lucas wasn't next to me, but the sheets still held the warmth of our bodies. I glanced at my watch. It was a few minutes past eight. I put on my robe and headed to the kitchen. Lucas was preparing breakfast, the coffee pot collecting the last drops of tea.

'Good morning.' A yawn cut in between the words.

'Good morning, honey.' Lucas turned from the counter. 'I woke you up; I'm sorry.'

'I know you can't sleep when we're seeing Chris.' I hugged him.

'Even though it's been half a year, your meetings still make me uneasy, and I need to do something to keep my mind off it. Hungry?' He kissed me.

'Please.' I snuggled into his arms. 'We agreed to these meetings to avoid court. Do you remember?'

'Yes, but I still find it hard to believe in his good intentions.'

'I have a problem with that too,' I sighed, tilting my head to meet his gaze.

'I love you.' He stole a kiss and went back to preparing breakfast.

'I'll check on Harry.'

In the corridor, I passed the photos on the walls, the pictures locked in times that we still wanted to see. One was slightly crooked. I corrected the frame. This photo had been taken by the lake when Lucas taught Harry to swim. I thought Harry would scream at the top of his lungs, waving his arms and legs in panic, but he just lay in the water, following Lucas's instructions. When they were done, he cuddled up to him. I think that's when Harry's heart made room for Lucas.

'Harry, it's time. We're meeting Dad today, remember?' I sat on his bed, rubbing his back.

'Just a minute, Daddy,' he mumbled.

'How long did you play with Lucas on the console, eh?'

'A while,' he replied without opening his eyes, a slight smirk on his sleepy face.

'All right, my little spider. Get some rest, and I'll get breakfast.' I smoothed his messy hair. 'I love you,' I whispered, leaning over and kissing his temple.

'Me too...' he mumbled.

I returned to the kitchen, where the smells of tea and fresh bread wafted with avocado, tomatoes and a fried egg already waiting on the plate.

'Harry isn't coming?' Lucas was filling a mug with tea.

'He's still asleep. What time did you finish playing yesterday?' I smiled.

Lucas tilted his head and narrowed his eyes.

'We had to finish the sixth level.'

'Well...' I couldn't scold him, and my smile spread wider.

'Sorry.' He kissed me softly on the lips.

The meetings with Chris took place once a month in a public place. We'd decided it would be Schiphol Airport in Amsterdam. Because of the cameras and checkpoints, the airport offered us security in case Chris tried to kidnap Harry. Lucas got us passes to wait for Chris before leaving the gate.

I remembered our first meeting. Harry, seeing Chris from a distance, gripped my hand tighter.

'Are you nervous, honey?' I crouched down to hug him.

'Just a little,' he sighed, resting his head on my shoulder.

After a moment, he let go of my hand and ran as fast as he could to Chris, who crouched next to him and hugged him tightly. Standing up, he quickly wiped his cheek. The emotion seemed sincere to me. As he walked towards me, I was afraid, but this time not of him but of the emotions this would provoke in me. He asked if he could hug me. I nodded, then felt the warmth of his skin and the familiar scent of the eau de toilette he'd used for years. An image of the morning wash routine flashed quickly through my mind as the three of us brushed our teeth and made faces while laughing.

Harry took his dad's hand and unknowingly led him to the nearest gate, D5. I stood dumbfounded as they sat in the last row. I wanted to run up and scream that I absolutely disagreed, that there was no way, but Harry's eyes filled with joy, and the words jumped energetically from his mouth straight to his father. They both gestured for me to join them. Sitting in the row opposite, I realised that this place was just changing, taking on a new meaning, making room for something still difficult to define.

*

'Ready?' Lucas peeked into the room as I finished dressing Harry.

'Yes, Uncle,' Harry exclaimed enthusiastically.

'Let's go!'

Harry ran over to Lucas, grabbing his hand, and I fought with myself to get up and go to another meeting with Chris. I was tired of the memories of our life together, which I wanted to tear away, to erase as if they had never been there.

'Everything OK?' Lucas was looking at me.

'Yes,' I mumbled. I grabbed Lucas's other hand, and we headed for the door.

This time Chris's flight was twenty minutes late. I stood with Harry in front of the big glass wall watching the planes. I watched his delight as each machine soared into space.

'Daddy, when I grow up, I want to be a pilot,' he declared firmly.

I shivered. His dream scared me – so many dangers lurked at the airport. I wanted to protect him but knew I had no right to take away his dreams.

'And will you take me to Warsaw?' I asked, watching another plane take off.

'I'll give you the best seats with Uncle Lucas.'

'You are a dear.' I leaned in to kiss him just as the delayed flight from Newcastle was announced.

'Dad's arrived!' Harry jumped happily.

'Then let's go greet him.' I took his hand, and we walked towards the hall.

When Chris emerged from the corridor, I saw sadness on his face for a split second, but seeing Harry running towards him, he quickly covered it with a smile. I watched him during our meetings but never saw anything else.

‘Hi, Tom.’ He hugged me.

‘Hi.’ I hugged him back. ‘How was the flight?’

‘I slept through it. I’ve been a bit overtired lately.’ He immediately looked away. ‘Are you hungry, son?’ He looked Harry in the eyes.

‘No, Dad. Uncle made us breakfast.’

Harry’s energetic words were a slap to Chris, who immediately looked down.

‘I haven’t had time to eat anything.’ He looked at me shyly.

‘Didn’t Grandma make you something?’ Harry stared at his father in surprise.

Chris was silent for a long moment.

‘Son, now that...’ He hesitated, as if guarding his words. ‘You live here, Grandma went home.’ He stroked his head.

Harry grimaced and lowered his head. I immediately wanted to distract him.

‘Honey, Dad is tired after the trip. Let’s get him some breakfast, and we’ll buy some cookies.’ I took Harry’s hand, and we walked towards the nearest restaurant.

‘Chris?’ a woman’s voice suddenly sounded behind us. We stopped.

‘Helen! What are you doing here? I haven’t heard from you in so long.’ Chris walked over to her, and they hugged.

‘I’m returning from a business trip; I have a transfer here.’ She looked at me and Harry. ‘This must be your husband and son, whom you told me so much about long ago.’ She smiled at us.

I waved in greeting, and Chris looked at me uncertainly. I got the impression that he was ashamed to tell her that we were no longer together. I decided not to do anything about it. Let him keep his secret.

'Chris, excuse me, I have to be on a plane soon; we should meet and catch up sometime. I have so much to tell you.' She placed a friendly hand on his shoulder. 'Nice to meet you.' She turned to Harry and me in farewell.

At the restaurant, Harry excitedly recounted all the past month's events to Chris, and I let my mind wander, watching the people at the tables next to us. One couple fed each other pieces of fruit. Their gestures, smiles and longing glances didn't let me take my eyes off them. They didn't talk. He put his head on her shoulder, and she gently ran her hand through his jet-black hair like I did when Lucas rested his head on my chest.

'Tom?' Chris's voice got through to me.

'Sorry, what did you say?' I stared at my plate.

'Harry has questions for us, and I think it's time we answer them together.'

'What questions?' I looked at Harry.

'Daddy, why do we still have to meet at this airport? Why can't we invite Dad to our house or visit him?'

His words touched me with fear. I glanced at Chris, who was confused and looked down. I opened my mouth, but words failed me.

'Honey.' Chris took his son's hand. 'Daddy's closer to the airport. I don't like Amsterdam – it's too noisy for me – and I prefer to meet here.'

'Maybe I'll come to you next time?' Harry turned his head in my direction and begged with his eyes, and I fought with myself to say no.

'I think...'

'Daddy, please,' came Harry's desperate whisper. I looked into his eyes. They held a longing so great that it squeezed my heart. I took a deep breath.

'Harry can't go alone.' I exhaled coldly.

'Daddy, no...'

Harry grimaced, disappointment covering his face. For a moment there was nothing but the bustle of people around us.

'I understand,' Chris said resignedly, lowering his head.

'We'd both have to come,' I added after a moment.

Chris immediately looked up and shifted in his chair. Harry's eyes glittered like sapphires.

'Tom, thank you. It means a lot to me.' He placed his hand on mine, but I immediately took it away.

'If you're up to something, you'll never see us again.'

'Tom, I'll take care of you, you know that.'

'Daddy.' Harry jumped up from his chair and ran to me. 'I love you,' he whispered.

'I love you too, spider,' I whispered.

Lucas was waiting in the airport parking lot. He got out of the car, and Harry ran over and jumped into his open arms.

'Everything OK?' Lucas tried to find my gaze as I approached.

'Yeah, let's go home.' I quickly got into the car.

No sooner had Lucas started the engine than Harry burst out with the news that he would be visiting his dad with me for a weekend and could cuddle Judith's kitty. Lucas, as if struck by lightning, looked at me. We exchanged glances, but I quickly turned my head to the window. Harry moved on to the rest of the meeting and how Dad had promised him a new phone, but he needed my permission. This information must have escaped me as my thoughts wandered in the restaurant. Harry asked Lucas to intercede for me. I laughed, saying, 'Hey, I'm here, and I hear.'

Back at the apartment, Harry ran to his room, and I sat in the living room.

'Will you tell me what happened?' Lucas sat next to me.

'Harry asked a lot of questions. Why are we meeting at the airport and why can't his father come here and he can't visit him? I didn't have the heart to refuse him. Sorry. However, I made the condition that he won't go alone.'

Lucas fell silent and then hugged me.

'I don't blame you, but the idea terrifies me. You are the heart of this family; if anything happened to you, my life would lose meaning. I love you very much, and I want to protect you.'

'Maybe this time it'll be OK.' I hugged him tighter.

Harry asked me if he could see his father more often. I agreed, and we set up a new schedule of meetings every two weeks. The next time they met, Chris's face was pale, as if he hadn't slept for several nights. At times he coughed slightly, and he kept his hand on the tabletop as if it would help him to keep his balance. He had never been sick, and colds flew by like a snap of his fingers.

'Everything all right?' I asked, studying his face.

'Yes, I haven't been sleeping much lately. They gave me extra responsibilities at work, and I'm overtired.' He quickly looked away at Harry.

'Son, you mentioned recently that you want to go to a forest camp.'

'Dad, this isn't a forest camp, it's a survival camp for real men.'

'Ah, now I understand. Well, then you must definitely go.' Harry's explanation amused Chris.

'Tom, let me pay for this trip.' He turned to me.

'Provided we pay half.' I didn't want any presents from him. Even though he had promised not to go to court, I still wasn't sure whether he was gathering evidence to file a custody case for Harry.

Harry immediately began browsing the range of tents in an online store.

'How about you, Tom?' Chris found my gaze. 'How are you doing in your new country? Is it similar to England?'

'It's completely different, but you know that I adapt easily to new circumstances.'

'Yes, I know.'

I waited for him to ask about Lucas, but Chris carefully avoided the subject.

'Dad! Can I have this knife?' Harry waved the phone in Chris's face, interrupting our conversation.

'Harry! No knives,' I scolded him with a glare.

'Daddy, please.'

'Son, let's discuss this with Daddy later.' Chris winked at Harry and stroked his head.

Harry immediately beamed and jumped a few times in joy. A few seconds later, he buried his nose in the phone again.

'Chris, don't be angry, but we won't be able to meet in two weeks. I'm on a business trip to Warsaw.' Afraid of his reaction, I didn't look him in the eye.

'Do you still work for Pierre?'

'Yeah, they won't let me go.' I laughed nervously.

'I'm not surprised.' He smiled, but this time it was a friend's smile, not a husband's.

'I thought Harry and I could come to your place as soon as I return. If that is still on?'

He remained thoughtful. It was the first time I'd seen him so focused.

'Chris? Is everything all right?'

'Yes, I'm sorry. What did you ask?'

'Are we still OK to visit?'

'Nothing has changed on my part,' he said, perking up.

*

I missed Tom terribly when he went to work. He'd say, 'You'll see, you won't have time to miss me. Harry won't let you get bored,' he'd laugh. However, when evening came and the other side of the bed was empty, I'd suffer impatiently awaiting his return. Exactly the same as years ago, when I'd wait for him to appear in the airport corridor.

A merciless horn outside the window woke me one Saturday. I glanced at my watch; it was nine. Tom was coming back from work in Warsaw today.

'Jesus!' I jumped out of bed and ran down the hall to Harry's room. 'We overslept! If you don't get up, we'll be late to pick Daddy up from the airport. Today is his birthday!'

'Uncle, didn't you set an alarm?' Harry jumped to his feet.

'Your daddy always does it. Run to the bathroom; we only have an hour, including the drive to the airport.'

'Daddy always checks in the app if the plane is delayed.'

'Clever, I didn't think to do that.' I ran for the phone while Harry quickly brushed his teeth.

When did this child grow up so much? I thought while opening the app.

'We're saved,' I called. 'We have an extra hour; the flight is delayed! You're a genius.' I pecked him on the cheek.

I made breakfast, and then we stood in front of the mirror, making faces and adopting model poses. I showed Harry how to tie a tie and gelled his hair lightly, which caused him to look at himself in the mirror a bit longer.

'Now for some fragrance. Please close your eyes.' I gently splashed the eau de toilette on Harry's neck.

'Do I look smart?' he asked without taking his eyes off the mirror.

'Like a model! Daddy will be impressed.' I smiled. 'Are we going?'

'We are.'

He offered me his hand. 'Let's go!'

At the airport, people smiled as they passed us. We must have looked a million euros in those navy-blue jackets. We stood by the pillar and kept our eyes on the door, looking for Tom.

The first passengers began to emerge from the corridor into the main hall. I swallowed. Harry shifted from foot to foot. We didn't take our eyes off the exit. After a while, my heart jumped. Tom appeared. Seeing us, he stopped, his mouth slightly open, and at that moment, he only had eyes for us.

'Wow! What's the occasion?' He walked over, looking us up and down.

'Your return to us and your birthday,' I said. 'Happy birthday, honey.' I kissed him on the lips, and a kind smile appeared on Harry's face.

Tom crouched next to Harry and he immediately threw himself into his arms.

'I missed you so much, Daddy!' he said, snuggling into him and closing his eyes.

'I missed you so much too. Beautiful smell.'

'It's Uncle,' he muttered, a little embarrassed.

'Wonderful,' he breathed again.

He stood up and hugged me. I'd missed the warmth of his body.

'Welcome home, baby,' I whispered in his ear.

Tom tilted his head back and looked deep into my eyes.

'I missed you.' His gaze instantly warmed my heart. 'And how did my boys manage without me?' he asked, taking Harry's hand.

'Daddy, Uncle forgot to set the alarm today.'

'Harry!'

Tom laughed, and we headed to the car.

When we got home, the three of us sat on the sofa. We swapped stories from the last week and reported how the time had passed. Harry kept glancing at the suitcase. He was looking forward to his favourite sweets that Tom always brought from Poland: Ptasie Mleczko and Toruńskie Pierniki with apricot and chocolate.

'Daddy, have you forgotten?'

'Honey, of course I haven't forgotten, but we'll have dinner first, and then you'll get dessert.'

'And my dessert?' I started kissing Tom's neck passionately.

'You'll get it tonight,' he laughed, closing his eyes.

After dinner, Tom unpacked his suitcase and took out the candy for Harry.

Harry quickly opened the box, and within moments, a large smear of chocolate had gathered in the corner of his mouth, which I wiped away, smiling. I remembered wiping the same chocolate from the corner of Tom's mouth when we met at the airport.

'It's time for gifts.' I winked at Harry, and we took two boxes out of the closet and went back to Tom.

'This is for you, Daddy.' Harry handed Tom the gift.

'Thank you, babe.'

Tom opened the box and took out a framed picture of the three of us at an amusement park. His eyes shone joyfully, and he couldn't stop hugging Harry. Harry then looked at me knowingly and nodded, signalling it was time, before leaving the room.

'Tom?' I sat next to him on the sofa.

'Why so serious? I'm starting to get scared. What have you done?'

'This is for you.' I handed him a tiny navy-blue box, and he couldn't take his eyes off it. 'Won't you open it?'

He opened the box, and the sun's rays immediately danced on the rings.

'Lucas, you know we can't.' He looked at me painfully.

'I know you're not divorced yet, and we have to wait, but I need to know. Will you marry me?' I knelt in front of him.

Tom took my hands. He couldn't contain his emotions. He looked at me, tears flowing from his eyes. Then Harry entered the room.

'Won't you answer, Daddy?' he called from the doorway.

Tom turned to him in confusion, then looked at me, startled.

'Of course I'll marry you someday, silly,' he said, almost through tears.

I hugged Tom, and Harry joined us.

'Were you involved in this too?' Tom turned to Harry.

'Just a little,' he chuckled. 'I chose the box.'

'It's beautiful, like my son.' Tom closed his eyes, kissing Harry's temple.

The next day, when we returned from a Sunday walk and were preparing dinner, Tom's mother called. He put it on speaker.

'Good morning, Tom. Do you have a moment?'

'Hi, Mum. Is something wrong?'

'Tom, Chris mentioned that you and Harry are visiting him for the weekend. Is that true?' There was uncertainty in her voice.

'That's true, although I'm only doing it for Harry.'

'Tom, it's wonderful; you don't know how excited Chris is that you're coming. Do you think I could come too?'

'Mum, always. We haven't seen each other for so long. This will be a good opportunity.' He stopped slicing a tomato and walked over to the window.

'And do you know exactly when you will arrive?'

'We tentatively agreed with Chris that Harry and I will fly out next weekend.'

'I'm buying the train ticket right now, and I'll be arriving a few days early to help Chris with everything. I missed you so much.'

'Me too, Mum. And how are you? We haven't talked for a long time.'

'All good. Lots of business at the council. We're building a new park in the area, and it's a problem, but I won't bore you with work. We'll talk when you arrive.'

When he ended the call, he looked at me. I stood motionless at the counter, lost in my thoughts. Jealousy and fear fought within them.

'Everything all right?' He came to me.

'I'm afraid to let you go. I have a feeling that something will happen and you won't return to me.'

'Don't say that.' He hugged and kissed me, but it didn't calm me down. 'It's only two days, and we'll be back soon.'

'I know, but I'm so scared,' I whispered.

I woke up during the night. Tom stood motionless by the window. At first, I thought he was sleepwalking, but as I went closer, I saw his eyes were open, staring at the tree outside our window.

'Honey, what's going on?' I snuggled into his back.

'I'm scared too. You won't understand this, but I'm afraid of missing this place, not for Chris but for Mum and England. And when that happens, I'll feel guilty for you.'

'Tom, I really do understand. You are a fantastic father. Nobody would do what you do for Harry.'

'I'm sorry,' he cried.

'Don't be sorry, we'll survive this.' I kissed him on the mouth, and we stood in the window for a long time, cuddled up to each other, Tom's warm tears touching my skin.

*

It was Friday evening, the day Tom and Harry were leaving. Waiting silently, Tom and I sat on the sofa in the living room. After a while, we heard the noise of the suitcase wheels as Harry dragged it to the front door.

'Where will you sleep?' I whispered, the words coming with great difficulty.

'Harry in his room and me in the guest-room, or with Harry. I don't know yet.'

'Can I write?'

'Absolutely! You know that.'

At the airport, I waited with them. Tom and I sat at the gate silently, and Harry, excited about the trip to see his dad and grandma, ran between the seats. His hand got caught in the croissants spread on the chair, which fell to the floor. I don't know why I couldn't control my anger.

'What the hell are you doing!'

Harry stopped, and his eyes widened. I'd never addressed him that way. Tom looked at me, confused.

'I'm sorry.' I walked over to Harry and hugged him tightly. I felt guilty. 'Sorry. I'm nervous. I didn't mean to do that.'

Boarding was announced.

'It's time,' I sighed.

'I'll call you as soon as we land.' Tom hugged me.

'And me?' Harry held out his hands. I'd been scared he wouldn't want to after I scolded him.

I knelt beside him, hugging him tight. I closed my eyes and thought, *I don't want to lose you.*

'Uncle, won't you be sad alone at home?'

'Very. I miss you already, and I don't know how I will last these two days without you.'

'I'll miss you too, but tonight...' He lowered his voice. 'I'll text you when everyone goes to bed.'

'OK,' I whispered, and my heart must have been huge because I felt it in my chest.

'I heard that,' Tom laughed.

'Daddy, I'll have you by my side.' He tilted his head with an innocent smile.

I went to Tom. His hands were slightly damp. He was nervous but said nothing. I looked into his eyes and couldn't say a word. I saw sadness in them, and then tears welling up. I hugged him tighter.

'Daddy, everyone's going through.' Harry pulled my hand. 'We have to go.'

After a kiss, Tom and I exchanged longing glances. He took Harry's hand, and they walked towards the gate. Before entering the sky bridge, Tom turned around, and Harry waved at me. Tom and I exchanged a silent *I love you*.

*

On the plane, Harry watched intently through the window as the baggage carts arrived, and then the pilot, who stood for a moment in the aisle. I witnessed the airport world stealing his heart, and images of fear jostled through my mind. An explosion, a plane crash or a madman trying to kill everyone. I fought these images, trying to push them out of my head. I thought Harry would someday transport people whose paths might meet at the airport. Maybe he would unknowingly help souls who had been looking for each other all their lives. Initially, the airport was a shelter where I could go unnoticed. Then it became a home, until it finally turned into a nightmare from which I ran away for a long time. When I return to it, I see the story of my life, a piece of me left here.

These tiring thoughts made my eyes fail me and took my mind into an imaginary world, bringing sleep – the same one that used to come to me when I had lost my memory. The man was calling my name and reaching out to me. But this time, I saw his face. Lucas. I ran as fast as my legs could carry me, and when I got close, there was an explosion, and the collapsing wall cut off my path.

I flinched, waking up in the chair, but luckily Harry didn't notice. With his nose glued to the window, he watched the tiny towns we flew over and the clouds fluffy as snow that reminded me of Cumbria.

We landed on time. It was after nine in the evening in Newcastle. I turned on my phone.

We've landed safely and are about to go through passport control.

I'm wandering around an empty house, and I miss you terribly.

Maybe you can catch up on movies?

I don't know if I can concentrate. Love you. Lucas.

We will be back soon. We love you. Tom and Harry.

We were just exiting the baggage hall, approaching the door, when I stopped because my legs gave out. I grabbed the railing.

'What's happened, Daddy?' Harry grabbed my hand and looked at me with concern.

'Let's wait a minute.'

'Are you feeling unwell?'

'It'll be over soon. Daddy isn't as young as he used to be.' I laughed nervously.

After a while, Harry's phone rang.

'It's Dad!' he exclaimed cheerfully, quickly answering the call. 'Dad, we'll be right there; Daddy just had to rest for a while. No, it's OK, we're coming now.'

He put the phone in his pocket.

'Shall we go?' I extended my hand. 'I'm better now, honey. Let's go. Dad is waiting.'

The doors to the arrivals hall slid open. The airport hubbub reached me, and with it, the past, waving its hand at us.

'Tom, are you OK?' Chris ran over to us. 'Are you OK?' He greeted me with a hug.

I looked at a woman who was probably picking up her husband. Their longing expressed in a kiss was so real...

'Tom?'

'It's just tiredness; I need to rest.'

'You shouldn't be flying so late.' He took the suitcase from me.

Harry hung around his father's neck, and he lifted him, hugging him tightly.

'Let's go home. Grandma's waiting for dinner.' He offered me his arm. 'Can I?' he asked uncertainly.

'Yeah.' I took his hand, and we walked towards the parking lot. *I can handle it. It's only two days*, I thought.

The wind brushed my face with the familiar moist air as I exited the airport. Memories of my arrival and being picked up by Chris said hello. On the way to the parking lot, Harry kept glancing at me.

'Son, how was the flight? How are you feeling?'

'OK, Dad.'

'Is everything OK at school?'

'Yes. Uncle Lucas taught me maths.' The words came so naturally from him, and Chris kept quiet.

However, I had doubts about whether this kindness was a game or a ruse to take my child away from me. I glanced at Chris's happy face but couldn't read it.

All the way home, Harry told his dad about the past weeks: school, friendships and how he was doing in the new country. When he confessed that he would like to become a pilot, Chris initially fell silent, as if searching for something in his mind. He immediately stated that his grandmother was looking forward to seeing him, thus changing the subject. But when Harry let it slip that Uncle Lucas was teaching him how to roller-skate, Chris's smile quickly faded. I noticed that he tried to restore it but to no avail.

'Look at the birds!' I interrupted Harry's monologue, his blue eyes fixed on the window to take in the sky. I looked at Chris. In this light, I noticed that he seemed more tired than the last time I saw him.

When Chris pulled up to the house, the light in the hall came on, and a moment later, Mum appeared in the doorway.

'My Harry!' she cried, holding her hands out to him.

Harry quickly unbuckled his seat belt and jumped out of the car, throwing himself into Granny's arms. I couldn't help but smile. Now I was sure that despite my prejudice against Chris, I had done the right thing.

'There's my son.' Mum kissed me in greeting.

'Mum, let's take care of Harry. Tom needs to rest,' Chris interjected as he took our suitcase out of the boot.

'Has something happened?' She looked concerned.

'I'm getting old, Mum,' I said with a laugh.

'And what am I supposed to say?' She also laughed. 'Come on; I've prepared your rooms.' She embraced me, and we went inside.

Nothing had changed in the house; it remained as we had left it. In Harry's room, there was still an open notebook on the desk with a drawing he hadn't finished. I had to watch my feet to avoid stepping on toys. This further fuelled my concern that Chris was still getting his hopes up.

'Oh, Dad!' cried Harry, running up to the desk. 'A new computer!' He stared at him.

'The other one was getting old; I wanted you to have a new one.' He blushed.

'Dad, thank you.' Harry threw himself into his arms.

'Now I'll be able to talk to you on camera when you get back... to Amsterdam.'

He struggled to get past the word *home*.

'I love you.' Harry kissed him on the cheek, and a look of pride and contentment came over Chris's face.

'Chris, can we have a word.' I interrupted the idyll.

'Yes?'

'If you're trying to keep him with this computer, it won't work.'

'Tom... I wouldn't even try... I promised you, after all.'

'Your words never meant anything; how can I believe them now?'

'You have to try, trust me.'

I didn't answer. Mum took my hand and stroked it. For a moment, I felt as if we were still living here. I stuck my gaze into the carpet and took a deep breath.

'You can rest while we take care of Harry,' Mum said. 'As long as you're still awake, I'll just be after you for gossip.' She winked at me.

'OK, Mum.' Kissing her on the cheek, I noticed Chris's surreptitious gaze, which exuded longing.

Half an hour later, when Harry was asleep, Mum appeared in my room. She sat down on the edge of the bed.

'Tom, are you happy?' She shyly looked into my eyes.

'Yes, Mum. Very happy.'

In that moment, I could see her joy hugging her sadness.

'I don't want to lie to you. It was difficult for me for a long time. Chris is my son, and I saw how much he suffered when you two split up. He is better now. He is recovering, and I hope that one day, like you, he will find someone to build a happy relationship with.'

Tears appeared in her eyes, and she quickly wiped them away.

'Tom, you are like a son to me, and your happiness is as important to me as Chris's happiness. And now you have to tell me everything in detail.' She laughed, and I joined her.

Initially, I quite timidly outlined my relationship with Lucas. I stepped very carefully, afraid that any word might hurt her. Of course, we were happy. We did lots of cool things together that I never did with Chris. Cooking, going on trips and watching movies together. Lucas would dim the lights, light the candles and put two glasses of wine before us. I didn't mention Harry immediately, but I could see that he was the one my mum was primarily concerned about.

'Lucas and Harry have grown closer; they have their own little world.' I lifted my gaze. 'Everything is just as I always wanted it to be. Simple and warm...'

Listening to the story, she tried to accept the new situation with a smile. She said she would like to see Amsterdam one day and then told me about Judith. She'd met a man in Whitehaven, and they had been inseparable ever since.

'I told her you're going to divorce, and now you're living with Harry in Amsterdam.'

'How did she take it?'

'She was silent at first, thought for a long time, then said that sometimes the universe has another way for us.'

'That doesn't sound like her.' I furrowed my eyebrows.

Mum suddenly stood up and walked to the window. She looked straight out.

'Do you think Harry could come here more often?'

'That depends on Chris.' I ran my gaze down her back.

'He's trying; he really is.' She turned to me. 'Chris has changed a lot since you moved out.' Mum came back over and sat beside me, taking my hand.

'Mum, we both know that Chris doesn't change for no reason. There's something at stake here.'

'It's different now...'

'So I'm going to watch him.'

'Give him a chance to make amends to you for all he has done.'

I opened my mouth, but Chris came into the room just then.

'What are you two gossiping about?' he whispered.

'I was telling Tom about Judith,' laughed Mum. 'I'm going to bed now, Tom.' She kissed me and got up quickly. She momentarily stopped at the door and put her hand on Chris's shoulder.

'Good night.' She left the room.

'Tom, I'll just be a moment. I'd like to thank you for coming with Harry.' Chris hesitantly approached the bed and sat down on the edge of it. I moved over, keeping a safe distance. 'I can imagine how difficult this must have been for you, but I want you to know that... I'm trying.' He lowered his gaze.

'Do you understand that, after what happened, it won't be easy to believe you?'

'I know. I wish I could turn back time.' He touched my hand, and I immediately moved it away.

'Chris, we have a son and should focus on his happiness. Harry doesn't have to choose between us; he can have both of us and be happy.'

'I will prove to you that I deserve your trust.' He stood up. 'I'm going now. Good night, Tom.'

'Good night, Chris.'

At the door, he stopped and turned around.

'You have given me a huge gift with this visit. Thank you.'

The next morning, we went to the fair in Keswick. Harry and I loved the place. It had a kind of magic about it that drew us in every Saturday. Harry winked at me, pointing to the chocolate shop, which made my mum laugh.

'You guys go. Chris and I will go to the market to shop for lunch. We'll come and get you.'

'OK, Mum.'

We entered our treasure cave, where we disappeared between the shelves. We leaned out between them occasionally so as not to lose sight of each other.

At one point, Harry approached me and pointed to some mint chocolate chip cookies, perfect for Lucas. I reached for the packet, and at the same moment, a message arrived from him, as if he could tell we were thinking of him.

How are you doing? I miss you terribly.

We're at the Keswick fair.

I wish I could be there with you now.

We're coming back to you tomorrow night.

I can't wait. I love you.

We more.

We left the shop with a bag of jelly beans and some chocolate, which we snacked on repeatedly.

'That's your trademark,' Mum laughed, pointing to the candy-filled bag I clutched. Harry bared his chocolate-painted teeth.

'Come on, my prince.' Mum gently pushed him towards the car. 'Let's go home.'

On the way back, we got stuck in traffic in Workington. There had been an accident of some kind that blocked the main road. We waited to be allowed to drive through, and I was reminded of the day Chris drove me to Tracy's for therapy. The situation was identical, except I couldn't look at what was happening on the side of the road. The police showed up almost immediately, just as they did then.

I looked at Chris, and he glanced at me.

'Chris, do you remember when there was an accident here once, and we passed it without waiting?' He glanced at me, puzzled. 'Turn into Gray Street,' I managed.

Chris turned, and we drove down a narrow side street, escaping the gridlock.

'Just like old times,' said Chris cheerfully.

We parked up in front of the house. Chris and Harry were getting the groceries out of the boot and I was helping Mum out of the car when I spotted Judith running to the fence.

'You're here!' she called out, stopping, as usual, at the fence.

'Now she won't let us leave,' laughed Mum.

'Tom, how are you? It's been a long time.' She scanned me with her eyes as we approached the fence.

'Same old, really.' I didn't feel like talking.

'Harry, how you've grown!' she exclaimed, gazing at him. 'You'll be a man soon.'

Harry smiled, embarrassed.

'Judith, I hear you've had a big change of heart! Will you tell us his name?' I looked her straight in the eye.

'Ohh...' A blush appeared on her face for the first time. 'His name is Harold; he's an extraordinary man.' Her gaze grew dreamy. 'It was fate; I was in the shop and—'

'My dear, I'm sorry, but Harry is hungry,' Sue interrupted. 'I've got to make dinner. We'll arrange a chat another day.'

We said goodbye to Judith and headed for home.

'She'd never have stopped.' Mum lowered her voice, and we all burst into laughter.

In the evening, Chris knocked on my door.

'Can I come in?'

'Come in.' I corrected myself on the bed by covering myself with the duvet.

He walked in uncertainly and sat down on the foot of the bed.

'It was a really nice day, Tom. Thank you.' He looked deeply into my eyes. 'Do you think I could see Harry more often?' His pleading gaze did not relent.

'If you keep your promise not to try to take him away from me, we can try. However, I don't know yet if he will come alone.'

'Thank you, and remember that you are always welcome here.'

Since that trip, Chris has been a presence in Harry's life. Their evening conversations before bed became an integral part of each day. I enjoyed his involvement in his son's life. He even tried to make a connection with Lucas when he unknowingly walked into Harry's room during their conversation. Lucas tried to be nice but couldn't quite break through. He said he didn't trust him and could feel trouble coming.

Another meeting at the airport was coming up. In the middle of the week, Chris called, informing us that he had caught some kind of cold and didn't want to infect us. He asked for the meeting to be postponed. There was something in his voice that did not make me feel at ease; the thoughts screamed to me: *He is lying! He is up to something!* I tried to silence them, explaining to our disappointed child that Dad was just sick and they would meet next week. I asked Chris to talk to his son. I stood outside the door, listening to their conversation.

'Hi, honey, how are you?' Chris asked.

'Dad, I've been waiting for your call; what's wrong?' Harry was clearly concerned.

'I caught some nasty virus; I'm running to the bathroom all the time.'

'That's a shame. When will I see you again?'

'Next weekend. I promise.'

'Harry! Dinner's ready!' Lucas called from the kitchen.

I returned to the living room and quickly sat on the sofa to avoid getting caught.

During dinner, I glanced at Harry, whose sadness had set in. He declared that Dad was ill and would see him in a week, then let out a disappointed sigh into his plate. Lucas and I exchanged glances.

'So, since you've got the weekend off,' Lucas began, 'why don't we take Daddy out for some roller skating?' He looked up at Harry's newly formed smile.

'Ohh no! Don't even think about it!' I said to Lucas.

'Yeah, Daddy, please.'

'I don't think we have a choice.' Lucas gave Harry a meaningful look, and they both got up from the table. They turned their heads and approached me like zombies, stretching their arms out in front of them.

'Agree, agree...' they cried out in squawking voices, knowing I hated it.

'No, don't! Lucas, stop it! Please!'

I sprang up from my chair and ran towards the living room. They caught up with me by the sofa, climbing on it and moving their jaws gruesomely. I laughed and tried to fend them off with my hands, but they didn't stop. After a few minutes, I succumbed.

'I agree; just stop!' I shouted. They high-fived each other and hugged me. Lying in silence, we stole a moment from time in which we listened to our breaths.

9. Chris

On Friday, I stopped twice on my way home from work and jumped out of the car at the last minute, vomiting at the side of the road. At night, I covered myself with a blanket and a duvet, which didn't help me stop shivering from the cold. The faces of Mum, Tom and Harry appeared before my eyes in turn. Much younger than she was now, Mum chastised me for coming home late. Then Tom's disappointed eyes when I didn't go to the fair with him. The tears came to my eyes when I didn't go for a bike ride with Harry. He spoke so little that first night he came home with us. *You must be strong,* Tom kept telling me that first week. I got out of bed and ran to the bathroom. I hadn't eaten anything that day and still couldn't stop vomiting. I spent Sunday on the sofa, and on Monday, I took a week off, completely ignoring the household chores. The backlog piled up at home and work, and litres of guilt about neglecting it all flooded over me.

On the Monday before work, I got ready for an appointment with a psychotherapist. I had been going to her for a while, hiding it from everyone. As I was still weak with shaky legs, trying to tie my shoelaces, Tom's voice continued to ring in my ears: *You have to be strong.* Now all I needed was some hope of getting my family back.

I dashed across the yard and hurriedly got into my car, hoping Judith wouldn't notice me, but as I drove out of the gate, I saw her face firmly focused on me in the window. Surely she would call my mother, and they would gossip. My mother would say that her outcast son never calls her, and Judith would confirm this and add, *You see how they all are. Only Tom knew how to deal with this meddlesome whiner.* I had tried to be nice, but only for Tom's sake. It didn't matter now, and she must have sensed it because she hadn't even come near the fence since Tom moved out.

Out on the road, I passed the first and second flocks of sheep giving themselves entirely to the grass. There was no one else around. I sped up.

Why did I agree to move here? Apart from the views, there was nothing in the area. I had to travel tens of miles to do the big shops. And the rain. I was better in Reading; I could always go out and meet people. This was like being in prison, in a cell I no longer shared with anyone.

I parked outside the therapist's house. It was raining mercilessly, like it always was when I had something to do. I got out of the car and ran to her door. I shook off the raindrops in the corridor and went into the study.

'Hello, Chris.' Emily shifted in her chair.

'Sorry I'm late. For some reason it's been hard for me to get on top of everything today.' I sat on the sofa and took off my jacket.

'Would you like something to drink?' She stared at me.

'No, thanks. We'd better start,' I grumbled.

'You've missed a few sessions recently. What happened?' Her gaze pinned me to the wall, and I tried to find some explanation on the fly.

'It's been a while. First Tom visited me with Harry—'

'Tom and Harry were with you?' Her disbelieving expression indicated that I was falling into paranoia.

'You wouldn't believe it, would you? And here's the surprise. Mum also came, and we had a great weekend. I felt like before, as if we were still a family. What am I saying? We're still here; they're living elsewhere for a while, and then—' I broke off, barely holding back my words. 'I had the flu and was in bed.'

'Has Tom come to sign the divorce papers?' Squinting slightly, she tilted her head.

'Of course not.'

'I remember that Tom wanted a divorce.'

'He wanted to... Maybe now he doesn't want to at all.' I dragged my hand over my trousers as if I wanted to wipe the dust off them.

'Chris, I remember that you came to me because you wanted to come to terms with the fact that Tom has made a new life for himself.'

'He will come back!' I yelled. 'We're just having some temporary trouble.'

There was silence, and Emily made a note. I wondered if Tracy took notes when Tom went to therapy. It was so irritating.

'I want you to take a deep breath. You have a lot of emotions in you. A lot of anger. It's quite normal. Divorce is a process that can be compared to mourning—'

'Fuck!' I shouted. 'What divorce! What grief! I've told you, these are temporary problems that we will deal with. We've done it once, and we'll do it again.'

'Try to control your emotions,' Emily said calmly. 'If this happens again, we'll have to end our meetings.'

There was silence, and I felt ashamed of my behaviour.

My voice dropped to a whisper. 'I'm sorry, it won't happen again.'

'Let's go back to your husband and son's visit,' she went on after a moment. 'How did you feel when they visited you?'

'It was the most wonderful two days. Their presence made me forget for a moment that... that they live in another city. I thought I could keep them at one point, but I knew Tom wasn't ready for that yet.'

'Keep?' I heard fear in her question. 'What exactly did you mean by that?'

'I didn't mean anything bad.' I shifted on the sofa, sliding deeper into the backrest. 'I thought maybe if I told them... maybe they'd stay with me.'

'What would you like to tell them?' She scribbled something mechanically on her notebook, then looked back at me.

'Nothing... It doesn't matter.' I reached for a mug of tea.

I don't really know why I didn't want to tell her. Maybe because I thought it was a temporary problem that would soon disappear and I wouldn't have to tell anyone about it.

'Chris, losing your family is a stressful situation, but—'

'I said—' At the last moment, I managed to stop my raised voice. 'I'm sorry. I meant to say it's temporary.' I got up. 'I can't.' I grabbed my jacket and headed for the door. As I crossed the threshold, I heard Emily calling me to come back, but nothing could change my decision. This therapy was useless. Nothing made sense anymore.

Furiously, I jumped into the car. I didn't even glance in Emily's direction as I drove away. I went to work and sat at my desk, not speaking to anyone. At the end of the day, after everyone had left the room, my boss approached me.

'Are you staying late?'

'Yes, I wanted to finish these documents.'

'Don't stay too long; you've been ill.'

'Yes...' I sighed.

I didn't know what to do with myself when I got home. I wandered around, peering into empty rooms that echoed the sounds in my head of Harry running around in his Spider-Man costume and Tom chasing after him. When he caught up with him in the living room, they tumbled to the floor, and Tom shouted some magic spells to stop Harry. I watched them from the sofa, unable to stop laughing.

Then I went into the kitchen, where my mother would usually be, cooking. I smelled the cake she was baking. Seeing me, she would cut a large piece of apple pie for me. I returned to the living room with the cake, but the guys tried to take it from me. They chased me halfway through the house, then we rested on the sofa, panting. I missed our life together so much.

Tom's things were still in the bathroom. Sometimes I would smell his cologne, and it seemed to me that he was next to me, and when I went to bed, I had the feeling that he would get in, cold, and I'd hug him. Now that I was alone in that big bed, I couldn't sleep. I turned from side to side, wondering how they were doing. What were they doing? Did they ever think about me? Tom was such a stranger during our meetings at the airport that his mind wandered off. I'd like to know where it disappeared to.

The next morning I called Emily. I apologised to her for my impetuous temper, and we agreed that I would come to the session before work.

'Sorry again about yesterday,' I said as I entered the office. I removed my jacket and sat on the sofa, staring at the floor.

'I'd like to clear something up.' She looked at me sternly, like a schoolteacher, and I felt like a scolded child. 'I don't allow this behaviour in my office. If this happens again, we won't be working together.'

'Sorry. I couldn't control my emotions.'

'What are these emotions? Tell me about them.'

‘Helplessness.’ I raised my eyes. ‘I wish so much that Tom would forgive me and come back with Harry. I can’t manage without them. I feel pain every day that I can’t get rid of. I wish it would stop.’

‘Chris, breaking up is a long process. From what you said a while ago, Tom asked you for a divorce. What did you feel then?’

‘At first, I thought he was teasing me, but his seriousness made my heart ache. I didn’t know what to do.’ Suddenly I felt a strong scratch in my throat and coughed.

‘Are you OK?’

‘Yes, it’s just a cold.’

‘Chris, I understand that this is difficult for you.’ She reached for a glass on the table, next to which was a water decanter. ‘I’m here to support you.’ She filled the glass and placed it in front of me.

‘I still feel like they’re coming back.’ I burst into tears, but I quickly managed to control it. *Pathetic*, I thought.

Emily pushed the box of tissues towards me.

‘You mentioned that you have contact with your son. How do you feel about that?’

‘Tom is slowly opening up to more frequent meetings. I am grateful to him for that. I was afraid I wouldn’t be able to see them. I miss Tom, but he doesn’t trust me after what happened and comes to the meetings with Harry.’ I reached for my glass of water. ‘And I’m glad to see them, if only for a little while.’

‘The situation is difficult for both of you, but I can see you are trying. Any married couple would have trouble with this.’

‘It’s thanks to Tom. He always knows what is right. I didn’t feel lost with him. He could organise everything.’

'Do you feel lost?' Emily folded her hands.

'Yes. I don't know what I should do. When we were together, we had our schedule and responsibilities. Now I don't know what I'm supposed to do and when to do it, when I should go to sleep and when I should eat. I get lost. I miss them so much.'

'You mentioned that you like working in the garden. You haven't had time for that lately, have you? What do you think now?'

'I don't know...'

'Imagine that your garden is a reflection of your life. It's a mess, with sticks strewn about, dead plants and weeds, but if you start cleaning it up, you'll give new plants a chance to grow before you know it. I'd like that to be your assignment for the next week.'

'I'll try,' I sighed unconvincingly. I didn't know how to tell her I no longer had the energy and enthusiasm to work in the garden like I used to.

At work, I sat down at my desk. I could feel my co-workers' eyes on me. They probably gossiped about me in the kitchen, making fun of me, but I didn't care.

'Chris, I'm worried about you.' The boss had noticed that I was staying late again.

'I'm almost done, literally ten minutes.'

'I'm glad. You need to rest. Go home.'

What home? I thought as he left. *I don't have a home anymore.*

I got back late in the evening. There were letters on the kitchen floor, and one was still stuck in the door. I took it out of the slot. I kept getting Boots coupons addressed to Tom. I put them back in the compartment where I kept his correspondence and turned on the TV. I thought if I stayed up until midnight, I would fall asleep more easily, but I didn't until the morning. The phone woke me up.

'Chris?'

'I'm here.' I could barely get the words out.

'Come in today; your results have come. I want to speak with you.'

'I'll get myself sorted and be right over.'

I jumped out of bed and ran to the bathroom. The toothbrush slipped from my hands several times, staining the floor and my pyjamas with toothpaste. I gave up on breakfast because after approaching the fridge, I stopped feeling hungry. Instead, there was a tightness in my stomach and an uncertainty about what to do next. I pushed my dark thoughts away, hoping it wouldn't be so bad. I drank a glass of water while getting dressed in the hall. I put it back on the dresser, then stopped and looked at it again. Tom would have told me off for that. I took my shoes off and put the glass in the kitchen.

In the car, I turned my attention to my hands on the steering wheel. They were shaking, like when I took my driving test. I inhaled and exhaled several times like Emily had advised me. I set off.

At the hospital, I went directly to the doctor's office.

'Hello, Chris.' He got up from his chair as I opened the door.

I immediately sat in the chair before his desk, awaiting the verdict. His serious face showed no emotion, and his eyes touched me with coldness.

'Chris, the tests have shown two metastases in the stomach area.'

'Has it gotten worse?' My heart pounded so hard that shadows appeared in front of my eyes.

'The chemo didn't help,' he said resignedly.

'So, what now? Some radiation, more chemotherapy? We keep treating it, right; there are new drugs, therapies...'

'Chris, listen—'

'For God's sake! I did everything you said. All of it!' I jumped out of the chair.

'Chris, there was no guarantee. You knew that.'

I couldn't control my rapid breathing. My legs refused to obey me, and I sat back down.

'I'm sorry, Chris, but there is nothing more that can be done. I don't think you should delay telling your family.'

I looked out the window and tears came to my eyes. All I could think about right now was Tom and Harry.

'Right. I have to go now.' I stood up, wiping my cheek and extending my hand in farewell.

'Chris, talk to them.'

'Once again, thank you for everything. I'll be in touch.'

I left the hospital in a hurry. In the parking lot, I couldn't contain it and kicked the car's front tyre with all my might. People passing by quickened their pace. I got into the car, closed the door and opened my mouth, from which a piercing scream erupted. I grabbed the wheel. Now it was certain that I would not be able to get my family back. Maybe if I told them, they'd return, but I didn't want their pity.

At home, I couldn't sit still. Aimlessly, I wandered from room to room, blaming life for what it had done to me. Finally, I entered the garden, where the wind pushed Harry's swing. I missed them so much. I wanted to tell them everything and even made up scenarios in my head about how

I would do it, but every time I reached for my phone, I was filled with fear and the words were lost in the chaos of my mind. I dialled Tom's number several times before I finally found the courage.

'Tom? Do you have time to talk?'

'What's up?'

In the distance, I could hear the TV and Harry talking to Lucas. That squeezed my heart tighter.

'I'd like to meet with you to talk.'

'What's happened?'

'It's time for us to... We have to finish our unfinished business.' I couldn't control the trembling of my hand, and I held the phone with my other.

'I don't understand what you're talking about. If you're trying—'

'Tom,' I interrupted him. 'I'm not trying anything. Don't be afraid of me. I just want to meet with all of you and talk. Wherever you want to.'

'With all of us?

'Yes, Tom. With all of you.'

'You have to give me a moment; I'll call you back.' His voice sounded lost.

'Sure.'

*

I hung up and looked at Lucas, who was walking towards me. Among all the thoughts that swirled in my head, one gnawed at me like a worm. Chris had found a way to take Harry away from me. I tried desperately to dismiss the thought, telling myself that despite his evil, despite all that he had done to me, there was good in him. He probably wanted to take Harry on a trip and was going to ask for my permission.

‘Who called?’ Lucas asked, cuddling up to me.

‘Chris,’ I sighed.

‘What did he want?’

‘He wants to meet.’

‘Again?’ He tilted his head and looked me in the eyes.

‘This time with all of us. He wants to talk about something.’

‘What’s he up to now?’

‘Something good this time?’

‘Him? That’s rather hard to imagine.’ Lucas went to the fridge and took out a juice.

‘Maybe we should invite him here and listen to what he has to say. Harry would be happy.’

‘Here?’ Lucas almost spilt the juice on the counter. ‘He’s going to destroy us again.’

‘He’s been trying so hard lately. Maybe this is a good time to bury the hatchet?’

Lucas thought momentarily, then approached me and took me in his arms.

‘You know I love you, and if you think it’s good for Harry, let’s do it, but I will never be able to trust him.’ He kissed me and left.

I went to the window and looked at the tree. I wanted to ask it what I should do, but it wouldn’t answer. I dialled his number.

‘Chris?’

‘Yes, Tom.’

‘You can come and visit us. I hope I won’t regret it.’

‘Never. Thank you.’

‘I’ll send you the address.’

*

When Tom ended the call, I forgot about the whole world. The happiness of seeing them immediately filled me with warmth, but only for a short while because right after that, I realised that this might be the last time. I should fix everything before... The phone rang. Mum.

'I couldn't get through to you. Who were you talking to?'

'Tom.'

'I hope you didn't fight again?'

'No, Mum...' My throat went dry, and I couldn't stop coughing.

'What's wrong? Are you sick?'

For a moment I had a feeling that my mother was going to catch me out. She'd sniff out the lie and then panic and come over. I sat down at the dining room table.

'Why are you interrogating me? I'm not a child anymore.'

'To me, you will always be a child, and I will worry about you for the rest of my life.'

I couldn't drown out the sarcasm ringing loudly in my head: *You won't have to for much longer.*

'Mum, we haven't talked for a long time, why not tell me how you are? How're things going at the council?'

'Chris, don't change the subject.'

'I've caught a cold and can't get over it.'

'Because you don't take care of yourself. You should come to your mother. I'll take care of you. We haven't seen each other for a long time.'

I tried to occupy my hand and started to play with the tablecloth. At that moment, a memory of Harry doing the same thing came to me, and Tom admonishing him.

'Chris? Are you still there?'

'Yes, Mum. I'll come, but I can't right now. I have to visit Tom and Harry.'

'Visit how? Are you going to Amsterdam?'

'Yes. They invited me.'

'That's great, that you'll get to see them... but are you ready?'

'Yes, Mum. I'm ready to meet Lucas.'

'I'm worried this will hurt you.'

'It's past time to put things right. Life doesn't wait for us.'

'That would be great. I will keep my fingers crossed for you.'

A week later, I was getting ready for a Friday night flight. I wanted to surprise Harry and asked Tom to keep my arrival a secret from him. I decided to come from the airport alone.

*

Harry was in his room, sulking. I hadn't let him go to a friend's that evening. I barely held my tongue so as not to spoil the surprise. Doubts about whether I had done the right thing attacked me constantly. Lucas couldn't sit still on the sofa and paced the living room nervously while I shelled nuts.

'What if he wants to take Harry away from us? Maybe it's a trick?' Lucas whispered.

'Honey, I'm sure that won't happen. We're both on our guard right now, and we'll react immediately if Chris makes one suspicious move.'

When the doorbell rang, I jumped, and the nutcracker fell from my hands. Lucas picked it up.

'We'll be fine,' he whispered, and kissed me.

'Harry, will you get the door?' I called as I walked into the corridor with Lucas.

Harry, still annoyed with me, passed us, looking ahead and going straight for the door. He released the bolts, tugged vigorously on the handle, and moments later, he was screaming with joy as he threw himself on Dad's neck.

'You're here!' he exclaimed, kissing Chris.

'Hi, son.' Chris hugged him hard.

I walked over to Chris, and his pale face and the dark circles under his eyes caught my attention. When he removed his cap, it seemed his hair no longer had its former shine and was visibly thinned. I hadn't noticed before.

'Hi, are you OK? You are very pale.'

'Hi. It's leftover from the flu.' He looked away. 'I can't shake it off.'

Then he saw Lucas. He hesitated but walked over to him, extending his hand.

'Hi.'

'Hi,' Lucas replied coolly, ignoring his hand.

'I'm sorry, Daddy.' Harry hugged me hesitantly.

'Nothing to be sorry for. Show Dad your room.' I kissed him. 'I'll get dinner ready.'

'Daddy, come.' Harry tugged at his hand.

As Chris and Harry walked down the hall, Chris's eyes wandered over our pictures hanging on the walls. I wondered what he was thinking now. This visit must be difficult for him, but why did he come? I noticed a large piece of lint on the floor and picked it up, and on the way to the kitchen, passing the living room, I adjusted the sofa cushions several times. I don't know why because they didn't need to be corrected. I walked into the kitchen, where Lucas was preparing the plates.

‘I’m sorry, but I couldn’t shake his hand.’

‘I don’t blame you.’ I hugged him and kissed him on the lips. ‘We’ll soon find out what he came for, but for now, let Harry enjoy his dad.’

During dinner, the conversation was dominated by Harry, who was so excited about Chris’s presence that his mouth wouldn’t stop for even a second.

‘Dad, do you know that I am the best in the class, and the lady said that I lost my accent quickly?’

‘That’s great, son.’ He stroked his head.

‘And my friends from school and I play football together, and I’m on the team with them.’

Harry tried to summarise each event for Chris, but Chris’s eyes kept losing focus. I couldn’t stop watching him. I tried to read something on his face, but I couldn’t.

‘Eat something,’ Lucas whispered, leaning into me.

I tried to calm the raging tension and uncertainty that filled my insides. I couldn’t.

‘What did you want to talk to us about?’ I turned to Chris.

Lucas put his hand on my trembling knee, under the table.

‘I’d prefer to discuss it when Harry has gone to bed.’ Chris held me with a longer, pleading gaze.

By the end of dinner, I couldn’t swallow anything, and even though Lucas kept shoving food at me, I felt like I was about to vomit.

Chris put Harry to bed, and I sat down with Lucas in the living room, exchanging nervous glances.

‘What do you think he came for?’ Lucas whispered.

'The only thing I can think of is that he wants to leave somewhere with Harry and will ask me for permission. They've never actually gone away together, and Chris likes to travel.'

'Hope you are right,' he sighed.

When we heard him close Harry's door and head towards us, I held my breath and squeezed Lucas's hand tighter. Chris entered the living room, took a chair and placed it before us. Lucas immediately moved closer to me. Chris sat in silence for a moment. When he finally looked at me, I saw despair in his eyes, like that day when he first drove me to therapy at Tracy's.

'The most precious gift you can receive in life,' he began, 'is knowing you love someone. Someone who returns your affection. You gave it to me and I... Tom, I'm sorry I was selfish. I have hurt you with words and deeds all these years instead of loving you. I didn't support you. I don't even know when I became so possessive and selfish. I hope you can forgive me someday.'

Lucas stabbed his gaze to the floor. Chris hung his head and took a deep breath, words coming to him with difficulty.

'I fell in love with you in our first conversation on the internet, and ever since then, I have always wanted to be with you. I know I've made many mistakes that I should never have made, but I was just a weak, stupid man who loved you. Now that I see you're happy and Harry's happy, I rejoice together with you.'

He looked at Lucas, but it wasn't a look of hatred, more sadness, because I saw tears in his eyes.

'I know you hate me, and you'll probably never forgive me, but I want to apologise to you too.' Lucas looked at him. 'For everything. For stalking you like a rat because I didn't want you to take Tom away from me. But it was inevitable. I only ask for one thing – take care of my boys. Give them what I couldn't.'

He cried, and so did I. I got up and hugged him, but he kept sobbing, repeatedly repeating, 'I'm sorry.' I stroked his hair, which wasn't as thick as it used to be, and he closed his eyes.

'We've been through a lot together, Chris – a lot. We have a son, and I would like you to be present in his life. Harry loves you very much and needs you.'

'Thank you, Tom. That means a lot to me.'

I looked at Lucas, whose glassy eyes were trying to hide tears. He got up and came over to us.

'It's been a long evening. We should all rest.'

'I'll make your bed, and you take a shower,' I told Chris.

'Tom, wait.' He grabbed my hand. 'I'd like to sign the divorce papers. It's time.'

Lucas abruptly grabbed his shirt pocket as if to find a pen. We looked at him, and after a while, we all burst out laughing. We couldn't control it for quite a bit, which made us forget about all the bad things that had happened.

I heard Harry running from his room down the hall in the morning. His bare little feet hit the floor hard, making a wooden groan. Then the melodic sounds of his conversation with his father leaked into our bedroom, and they must have fallen asleep because after a while there was silence, and I fell asleep too. Chris and Harry were inseparable at breakfast, like two little boys whose laughter filled the kitchen. Lucas made scrambled eggs, and I couldn't stop staring at Harry.

After breakfast, we walked, showing Chris a bit of Amsterdam. He watched people intently and winced at the sound of the Dutch language as Harry spoke to Lucas.

'He's doing well, becoming a native Dutchman.' He glanced at me. 'Learns fast.'

'And you?'

'What about me?'

'How's your Dutch?' He looked into my eyes.

'It's slower for me.' I chuckled, looking ahead. 'I definitely prefer English.'

'Can you do it? You've always been like that.'

'Yes...'

After a while, Harry ran over to us.

'What are you talking about?' He tried to find my gaze.

'Daddy was telling me how fast you learn a new language,' Chris responded immediately.

'It's not difficult, Dad.' He took his hand, and they led the way.

Lucas came over to me. 'Everything OK?'

'I think so.'

It had been a long time since I'd felt as peaceful as I did that day when we returned from our walk and Harry and I watched cartoons together in the living room. Chris cuddled his son, kissing him now and then, and I felt relieved that we had finally found understanding.

In the evening, Chris packed his carry-on suitcase, and Harry wouldn't leave him for a moment.

'You'll come again, Dad, won't you?' Harry looked pleadingly at Chris.

‘If I can,’ Chris replied, looking straight ahead, his gaze lingering somewhere between the things he was putting in the suitcase.

‘We’ll drive you to the airport.’ I touched his shoulder. ‘You’re not going alone.’

He just smiled.

For the rest of our evening, Harry stuck to his father’s side the whole time. In the lobby, Lucas grabbed Chris’s suitcase, which surprised me. We exchanged warm glances.

On the way to the airport, Harry planned a camping trip in the woods with his dad, which they had been putting off. I watched them in the mirror, but there was a sadness in Chris’s face.

‘Dad, we’ll see each other soon, right?’ Harry grabbed Chris’s hand as we walked him to passport control.

‘Yes, son,’ he said, his voice trembling. I studied his face, trying to see the familiar spark of joy, but I couldn’t find it.

He crouched next to Harry and hugged him as if he were leaving forever. Then he approached Lucas.

‘Thank you.’ He extended his hand to Lucas in farewell, and this time Lucas took it. Then he came over to me.

‘Tom, thank you again for letting me come. It means a lot to me.’ He hugged me, and I immediately felt his warmth. We held the embrace for a long time. Memories of all our goodbyes greeted me. After a moment, Chris grabbed his suitcase and headed for the gate.

‘Chris! Wait!’ I called after him.

He turned and stopped, a curious look on his face.

‘Perhaps you would like to spend a weekend with your son? Harry would be very happy. We’ll take care of everything else.’

'Thank you, Tom,' he whispered, and hugged me again, but I felt despair and fear in his embrace this time, as if it was our last meeting.

'Are you OK, Chris?' I found his gaze.

'Yes. Now that's it.' He smiled and kissed me on the cheek.

When he left, I felt like before. I would walk with him to the airport, and he'd pick me up next week. At the gate, he turned and waved to us one last time. His eyes still glowed with sadness. Maybe he had problems at work. No, it couldn't be work. There was something poignant in his gaze, something that seriously bothered him. I decided that at the next meeting, I would ask him about it.

At home, I bathed Harry, and while I changed him into his pyjamas, he cuddled up to me.

'Thank you, Daddy,' he whispered.

'For what, honey?'

'For the surprise. And sorry for my stupid behaviour.'

'I'm not angry, and you know what? I talked to your dad. You can go to him for a weekend.'

'Really? I can? Daddy?'

'You can, honey. We need to work out the details with Dad.'

Harry jumped up and down on the bed a few times, and I couldn't stop laughing.

'Well, it's time for bed, baby.' I kissed him good night. 'Leave it on?' I pointed to the bedside lamp.

'Daddy, I'm not a baby anymore.'

'No?' I laughed.

'In case you haven't noticed, I've been turning off the light for a long time.'

'All right, my man. We turn it off. Good night.'

Lucas was already in bed when I entered the bedroom. The starlight streaming in through the window gently illuminated his face. I slipped under the duvet, and he immediately snuggled up and kissed me.

'Was all that with Chris real?'

'I think so. He's been through a lot and understands it all now, and that's the most important thing.'

'I don't know what to think about it.'

'Think positive.'

'You know, I don't want to say anything...' He modulated his voice theatrically. 'But that long hug and kiss in front of my eyes...'

'What kiss? It was just a goodbye. Come on? Are you jealous?'

'Maybe.'

'Really?'

'I think you'll have to make it up to me somehow.'

'Oh yeah,' I laughed. 'And what does that look like?'

'I'll show you.' He took my hand and started kissing me.

10. Reconciliation

Amsterdam was cradled in the arms of a lazy Saturday. The sleepy streets were washed by a gentle breeze that caressed the leaves on the branches of the trees. The apartment joined us in sleep, making gentle noises. Here and there a rustle, a soft crackle or the murmur of water in the pipes, reminiscent of swallowing saliva. Harry slept between us. He had come in during the night and cuddled up to me. I felt his warm breath on my neck. This bliss was suddenly interrupted by the loud ringing of my phone. I grabbed it so it wouldn't wake anyone up. Mum.

'It's seven in the morning,' I whispered.

'Tom, I'm sorry to wake you, but Chris is in hospital.' Her voice wavered.

Stunned, I sat on the edge of the bed as my mother continued.

'They called me yesterday. He lost consciousness. I came immediately.'

'Wait.' I stood nervously, glancing at Lucas's and Harry's faces. They slept. Treading like a thief on tiptoe, I left the room, closing the door almost silently behind me. I went to the living room.

'Tell me what happened?'

'He was hiding cancer from us. How could I have missed it?' There was terror in her voice. 'Now I remember him coughing. He was very pale, but I believed him that it was a cold. He's dying, Tom.'

The words sent an icy shiver down my spine.

'Mum, I didn't notice either. It's not your fault. How is he feeling?' I sat on the sofa.

'It's not good. The doctors say there's not much time left. He was talking about you and Harry. He would love to see you.'

I fell silent, losing my thoughts and falling into the void.

'Tom? Are you there?'

'Yes.'

'Will you come?'

I got up and walked to the kitchen counter where Harry's mug was sitting. I looked at it and wondered how to explain this to a child.

'Of course we will, Mum,' I replied after a moment.

'I'll be waiting for you.'

I hung up and stayed still. I watched a tree in the deserted street shed its yellowed leaves for a long time. They tumbled helplessly to the pavement. I returned to the bedroom, and Lucas woke up and propped himself on his elbow.

'What's happened?' He squinted his sleepy eyes, the seam of the pillow imprinted on his cheek marking his face. I looked at Harry, who was still sound asleep.

'Let's go to the living room. I don't want to wake Harry.'

Lucas grabbed a dressing gown off a chair and hurried out with me.

'What's going on?' He tried to find my gaze.

'Mum called.' I swallowed and took a breath. 'Chris is in the hospital. He's dying.'

'What?' Lucas froze.

'He was hiding cancer from us.'

There was a silence in which neither of us knew what to say.

‘I’ll go with you,’ Lucas said after a moment. ‘Harry should be there.’ He came over and hugged me. ‘I’ll make breakfast, and you wake Harry up.’

I made my way to the bedroom with a knot in my stomach. Nobody had prepared me for how to tell a child that his father was dying. I went into the bedroom; he was asleep. I sat next to him and gently stroked his back.

‘Honey, wake up. We have to go to the hospital. Dad is sick.’

His eyes were still asleep, but his body jerked nervously.

‘What’s wrong?’

‘Son, Dad didn’t tell us that he has cancer.’ The words came out of me with great difficulty. Harry froze momentarily, then his chin quivered slightly, and I saw him grip the duvet tighter.

‘But they’ll cure him, won’t they?’ His eyes filled with tears.

‘No, son,’ I whispered, my breath uneven. ‘They can’t help him anymore.’ I tried to control my tears.

‘But they can’t! They have to heal him!’ He rushed into my arms, crying.

‘I know how hard it is for you, but we should be with him now.’ I hugged him tightly. ‘He’ll want to see us.’

Harry snuggled into me, his warm tears touching my shoulder. I stroked his back in a slight rocking motion, trying to calm his racing emotions.

In Newcastle, we hired a car and set off for Cumberland Infirmary in Carlisle. Harry cried the whole way. I sat in the back with him and stroked his head while cuddling him. Every so often, Lucas and I exchanged glances in the mirror.

‘Why didn’t Daddy tell me?’

'Honey, Dad didn't tell anyone. He didn't want to worry us.'

'But he should have told me.' He was sobbing, and I didn't know how to help him.

I didn't stop stroking him and hugging him. He'd only calmed down slightly by the time we got to the hospital. Lucas parked, and we went through the main entrance. In the emergency room, we were directed to the first floor, where I spotted Mum at the end of the corridor. She sat in a chair, her blue face pressed against the cream-coloured wall.

'Grandma!' Harry rushed towards her.

'You've arrived.' She rose briskly from her chair and caught him in her arms.

Lucas and I walked over and greeted my mother. We fell into each other's arms. She had lost a lot of weight since we last met. Her face was full of fatigue, as if she hadn't slept for several nights. Spidery red veins obscured the whites of her eyes. She stared at me for a long moment.

'Mum, this is Lucas.' I turned to face him.

She approached slowly, her gaze greedy, not wanting to miss any details.

'Nice to meet you.' He held his hand out to her, which she ignored, and moments later, she hugged him tightly.

Lucas stiffened. I nodded to him as a sign that everything was OK, and he gently reciprocated her hug.

'Do we know anything?' I looked towards the door of the room.

'He has a doctor with him now. He'll be coming out to us soon. Let's sit down.' She gestured to the chairs along the wall.

We took our seats, and Harry immediately cuddled up to Grandma.

'I was afraid you wouldn't make it,' she whispered.

'How could we not notice it?' I covered my face with my hands. 'I should have known Chris didn't change for no reason.'

Tears squeezed between my fingers. I took a breath, trying to stop them. I had to be strong for Harry. When he met us at the airport, I remember he seemed tired and sleepy. When he visited us in Amsterdam, I noticed his pallor and the dark circles under his eyes. He said it was from the flu. I didn't think about it then, but he was always healthy. He got over colds so easily.

After a while, the doctor appeared at the door. We jumped out of our chairs.

'This is Tom, Chris's husband,' Mum said immediately.

'How is he doing?' I shook the doctor's hand.

'I will not hide that it isn't good. He has been ill for a long time. Chemotherapy did not give the results we hoped for.'

'We didn't know he was sick.'

'I asked him to talk to you, but he wouldn't.'

'How much time does he have left?'

'The cancer has already attacked his bones, lungs, liver and intestines. It's a miracle he's still alive – it's as if he was waiting for something.' The doctor looked deep into my eyes.

Mum sat in a chair and covered her mouth with her hands. She sobbed. Harry looked at his grandmother in fear, and Lucas immediately took him on his lap and hugged him tightly. I knelt by them.

'Honey, do you remember how I told you about the angel who comes to take people to heaven?'

'Yes, I remember.' He barely managed to get his voice out.

'Dad is now waiting for such an angel, who will take him to heaven so that nothing can hurt him anymore.'

'But I don't want him to take him.' His breath fought the tears streaming down Lucas's sweater.

'Honey, if you don't let Dad go with this angel, he will suffer very badly, because the disease inside him is causing him great pain.'

Harry didn't answer, just cried.

I looked at the doctor. 'Can I see him?'

'Yes, just talk quietly. He is sensitive to loud noises.'

'Thank you, Doctor.'

I hugged Harry, kissing his temple, and then my mum, who continued to sob. Stroking her hand, I looked into her eyes, which now expressed only pain. I walked over to the door and gently pressed the handle. The silence of the room was disturbed now and then by the short beep of the vital signs machine. Chris lay motionless in bed. Oxygen was supplied to his nose through transparent tubes, and plasters held a needle with a drip stuck in his hand.

'Chris, it's me, Tom,' I whispered.

He moved his head slightly, and when he looked at me, I saw his blue and emaciated face with heavily sunken eyes. His aching body controlled the smile that appeared on his face.

'You've come.' He sounded as if his voice had stuck to his larynx. 'Where's Harry?'

'He's here, waiting in the corridor with Mum.'

'I'd like to see him.'

'I'll bring him in soon.'

I walked closer and sat on the chair next to the bed. He raised his hand slightly, trying to touch me. I brought mine to him.

'I'm sorry, I'm so sorry for everything.' Tears immediately flowed down his cheeks. 'Will you forgive me?'

The screech of the machine pierced my ears now and then, and I moved closer, leaning over it.

'Chris... of course I forgive you. You will always be in my heart, and Harry's. That will never change. We love you.'

He smiled, and I wiped a tear from his cheek.

'Do you remember when we planted flowers in the garden?' he began. 'You put them in pots, and I splashed you with the watering can. You jumped back and grabbed the hose from the wall. You turned on the tap, and the stream shot out at me. I chased you until we fell to the grass. To this day, I remember its smell and the coolness of the dampness. I kissed you, and the rain poured down on us. You wanted to get up, but I figured we were already wet, so we stayed on the grass. Water dripped from our hair and faces, and I couldn't stop kissing you.'

I almost smelled wet grass at that moment, and I started to talk about how we met. About the driver of our wedding limousine who got the times wrong and arrived too early, and Chris answered the door in just a shirt and underpants. Those memories were still alive in me.

Chris laughed, but it quickly turned into a cough. I was scared. No matter what he had done, he didn't deserve this fate. I lifted the oxygen mask and brought a glass of water to his lips, helping him drink. After a while, his cough subsided. As I wiped his mouth with a tissue, I noticed how long he looked at me.

'We were so happy.'

'Yes, it was a good time.'

'Tom, I really tried, but I was already such an idiot.'

'I can't deny it.' We both laughed.

'Will you hug me?' He looked at me pleadingly.

'Of course.'

I gently laid my head on his chest. My tears ran silently down his pyjamas. I could hear his heart beating and how hard he was taking air into his lungs. He awkwardly put his hand on my head and stroked it. I closed my eyes, and for a moment, I felt like we were getting to know each other again.

'I'll get Harry.' After a while, I freed myself from his embrace, discreetly wiping my cheek.

I opened the door and nodded at Harry, who immediately got up from his chair.

'Dad!' He ran to the bed, crying, but seeing Chris's pale face with the oxygen mask, he stopped and looked at me, terrified.

'You can hug Daddy.' I nodded.

He gently lay down next to Chris, who, fighting a shaking hand, placed it on Harry's head, closing his eyes.

'Are you dying, Dad?' Harry's voice wavered.

Chris didn't say anything for a moment, then looked at me, and I nodded as a sign that he should tell him the truth.

'I'm going to heaven, my son.'

'But that means I'll never see you again.'

'Just because you can't see me doesn't mean I won't be there.'

'Where will you be?' He raised his head.

'Here.' He touched his finger to Harry's chest. 'Whenever you think of me, I will feel it in heaven. It will be like a secret sign you send me.'

Harry laid his head on Chris's chest and hugged him tightly. I couldn't control my tears, and when I reached for a handkerchief, I noticed how Chris's hand slid inertly from Harry's head to the bed. The machine immediately roared in a monstrous, continuous sound.

'Chris?' I called, and ran over to the bed.

He didn't answer. His face had frozen.

'Daddy, what's going on?' Harry looked from me to Chris, terrified. 'Not yet, please.' He snuggled into me and cried.

The door opened, and the nurse and the doctor ran into the room.

'Please wait in the corridor,' they told us.

Lucas took my hand. Behind the closed door was shrill silence. The machine no longer made any sound. We fixed our gaze on the door in suspense until the doctor appeared.

'I'm very sorry,' he said. 'He's gone. You can come in if you want to say goodbye.'

Waterfalls of tears began to cover Mum's and Harry's cheeks. I hugged them, took their hands and entered the room. Mum leaned over Chris, kissed his pale forehead and immediately ran out into the corridor. Harry struggled to catch his breath as he looked at his father.

'Let's say goodbye to Dad.' I kissed Chris's temple, followed by Harry, whose tears instantly clung to Chris's pillow. In the doorway, I took one last look at him. That view was like a photo album I had just finished looking at. We left.

Mum was calming her emotions in Lucas's arms. Harry held my hand tightly.

'My goodness!' Mum suddenly raised her head, quickly wiping the tears from her cheeks. 'I brought lunch. Everything will be wasted, and I don't remember if I turned off the kettle. We have to go home and...' Her eyes were like a beaten dog's.

'Mum.' I put my hand on her shoulder. 'Everything will be fine, I promise.'

On the way, Harry cried occasionally, and Mum, trying to drown out her pain, did not stop talking.

'Tom, Chris didn't pick up the laundry. The receipt is still on the dresser in the hallway, and we have to get a new pot; the old one was cracking, and he wanted to replace it. He also said about having the car inspected and that the policy expires at the end of the week—'

'Mum, I'll take care of everything. Don't worry. Rest, you're tired.' I reached out and stroked her cheek.

I exchanged a quick glance with Lucas, who was driving. It's terrible, but I don't know why I felt sad and relieved at the same time. I was worried about Harry. The separation had brought them closer, and I didn't know how he would deal with it now. *I need to talk to Tracy about this*, I thought.

Lucas parked outside the garage. We got out of the car and Judith ran to the fence.

'How is he feeling?'

'Chris has passed away,' I replied quickly.

'Oh my God! I'm so sorry.' She held out her hands to my mother. 'Do you need anything?'

'No, Judith. Thank you,' she replied coolly.

When we entered the house, Harry ran to his room, and Mum disappeared into the kitchen. Lucas hugged me in the hall.

'Are you holding up?'

'Yes, but I'm worried about Harry. I'll go to him, and you see my mother. If you can, help her in the kitchen. She will pretend to be strong, but she is hurting a lot inside.'

I stood before the bedroom door and listened, but no sounds came out. I knocked and opened the door. Harry stood at the window, watching the tree. I walked over and we held hands.

'Everything all right?'

'It hurts so much, Daddy. Here, in the middle.'

'I know, son. It will be like this for a while, but the wound in your heart will heal. It won't go away but won't hurt as much.'

We stayed silent for a while, looking at the branches being caressed by the wind. My mind went to memories of Chris bustling around the garden. He turned to me and smiled. I decided to keep these scraps of memories for Harry.

'Come on, let's have something to eat. Grandma is waiting for us.'

'OK, Daddy.'

As I walked down the hall towards the dining room, the house brought back memories. I saw Chris sitting on the sofa with the remote control, and after a while, our stunned eyes met when Harry said the words to me for the first time: *I love you, Daddy.* In the dining room, Chris sat in his chair. He toyed with his fork, impatiently waiting for his meal. Every nook and cranny of this house had a story that played through my head one by one.

'Take a seat; let's eat.' Mum laid out the plates.

'I'm not hungry, Mum. You guys have a bite to eat. I'm going to have a look upstairs.'

I went up the stairs. I remember Chris didn't want to renovate them. He said to leave them as they were but finally gave in. I stopped in front of our bedroom and slowly opened the door. He hadn't changed anything or even removed my stuff from the nightstand; my dusty box of tissues was still there. Everything was exactly as I'd left it. I sat on the bed and looked at our wedding photo.

'Can I come in?' I heard my mother's voice outside the door.

'Yes.'

She sat down next to me, and I felt her warm hand on my arm.

'What now, Tom?' She looked ahead.

'I have no idea.'

'Maybe you could live here?' She tried to find my gaze.

When I looked at her, I saw her helplessness and confusion instantly.

'There are a lot of memories here...'

'Yes...' Mum sighed.

'But that doesn't mean we won't see each other. Come and visit us. Harry will be pleased. He misses you.'

'You'd better come to me first.' She stroked my hand.

That evening, we all sat in the living room in front of the TV, staring at some movie, like Mum used to do with Chris. They liked to watch game shows, contests, reality shows and series that only required a little attention. I joined them sometimes, although I was always frustrated by the entertainment. But now I missed those moments. They seemed to exist somewhere outside our complicated lives. Moments when we laughed at absurd answers to trivial questions while eating reheated pizza or some crisps that Mum dug out of the kitchen cupboard. I automatically turned my head towards the door, but Chris wasn't with us. Harry laid his head on my lap, and I continued to stroke him. Lucas was sitting close to me, clearly refraining from showing me feelings.

'I'll make the bed for you in the guest-room,' Mum told me. 'I will sleep in the bedroom.'

'Mum, rest. I'll do the bed. I know where everything is.' I hugged her and kissed her.

'Let me put Harry in his room.'

'OK.'

'Goodnight, Daddy.' Harry kissed me on the cheek, then did the same to Lucas. Mum stared at that for a moment. This was a new situation for her, but her eyes accepted it. Harry took her hand, and they left the living room. I wanted so badly to protect him from the evils of this world. However, I could not protect him from the greatest tragedy, losing his father.

'Honey, how are you feeling?' Lucas took my hand. 'Are you holding up?'

'Let's go home tomorrow. This place is bringing back too many memories.'

'OK. We'll leave in the morning.'

'We'll take Mum to the station. I'm not leaving her here alone. You know...' I took a breath and stopped myself. 'Let's leave as early as possible.'

'Of course.'

I made up the bed in the guest-room – a room soaked in my story. I couldn't explain it, but this place had always been closer to me than the bedroom I shared with Chris. I used to come here often when he was sleeping.

The first night after his death, I couldn't sleep. I gently removed my hand from Lucas's and slid out of bed. I went to the window. He was still there. He waved his big branches at me in a gesture of understanding. I felt as if he wanted to hug me. I crossed my arms over my chest and swayed along with him.

'Honey, what's going on?' Lucas's sleepy voice snapped me out of my reverie. I turned around.

'I can't sleep. Sorry.'

Lucas got out of bed and walked over to me. He snuggled into my back, and after a moment in complete silence, he started rocking along with me.

In the morning, right after breakfast, we left the house. I closed the door and took one last look around the yard. It was so quiet. Only the wind hummed its tune for us to say goodbye. I didn't notice when Judith approached the fence. She waited in silence until I turned around.

'Were you going to leave without saying goodbye?' Her sad gaze slid across our faces. I went to the fence, and my mother joined me after a while.

'We were going to check on you, but you beat us to it.' I hugged her. Judith's arms gripped me tightly.

'I'm so sorry, Tom.' She kissed my cheek. 'What about the house now?'

'I'll sell it, and we'll put the money aside for Harry's studies.'

'That's a good idea. Will you call me sometime?' There was longing in her eyes.

'Of course, we'll be in touch.'

A few seconds later, Mum and Judith were frozen in a long, friendly hug. Tears glistened in Judith's eyes. For the first time, I had doubts. Maybe I shouldn't sell our house? What would Mum do now? Did she have other friends? I looked behind me. No, I no longer saw a house, only a cold building where ghosts wandered. I had to free them and give them a new life. Sell a home that would open its doors to other stories.

'Sue, promise me you'll call me every day.' Judith's words appeared like a blessing for my decision. My muscles relaxed and I reached for Mum's hand. She nodded.

'How could I not call?'

Lucas started the engine, and we were on the road. Judith waved until we were out of sight. No matter how many times I opened my mouth, no meaningful words came to mind. The other three were also silent. Time seemed to press against us, expecting something important. Now I realised that death could come at any time and interrupt what we had planned. A new fear crept into my heart. One day I would lose everyone.

While we waited for her train, my mother and I sat on the platform.

'Call me when you get there. I'll be waiting.' She took my hand.

'OK, Mum.'

'And visit me.' She tilted her head to meet Lucas's eyes.

'Or maybe you will visit us?' Lucas reacted by catching her gaze.

She smiled.

The train arriving at the platform lifted us from our seats. Mum hugged me, and Harry went over to Lucas. Her piercing gaze brought a blush to his face. Hugging him, she whispered something in his ear, and he nodded. I didn't hear. I was too far away.

As the train started to move, I turned around, unable to watch my mother's retreating figure. I was afraid that I would lose her too. That she would disappear like that departing train.

'Let's go home,' whispered Lucas, grabbing mine and Harry's hands.

'Yeah, let's go.'

11. Amsterdam

Six months after Chris's death, Tom would often wake up at night and stand by the window. I would join him and we would stay in an embrace for a long time. He was still working for Pierre. He worked remotely, but he flew to Warsaw once a month for meetings. He liked his job. He often tried to figure out problems in the evenings, and when he succeeded, a winning smile appeared on his face. He felt needed, and that was the most important thing. So I helped him prepare for these trips well in advance, although it seemed piercingly cold every time I said goodbye to him at the airport and returned to the apartment. However, I wanted to add a drop of excitement, joy and hope to this ocean of difficult emotions.

Tom was slower than Harry to adapt to the new country. I remember one of the first days after we moved, he went out to get some bread and didn't return for a long time. I wanted to call him, but I spotted his cell phone on my way to get mine. It was on the hall shelf next to the umbrella. I looked out the window. Clouds had gathered in one area as if conspiring to rain. I asked my neighbour to stay with Harry and ran into the street. At the second block, I slowed down. He was sitting on a bench, lost in thought. When I approached him, he threw himself into my arms. He said he got lost in the alleys and couldn't find his way home. I could see that Tom was ashamed that Harry would sense some weakness in him, so we went to the local bakery and bought a bag of doughnuts. We went home cuddled up to each other, and I knew I would always want to protect him.

Dutch was very difficult for Tom. He often got the names of stores wrong, as if forgetting that he no longer lived in England. Harry corrected him, embarrassing him. I would comfort Tom, afraid that he would lose his enthusiasm and stop learning, or worse, he would decide that Amsterdam was not for him.

I did everything I could to relieve him of any duties. I took over cleaning the flat and the shopping, drove Harry to school and later helped him with his homework. Tom resisted my help for a while, but as he dug deeper into his work, he thanked me. I appreciated the time I spent with Harry, and when he called me Dad one day, my heart skipped a beat, even though he probably did it by accident. I had never seen myself as a father before, and now I wanted nothing more than to be a father forever.

Tracy was in our lives every Wednesday. Sessions were held online. First, Harry sat at the computer in the office while Tom and I waited in the living room. Right after that, I took Harry to Emma and Sven's so that Tom could have some privacy. They had a session together once a month, and when I came home, I often found them crying in the living room. I didn't ask for anything. Knowing that their pain had found an outlet was enough for me. Tom would then hug me tighter than usual. He apologised even though I told him he shouldn't feel guilty. I understood that he and Chris had a difficult history, but even so, there was a lot of love.

We Skyped Sue every Sunday afternoon, but Harry always took over.

'Daddy, we're waiting!' he called to Tom, squirming in his chair.

'I'm coming!' Tom's voice echoed down the hall as he carried a tray of tea and biscuits.

'Daddy, hurry up; we're connecting now.'

Tom would sit next to me, and we would exchange warm glances, and I would take his hand. When I felt his warmth, I lacked nothing.

'Grandma!' Harry would call as soon as Sue appeared on the screen, and it seemed to me her eyes were glassy every time she connected with us.

'What's up, darlings? How are you?'

'Fine, Mum. And how do you feel?'

'It's dark here and raining today. I'm always tired—'

'Grandma, when are you coming?' Harry couldn't wait any longer for his turn. 'I have so much I would like to show you!'

'Honey, Grandma isn't young enough to travel anymore,' Sue said, laughing nervously. 'It's better you come to me.'

'Grandma, do you know that I have an electric scooter? One with a real light.'

'Really? But do you wear a helmet?'

'Yes, Lucas even bought me pads.'

She looked at me with a warm smile, but I wasn't sure what she was thinking now. I repeated the invitation several times during our conversations, but she always diplomatically declined. Tom explained that she wasn't ready yet. I was afraid there would never be a place for me in her life, but I hid that fear from him.

'How's therapy, Tom? Are you sleeping better?'

'Yes, Mum, although you know... I've always had trouble with it.'

'I know, darling.'

'Grandma, when I come, will you bake me an apple pie?' Harry moved closer to the screen.

'Of course. You will get the first warm piece.'

'And lots of whipped cream!' he exclaimed, his eyes sparkling with joy.

Harry seemed stronger than Tom, and for a moment, I thought he had gotten over his dad's death more quickly, perhaps because he was busy with school and new friends. But one afternoon, when I walked into his room, he was sitting at his computer, staring at a picture of Chris on his desk. When he heard me, he quickly wiped his cheek and looked scared, as if he had done something wrong. I walked over and hugged him, stroking his head.

'Darlings, you'll have to excuse me, but I'm going to bed early tonight.' Sue yawned, covering her mouth with her hand. 'I'm falling asleep sitting up.'

'All right, Mum, get some rest.'

'Grandma, I haven't yet told you about—'

'Honey, Grandma is tired.' Tom planted Harry on his lap and kissed him. 'You'll tell her everything next time.'

Sue sent Harry a kiss and we said goodbye, and Tom continued to cuddle Harry for a long while.

It was one of those lazy Saturdays when we didn't have to rush anywhere. The three of us could spend the day in pyjamas, only waking up to eat.

I got up first. I gently closed the door and went to Harry's room to avoid waking Tom. He was sitting in front of the computer with headphones on, playing some games while talking with a friend. He didn't even notice me. I silently backed away and went to the kitchen.

I was making tea when my phone rang.

'Good morning. Am I speaking to Lucas Espen?'

'Yes, that's me.'

'Gert Dekker. We talked a while ago about an apartment. You were looking for something bigger, closer to the centre.'

'Yes, I remember.'

'This flat, which you liked then, has now been put up for sale, and I thought you might still be interested. Hence my call.'

My heart pounded harder. Secretly from Tom, I'd been looking at a spacious, large apartment overlooking the park. I'd liked it very much, but the owner was renting it out and the idea went out the window.

'Yes!' I screamed, then lowered my voice. 'Of course I'm still interested.'

'Great! So come to my office on Monday. I'll be waiting.'

I opened the bedroom door slightly and approached the bed. Tom was still asleep. I kissed his temple, and he opened his sleepy eyes.

'What time is it?' he mumbled.

'It's only nine.'

'Where is Harry?' Tom sat up.

'He's in his room, playing on the computer.'

'I should check on him.' He tried to get up, but I grabbed his hand.

'Wait. I want to tell you something.'

'What do you want to tell me?' His eyes immediately widened in concern.

'I have to confess something. I didn't tell you anything before, but I found a bigger apartment for us a while ago. I knew you'd love it, but someone was renting it, and I'd considered the matter closed. But an agent just called. This apartment has just been put up for sale. I thought I could sell the one we live in, and we'd start over in a new place. Harry would have a bigger room and be close to the school.'

At that moment, I saw a twinkle in Tom's eyes that faded as quickly as it had appeared. Harry entered the room and opened his mouth to say something. He and Tom exchanged glances, and Harry sat beside him, cuddling up to his daddy.

'Did you hear?'

Harry nodded shyly, and Tom hugged him tighter and kissed him.

'I want the biggest room!' Harry called, and started hugging Tom tightly.

'We'll see what we can do,' I told Harry, taking Tom's hand. 'And you? Do you have any special requests?' I looked deep into Tom's eyes.

'Yes, and they're huge.' He smiled mysteriously.

'I'm all ears.'

'You just need to be there with us.'

'Then your wish will be my command.'

The three of us froze in the embrace, our heartbeats synchronising into one deep sound.

On Monday afternoon, we went to see the new apartment. As I parked outside the building, I felt a mixture of excitement and anxiety. I wanted so badly for Tom to like the place. I switched off the engine, and by the time I turned my head, Tom was already out of the car, looking around.

'Ooh! There's a bakery downstairs,' he noted.

'You won't have to walk far anymore.' I kissed him. 'Let's go upstairs and take a look at the apartment.'

Harry ran ahead of us, rushing to the open door where the agent was waiting. He passed him and ran inside.

'Harry!' called Tom.

'That's OK. Good morning! Nice to meet your family.'

Tom looked embarrassed, but he smiled and shook the agent's hand. Harry was already snooping around inside.

'Welcome, come in.' The agent let us through the door.

I took Tom's hand, and we started walking around the apartment. First, right by the front door, was a large room with a recess. The window was so large that daylight filled the space completely. Harry started running around like crazy, and in my mind's eye, I saw him sitting bent over his desk, doing his homework.

'Daddy, can this be my room? Please, please say yes.' He hugged Tom tightly.

'If Lucas doesn't mind.' Tom looked at me.

'It's yours, Harry,' I replied without thinking.

'Thank you!' He jumped for joy and hugged me.

We walked down the long corridor to the living room, where the sofa was the first thing that came into my thoughts. The three of us sat on it, cuddling each other, watching a fairy tale known to Harry by heart. The wind blew through the window, moving the curtain, and Tom covered us with a blanket. Upon reaching the kitchen, which was completely empty, the smell of fresh, crispy pizza touched my nostrils. I saw us sitting together at the big table for a moment. Tom put our portions on our plates, and Harry demanded ketchup. Tom smiled at me, and I thought he heard my thoughts.

We stopped outside one of the bedrooms. Tom entered first and went to the window. A moment passed before he spoke.

'This could definitely be ours.'

I walked over to him, curious. On the other side of the glass, I saw a large tree spreading wide arms, which, moved by the wind, said, *Hello.*

'Would you like to live here with me, Tom?' I cuddled up to his back.

He froze and was silent.

'Say something...'

He turned to me, though his face still showed no emotion.

'I'm so sorry, Lucas.'

'You don't like it?' I felt like I'd failed an exam.

'Daddy, no!' called Harry, who had just appeared in the doorway.

There was silence; all I could hear was my rapid breathing. Tom looked at me and then at Harry.

'I'm sorry because we have to go back to our apartment.' He laughed, and I witnessed my Tom returning. His smile that I missed so much. 'This apartment is beautiful, but can we afford it?' He winced.

'You scared me.' I kissed him. 'It's not that expensive. We can do it.' I looked deep into his eyes. 'Do you agree?'

'Yes.' He kissed me.

I lifted him up, and we spun on the spot, Harry whistling and clapping his hands.

'I love you.' I couldn't stop kissing him.

'I love you too,' he whispered.

I looked at the agent, who couldn't take his eyes off us.

'We're taking this apartment!' I called. 'Please prepare the paperwork!'

We spent that evening browsing home furnishings catalogues. Harry wanted a bigger desk and wardrobe. He'd given up on Spider-Man gadgets because apparently they were embarrassing. I noticed that Tom had quietened a bit. He was present but looking through the catalogues in silence.

'Honey, what's up?'

'Nothing. I'm thinking about how much work we have ahead of us, and that worries me.'

'You have me. You live with a designer, remember? I'll take care of everything. Just tell me what you need.'

That livened him up a bit. He opened the catalogue of kitchen equipment and showed me his ideas. Then we chose furniture for the bedroom and office and shelves for the wardrobe. Around midnight I woke up. We'd all fallen asleep on the bed among the catalogues. One was imprinted heavily on Harry's cheek. I moved him to his bedroom, and Tom tidied up the bed.

Time flew by, and the next thing I knew we were packing for the move. Tom wrapped our things in bubble wrap, and I put them in boxes. Harry always filled the space, but his room was silent this day. We only realised it after some time. We put the boxes down and walked together to his bedroom. Tom opened the door slightly. Harry was sitting on the floor, putting Spider-Man merchandise into a large container.

He turned when he heard us. 'Daddy, can we send this to England?'

'To England?' Tom was surprised.

'To Aunt Julie. She will give them to the children.'

'If you want, of course. We'll call Aunt Julie and let her know.'

'You won't mind if I give them to other children? I don't need them anymore.'

Tom walked over to Harry and hugged him.

'Honey, it's up to you to decide what to do with it.'

'I've already decided, Daddy.'

'Then it's settled.' Tom kissed Harry.

Three days later, we spent the evening in our new apartment, with boxes stacked in the middle of the living room and echoes dancing between them. In our haste, we hadn't labelled the boxes; now, we were desperately looking for our things.

'Honey, do you know where we packed the toothbrushes?' I asked Tom.

He walked over to me and looked deep into my eyes.

'Yes, my love. The toothbrushes are in one of those thirty boxes.' He pointed at them.

I laughed, then sighed. We were sitting on the floor a moment later, opening more boxes and writing their contents on the lids with felt-tip pens. Harry was bravely helping us, but I knew what he was looking for. Tom had accidentally packed an iPad into one of these boxes. Lost in the search, we did not notice the evening that crept up on us imperceptibly. I was rummaging through more boxes when Tom took my hand.

'Lucas, it's late. We haven't found the bedding yet. We only have this blanket.' He pointed at it. 'We can start again tomorrow. Let's go to sleep.'

'You're right.'

'Where will I sleep?' Harry asked.

'We'll be your blanket. You sleep with us.'

Harry immediately jumped on the sofa, and we joined him. Pretty soon, our body heat enveloped us, and we fell asleep.

Harry was the first to wake up in the morning, trying to get out from between us.

'Get up! We need to find my iPad.'

'Harry, have mercy. We're barely alive.' I hugged him. 'You'd better make us breakfast.'

'I don't think you'd like that,' Harry chuckled. 'Only Daddy makes the best breakfasts.' He put his mouth to Tom's ear and whispered, 'I'm hungry.'

'Wait a minute, honey,' Tom mumbled. 'Give me five minutes.'

This move had given Tom a new life. I heard laughter again, and his head was immediately filled with a thousand ideas for the further development of empty spaces, which he implemented immediately after waking up. Almost every day, he and Harry went for a walk in the nearby neighbourhood, from which they always came back out of breath and flushed. With each passing day, I saw more and more similarities between them. Harry squinted his eyes the same way when he was trying to focus on something. Caught not listening to us, he'd smile sweetly, which meant I couldn't get angry. Every evening, nestled in each other, we felt like we had lived here forever. Our love permeated day and night, and I lost myself in it deeply.

A month later, Tom received an email with information about potential buyers interested in the house in England. Despite their enthusiasm, he postponed the meeting several times. I tried more than once to ask what was holding him back, but I was afraid I'd only alienate him.

One evening, I checked on him when he was working on the computer.

'Darling? Do you have a moment?'

'Always.' He turned his head in my direction.

'I know you don't want to go back to England, but the buyers won't wait long. You should go. It would help you to get closure.' I put my hands on his shoulders.

'Nothing is hidden from you, eh?' He lifted his head and looked into my eyes.

'I know your every concern.' I stroked his cheek.

'That's true.'

'We can go together if you want.'

'You are lovely, but I have to do it myself.' He brought his mouth to my hand and kissed it.

On Saturday morning, Harry and I drove Tom to the airport. He was absent from the car. He was wandering somewhere with his thoughts, and I was afraid to meet them. Harry sensed something as well, because we glanced at each other occasionally, but neither of us said anything.

We said goodbye at the gate. Tom and Harry held each other for a long moment.

'I'll be back soon, honey. I miss you already.'

'Daddy, we'll pick you up at the airport.'

'OK, darling.'

Tom got up and walked over to me. His face was sad, though his eyes tried to smile.

'You can do it. It's only a few hours. The agent will pick you up from the airport, right?'

'Yes. He's collecting me.'

'All right. If you need anything, call or write.'

'Go home.' He kissed me.

'What about me?' admonished Harry.

'The biggest kiss for you.' Tom squeezed Harry tightly, and he tried to pull away.

'Daddy, you're going to strangle me,' he laughed.

*

By the time Lucas left with Harry, our son glancing my way, I already missed him. I stood still for a while after the crowd in the corridor had completely swallowed them up. Lucas didn't like to see me leave. Maybe it was better, because I didn't want to tell him I was afraid of the memories. It would have worried him.

On the plane, I remembered the first time I flew to England. Panic had gripped me. Chris wasn't there. What if he didn't come at all? But finally, he arrived, completely soaked. It rained all week, and he didn't have an umbrella. I couldn't believe so many years had passed. I leaned my head against the window and closed my eyes. I fell asleep.

After checking in at Newcastle, I made my way to the exit. As the arrivals hall doors opened, memories flew past me. A crowd of people waited like fans for their idol who was about to appear. Some ran to their loved ones with shouts of joy; others cried with emotion, and still others headed straight for the exit with stony faces. I passed the crowd, and as I stopped a little farther on, I noticed an agent holding a piece of cardboard with my name on it.

'Tom?' he asked as I approached him.

'Yes, that's me.'

'Jeffrey Edwards.' He offered his hand. 'We spoke on the phone. Now we get to meet in person. Did you have a good flight?'

'Yes, thank you.'

'This way, please.' He gestured to the exit. 'I parked close.'

Crossing the threshold of the airport, a familiar moist breeze touched my face. It was weird being in England without Chris. He was an integral part of the country, and now something was missing.

'We found a buyer for the car very quickly. Did you receive the transfer?' the agent asked as we drove, snapping me out of my thoughts.

'Yes, thank you.'

'The Merchants are still childless, but it's probably only a matter of time. They like the house very much and want to buy it immediately without changing anything about it.'

'That's nice.'

'As you requested, photos and personal effects have been packed and sent to the address you gave me. Has it all arrived?'

'Yes, thank you. I received the packages a week ago but haven't opened them yet.'

'I see. If you accept the offer, we can close the deal today. How is life in a new country?'

'Good, thank you.'

He must have sensed that I didn't feel like talking because after a while he turned on the radio, which emitted the familiar sounds of my favourite station, Heart. It reminded me of Chris and me singing songs, shaking our shoulders. He sang terribly, but I didn't care.

When we arrived, it was a mixture of sadness, joy, hope and pain. The house felt different and strange, as if ages had passed since I had been there. I made my way to the garden Chris loved so much, but now it was obscured by grass, dead leaves and overgrown bushes. It looked more like a man who hadn't shaved for a long time. If Chris saw this, he'd start cleaning right away. I apologised to the agent and entered the house. I went to the room on the ground floor where I'd spent most of my time – memories of when I first entered surfaced immediately. I went to the window.

'Hello, friend,' I said loudly.

Its branches moved happily in the breeze as if glad to see me.

'Perhaps a family will live here and start their new story. Take care of them as you took care of me.'

It seemed to me that he smiled and reached out his arms, wanting to hug me.

I went upstairs and made my way to the bedroom. I looked at the shelves that Chris and I had painted together and the balcony without a railing. We were supposed to have breakfasts on it in the summer, but we never finished it.

At that moment, I heard a car pull up, followed by conversation. I went downstairs and stood in the doorway. The agent was leading the couple towards me. She, about thirty, came first, and he, not much older, followed her. Their hunger for this place made them unable to stop looking around, just like we did when we first came here.

When they saw me, they came over and briefly said hello. She complimented my house, and he nodded silently.

‘The house is beautiful,’ she said a little excitedly. ‘We were told these were your ideas.’

‘It’s true; I’ve changed a lot here. When my husband and I bought this house, it was very neglected. The renovation took a year, and we still haven’t finished everything.’

‘Tom, I’ll get straight to the point. We’ve seen this house five times already. The agent has probably had enough of us.’ She laughed and looked at the agent standing next to her.

‘Of course not. I’m glad I found the home you were looking for.’

She returned her gaze to me.

‘We have seen a lot of houses, but this is the only place where we would like to live. That’s why we made a higher offer, hoping you will choose us. We would love it if you did.’ Her pleading gaze stroked me.

‘Kirsty, answer without thinking, and honestly. How do you feel being here now?’

‘You might think I’m crazy, but I feel butterflies in my stomach; they’re fluttering their wings hard, as if they want to get out into the garden.’

I fell silent, and all eyes were on me. Memories of renovating every bit of this place smiled at me.

‘Did I say something wrong?’

I walked over to Kirsty and hugged her tight. Her body stiffened slightly in surprise.

‘The house is yours,’ I whispered.

‘Really?’ she almost screamed, and jumped joyfully, then went to her husband and hugged him with happiness.

'We are very grateful that you have chosen us.' For the first time, I heard her husband's low and warm voice. 'We'll take care of this house, I promise.'

'Thank you.'

'If everyone is agreed, let's sign the documents,' the agent said. 'Tom has to go home today. We're all set.'

'I see no obstacles. Shall we sign?' I turned to Kirsty and Stan.

'Yes,' Kirsty almost shouted.

The agent spread out the papers on the dining room table, and Kirsty and her husband signed them. My turn came. I walked over to the table, and it seemed Chris was sitting at the other end. Smiling, he nodded in approval. I signed, and then we shook hands. The agent escorted them to the exit, and I stared out the window at the garden, where the wind was pushing Harry's swing.

After a while, the agent came back.

'Tom, there's one more thing. We found something else in the bathroom behind the sink when we sent your personal items. I think this belongs to you.' He took a bundle out of his pocket and handed it to me.

I opened it and saw a medallion with a dragon that Chris once gave me, and then I gave it to Harry. I smiled. I felt like Chris was giving me a sign that everything was going to be OK.

'Thank you. This keepsake means a lot to me.'

'Do you want to go back to the airport now?'

'Yes, let's go.'

I turned the key in the door as we left and headed towards the gate. However, after a moment I stopped to take one last look at the house where I had left a large piece of myself.

'Tom?' I suddenly heard a breathless voice.

'Hello, Judith.' I turned to the fence.

'You didn't want to say goodbye to me.'

'Sorry, there's so much going on I didn't think of it.'

'Did you sell the house?' She was staring at me with the same curious gaze as always, but I also saw understanding this time.

'Yes, a lovely couple are going to live here. I think you'll be friends.' I touched her shoulder.

'I don't know. They've come several times. I tried to talk to her, but her hubby was kind of surly and ignored me.' She rolled her eyes.

'Maybe he just didn't hear you.' They must have been too excited about the home.

'Maybe,' she sighed. 'And how are you? You don't call at all. I don't know how you and Harry are.'

'Sorry, we've been very busy. Lucas found a bigger apartment for us, and we moved. We've been living there for a while.'

'That's great. We'll have to call on Skype, and you can show me everything. I'd like to see Harry too. He must have grown.'

'Oh yeah, and he's starting to get moody sometimes.' I laughed. 'Time is moving so fast, and my little boy will become a man soon.'

'I know something about that. I wanted my children to always be tiny.'

'Judith, excuse me, the agent is waiting. He's taking me to the airport. We'll call you, I promise.' I hugged her and kissed her goodbye.

Getting into the car, I glanced once more at the house, which touched my heart with the sadness of farewell. The agent started the engine and we set off, discussing the final details of the house sale on the way. The entire sum was to be deposited into an account I had opened some time ago. Lucas and I had decided to save money for Harry's studies and maybe enough for a small apartment.

'Walk you in?' the agent asked as he parked outside the airport.

'There's no need to. I appreciate your help with everything.'

'The pleasure is all mine.'

We shook hands, and I headed for the entrance to Newcastle Airport one last time. I checked in and sat at the gate. I took my phone out of my pocket and realised it had been turned off all this time. My heart jumped nervously, and I was out of breath. I turned on my phone, and immediately the messages started coming in one after the other. I dialled Lucas.

'Tom?' I heard his shaky voice, and in the distance, Harry calling me.

'Sorry, so much was happening that I forgot to turn on my phone after landing. I don't know how it happened. I'm very sorry.'

'Jesus, Tom. We were out of our minds.' I heard him let the air out loudly.

'I'll put Harry on now.'

'Daddy, are you OK?' His voice wavered.

'Honey, I'm sorry. I'm fine, I was just really busy and forgot to turn on my phone, but I'll be back soon, and we'll see each other then.'

'OK, Daddy. I can't wait. Here's Lucas.'

'Honey, just tell me, what's happened with the house?'

'Sold. All finished. I don't have to come back here anymore.'

‘I’m happy. We will celebrate when you get home.’

‘OK.’

When the plane’s landing gear touched the tarmac, I felt a relief that had long resisted visiting me. I got off the plane energetically, wanting to hug my son and Lucas as soon as possible. I spotted them by the pillar as I walked into the corridor. Seeing me, smiles appeared on their faces at the same time. The sight warmed my heart. Harry sprinted towards me.

‘Daddy!’ He threw himself onto me. ‘Don’t leave again,’ he whispered, and I felt warm breath on my neck. I kissed him.

‘What about me?’ Lucas came over.

‘That’s my saying.’ Harry began to laugh. ‘You need to find something else.’

We all burst out laughing.

‘There’s enough for you too.’ I got up from my knees and kissed him on the lips.

‘Let’s go home.’ Lucas offered me his hand.

Leaving the airport, I turned around one last time. I thought I saw Chris. He was standing on the corner, waving goodbye to us, full of joy. Harry was also looking at the airport, but then he glanced back at me. He didn’t say anything; he looked deep into my eyes and took my hand, which he didn’t let go the whole way home.

Harry and I sat on the living room sofa. He cuddled up to me, and we stayed there in silence. I stroked his head, and he closed his eyes.

‘Harry, do you remember waking up screaming at night?’

‘Yes, Daddy, but I don’t have nightmares anymore.’

‘That’s good, son. I gave you something then. Do you remember?’

'Dad's medallion!' He tilted his head back but quickly looked down. 'I lost it, Daddy. Sorry. I looked for it but couldn't find it.' He cuddled tighter into me.

'I guess Dad made sure you'll still have it.' I took it from my pocket and gently slipped it into his hand. He slowly opened his fingers and flinched when he saw the medallion; our eyes met.

'Daddy, thank you, thank you so much.' His voice was filled with emotion, and his eyes filled with tears. Seeing this, I couldn't stop mine. Harry hugged me tighter, and I looked at the door where Lucas was standing.

'How long have you been there?'

'Long enough. Dinner is ready; I've come to call my boys through.'

'Shall we go?' I asked Harry.

'Yes, Daddy.'

I got off the sofa, and Harry put the medallion around my neck. I held my hand out to him, he grasped it, and we headed for the kitchen.

12. Butterflies

The week drew to a close, and I was the first to leave the office, impatiently. Harry was staying with a friend, so Tom and I would have time to ourselves for the first time in a long time. On the way home, I bought wine, cheese, nuts and grapes. Romantic scenarios for our evening filled my mind. When I got to the apartment door, I tried to open it noiselessly, but in the corridor, I heard a faint conversation coming from its depths.

'Good morning, honey!' I called, listening.

'I'm in the kitchen,' replied Tom.

Excited, I made my way towards him, but when I stood in the doorway, I saw a tearful Emma cuddling up to Tom.

'What's going on?'

Tom and Emma exchanged quick, knowing glances, and then Emma suddenly burst out laughing.

'It's from happiness!'

'Happiness?'

'The place has become available!' she screamed, jumping up and down.

'The place? What are you talking about?'

'We have a wedding date – in three weeks! Can you believe it?' Her joy overtook me.

'Really? That's wonderful, Emma! How is this possible?'

'Some couple had to change their wedding date, and we got their place.'

'Emma! I'm so happy for you!' I started kissing her with joy.

'Come on. Don't just stand there. Set the table; dinner's almost ready,' ordered Tom.

'Where's Sven?' I looked around the kitchen.

'He's having a meeting or something.' Emma rolled her eyes. 'Get the plates.' She nudged me with her elbow and winked.

Emma's talk of the wedding dominated the dinner. She had waited a long time for this. Again and again, I glanced at Tom, whose face was frozen in a smile, although his eyes occasionally wandered. I didn't know if it was due to fatigue or the wedding chatter.

'I don't want anything fancy,' said Emma. 'A modest wedding, followed by dinner with family and friends. Maybe some dancing?'

'Dessert?' Tom got up and grabbed my cleared plate. Before Emma could answer, her phone rang, and then all we could hear was the squeals of joy from a friend.

'I'll help you.' I grabbed a plate and followed Tom towards the kitchen. 'Honey, what's up?' I set the plate on the table and hugged him.

'Nothing, I'm just a little tired. I finished the online meeting, and Emma came in. I couldn't tell her it was a bad time.' He grimaced. 'This is her important moment, and we should be part of it.'

'I must admit, I'd planned tonight a little differently too.' I kissed Tom and reached for the wine I had placed by the window.

'I don't think Emma will let us do that today,' Tom laughed, and snuggled into me.

'My apologies.' Emma suddenly appeared in the doorway. 'Lucas, you mentioned that you had the evening off, and I completely forgot about it in my excitement. I'll get out of your way now.'

'Wait! Take some cake for Sven. You can eat it together.'

Tom packed a large piece of cake, and soon the house was pleasantly quiet.

'I'll get the glasses. I'll be right back.' I kissed Tom.

When I returned, I pulled out a blanket, and we covered ourselves on the couch. We drank some wine while watching a movie, and I don't know when we fell asleep, cuddled up together. In the morning, we were awakened by the sound of a garbage truck.

'And after a romantic evening,' I sighed.

'It was wonderful,' laughed Tom. 'We were both tired. There will be other evenings.'

'And mornings.' I started kissing Tom passionately just as the doorbell rang.

'The morning is over.' We both burst out laughing.

'Open it; it's probably Harry.' Tom kissed me.

*

Halfway through the next week, I was finishing an online meeting with Pierre when the phone rang.

'Hello? Am I talking to Tom Anderson?' It was a female voice.

'Yes, speaking.'

'My name is Hylke Vos; I'm Harry's teacher. I'd like to meet so we can talk.'

'Has something happened?' I felt my heart speed up.

'It's not a big deal. I'd just like to discuss this matter in person. When could we meet?'

'I've just finished work, so if you have time, I could be there in half an hour. We live nearby.'

'Great. I will wait for you.'

After the conversation ended, my mind created questions that crowded in my head. Maybe Harry had a learning disability? But he had excellent grades. Truancy? No, that was impossible. He must have gotten in with the bad crowd, and something happened. *Don't worry, she didn't say it was a bad thing.* The intrusive thoughts, however, would not leave me until the meeting with the teacher. I entered the building and went to her office.

'Good afternoon,' I said, opening the door hesitantly. 'Tom Anderson, Harry's dad.'

'Good afternoon.' She got up from behind the desk. 'Come in, please sit down.' She gestured to the chair across from her.

'Has Harry done something wrong?'

'Harry is a wonderful boy. Very unique, I would say.'

'I'm so sorry, I've been busy lately and haven't given my son the time he needs.' The words burst out of my mouth, cutting her off.

'That's not what I meant. I wanted to ask you... How long has Harry been writing?'

'Writing?' I couldn't hide my surprise.

'Your son has written some wonderful stories. I had a chance to read them. He has quite a large collection. I offered to send them to an international children's competition, but parental consent is needed. Hence my call to you.'

Her words echoed in my head. I leaned back in my chair and looked at her in surprise.

'I can see your embarrassment.' She twirled the pen in her hand.

'Harry hasn't told me anything, and we've never kept any secrets from each other.'

'Children sometimes have secrets. He was probably embarrassed.'

'Looks like it,' I sighed. 'Of course I don't mind, if Harry wants it.'

'I'm glad.' She took a document out of a drawer and pushed it towards me. 'You have to sign here.' She pointed.

'Of course.' I took a pen from the desk and signed the form.

'And now I will take you to your son. I think he's just finished his last lesson.'

We walked down the long corridor. I looked around. A lot had changed since my school days. The interiors of schools had become more modern and child-friendly. Schools now taught you to understand the world, not just memorise rules and definitions. The children's creativity and passions are allowed to develop without them being punished for being different. However, one question kept gnawing at my mind. *Why didn't he tell me? Does that mean he's grown up and doesn't need me anymore? Doesn't he trust me?*

'Harry?' the teacher called.

'Daddy!' Harry shouted out with joy when he saw me.

'Hi, darling.' I crouched beside him, searching his eyes for an answer. 'Let's go home together.'

'I'll leave you now.' The teacher said goodbye and left.

Harry cheerfully gave me his hand, and we moved towards the door. Along the way, he told me about the kids at school and the new caretaker who shared funny stories with them during breaks. I looked at him, not knowing how to start a conversation. At home, as I was taking off my jacket in the hallway, he approached me and took my hand.

'Daddy, you're kind of sad. Did I do something wrong? Are you angry with me?'

'I could never be angry with you. I love you. I just felt a bit sad when the teacher told me about your writing. I felt left out.'

'It's not like that...' He lowered his gaze.

'I'm very proud of you, but I don't know why you hid it. After all, we've always told each other everything. You don't need me anymore?'

'I wanted to tell you, but you were always busy.'

'I neglected you, I'm sorry. I'll fix it.'

'I'm sorry too.' Harry snuggled into me.

In the evening, he brought me his notebook in which he had written his stories. I read them several times, and my heart jumped with emotion. He'd written the story about a tree boy that I told him the first night he came to live with me. I remember making it up on the spur of the moment, and he was continuing it now. I was so happy. The next night I went to Harry's room.

'May I?' I knocked.

'Come in, Daddy.'

I sat beside him on his bed, placing his notebook in front of him.

'This is beautiful. I enjoyed it very much. I hope you will let me read more.'

'Of course, Daddy.'

'But before that, a true writer should have something magical. Something to help him create beautiful, magic words.'

'What's that?' He opened his eyes wide.

I took a box out of my pocket and handed it to him. He took it carefully and opened it, and after a moment, the room was filled with sounds of joy.

'It's a fountain pen! Daddy, thank you! I love you!' He hugged me.

'Just one thing, please. Don't write at night.' I kissed him.

*

Two weeks later, the three of us stood in front of the mirror, dressed in suits and looking at our reflections.

'My two treasures and me,' said Lucas. 'I'm a lucky man.'

Harry smiled broadly, and I kissed Lucas.

'Ready? Emma is waiting for us.' Lucas took our hands. 'Let's go.'

Harry and I took front-row seats at the registry office, and Lucas sat on the left with the other witness. There were a lot of people gathered in the hall. Emma's and Sven's families, friends and people they worked with daily. The murmur of excited conversations spread among the guests, who glanced at the doors now and then. After a while, we heard them open. We rose from our chairs. Emma and Sven entered holding hands, and the glow radiating from their happy faces touched us with warmth. We exchanged happy glances with Lucas. I could see the emotion in his eyes. With a movement of his lips, he uttered, *I love you*, and I responded with the same.

'Daddy.' Harry squeezed my hand tighter in excitement. 'Auntie looks like a fairy.' He couldn't take his eyes off her.

'Yes, darling. She looks beautiful.'

Once we were seated, I wondered if Emma and Sven were as nervous as I was when Chris and I got married. Were they afraid of their voices getting stuck and not being able to get their vows out? When I heard Chris's vow, I couldn't control my tears, and then, in the photos, I saw that some of the guests were also moved. I have never forgotten my mother's words, when she came to us after the ceremony to announce that she now had two sons and kissed each of us individually. Despite everything, this brief moment was a wonderful gift from life. I glanced over at Harry, who continued to stare at Emma and Sven as they took their wedding vows. *You were my second gift*, I thought, looking at Harry.

'Did you and Dad have a vow too?' Harry suddenly turned to me.

'Of course. We came up with a very short one so that we wouldn't get the words muddled up from stress.'

'Will you show me the pictures one day?' He looked pleadingly.

'If you want.'

'Thank you.' He hugged me, and I stroked his head.

'You don't even know how happy I am for them.' Lucas, who had suddenly appeared next to me, kissed me on the cheek.

'Me too, when I see how happy they are.' I took his hand.

After the ceremony, we went to the restaurant where the reception was being held. We took our seats at the table, and Lucas held my hand as if someone was about to kidnap me.

'Honey.' I leaned into his ear. 'I love your touch, but my hand is numb.'

'Sorry.' He let go. 'I'm very excited.' He kissed me, and I saw that a guy sitting nearby was watching us. I felt uncomfortable.

During the dinner, the parents officially blessed the young couple. After them, it was the turn of the witnesses, who told funny anecdotes from the young couple's life, and the whole room burst into loud laughter. Then the music came on, and several couples timidly began to dance. At one point, a little red-haired girl came to our table.

'Will you dance with me?' she asked Harry bravely.

Frightened, he looked at me, his face flushed.

'Honey, you can't disappoint such a beautiful girl.' I stroked his back.

'Yes, Daddy.' He stood up, embarrassed, and the girl gave him her hand.

As he left, he looked back. I smiled at him, closing my eyes as a sign that everything was fine. Not long later, I was amazed at how he was swinging around with her on the dance floor.

'When did he learn to dance like that?' I asked Lucas.

'He practised with me before the wedding.' He smirked mischievously.

'Oh, and I don't know anything about it?'

'It was a secret, honey.'

Harry high-fived Lucas at the table and sat down, raising his head. I kissed him, laughing. I had just sipped some wine when moody music blared from the speakers.

'Darling.' Lucas stood up and held his hand out to me. 'Our turn.'

'Daddy, you can't disappoint such a handsome man.' Harry smiled widely.

'Cheeky.' I winked at him.

I rose, taking the napkin off my lap and leaving it on the table, and we walked out onto the dance floor. The guy from the table next to us kept staring at us. I felt its heat when Lucas moved close to me on the dance floor. We started to move gently to the rhythm of the music.

'If that guy sitting at the next table doesn't stop staring at you, I'm going to have to intervene.' Lucas kissed me.

'Honey, I don't think he's looking at me; he's looking at us.'

'That's some excuse.' Lucas kissed me on the lips. 'You know... I thought Harry could spend the night at Emma's next Friday, and we could...' His devilish eyes were smiling at me.

'That would be lovely, but you forget I'm going to Warsaw.'

'Ohh yes.' He sighed. 'In that case, we'll postpone it until you're back.'

*

A week later, I got off the plane and headed up the sky bridge to the exit. As I stood in the lobby doorway by the pillar, I spotted Emma holding Harry's hand. Waving at me, they tried to smile, but their faces betrayed their anxiety.

'Daddy!' Harry threw himself into my arms.

I lifted him and twirled him around a few times.

'Where's Lucas?' I looked at Emma, putting Harry on the ground.

'They called him in unexpectedly for work. That's why I came with Harry.'

'Do you know why?'

'Unfortunately not.' She averted her panicked gaze.

'Auntie, I need to go to the toilet,' Harry whispered to Emma, shaking her hand.

'Honey, I'll go with you.' I took Harry's hand, but he pulled it out slightly.

'Daddy, you're tired from your journey. Wait for us there.' He pointed to the gate. 'We'll be right back.' He pulled Emma towards the restroom.

I turned pale. Suddenly it dawned on me that the moment I had feared so much had arrived. Harry had grown up. I grabbed my suitcase and sat at the gate. I watched people go to a nearby stand for drinks and sandwiches. My stomach rumbled. I got up and walked over to the glass case. I scanned past the sandwiches until I settled on the spinach tortilla. I opened the window and was about to grab it when suddenly someone behind me got there first.

'Wait a sec,' I called, turning to face the intruder, and froze.

'If you don't mind, we can share it.' Lucas grinned.

'I don't think I have a choice,' I said, laughing. 'I'll buy the drinks. What are you having?'

'I'd like green tea, please. Shall we sit down?' he asked with a mischievous smile.

'Maybe there?' I pointed to Gate D5.

A moment later, like two strangers, we sat beside each other. Lucas slowly unwrapped the tortilla and handed me the second slice.

'Emma said you were called into work.' I could no longer pretend.

'I managed to get away early.' His eyes smiled at me.

'Harry went—'

'I know, Tom,' he interrupted, and when he took my hand, I felt his trembling. I looked at him, and he swallowed hard, then took a deep breath and let it out.

'Lucas, what's up?'

'Tom, when we first met here, you stole my heart.'

'You stole my sandwich.'

'Nobody interrupts me like you do,' he laughed. 'I love it. You and Harry are the best thing that ever happened to me. I've waited a long time for you, afraid you'd never be ready. Life has given us a difficult path, which we have overcome together. Today I'd like to ask you something, Tom.' He quickly got up from his chair and knelt in front of me.

'Lucas, what are you doing? People are watching.' I nervously looked around.

'Thomas Anderson, would you like to continue to share your life with me, every day, but as my husband?' He took a small box from his pocket and opened it. 'Will you marry me?'

I could barely see the sparkling wedding rings through the tears welling up in my eyes.

'I love you, crazy man. I'll marry you, but get up off your knees, please, before they show us on the news.' I laughed through my tears.

He kissed me, and I hugged him, and at that moment, I heard Emma clapping and squealing behind me. I turned around. Next to Sven, Harry was jumping up and down with joy. His eyes were laughing at me. In the distance, I noticed people stopping and clapping. I felt warmth on my cheeks and crouched down next to Harry.

'Don't you mind?'

'No, Daddy. I'm very happy for you.'

'Really?'

'Really.' He hugged me tightly.

'And that toilet trip was part of the plan?'

'I can't say anything,' he whispered in my ear.

'Ah, yes!' I chuckled and hugged him tighter.

'I'm so glad, Tom!' Emma kissed me, and Sven came over right after her and hugged me.

'Let's go home,' she ordered after a minute. 'We have a lot to talk about.' She smiled widely.

At home, Emma got completely carried away. She couldn't sit still. She circled the room, showering us with her endless wedding ideas.

'Lucas, maybe we should use something from your first wedding?' Emma walked over to him. 'I remember there was a—'

'I don't think that's a good idea.' He looked at her meaningfully.

I noticed his confusion, and his eyes hung for a moment. I tried to recall my wedding, which was a big event for me then. However, now that life had written a different script, I could no longer find that uniqueness.

Emma fell silent and thoughtful, resting her chin on her hand as she circled the room. At one point, she stopped, narrowed her eyes and was about to say something when the apartment was filled with the sound of the doorbell. I started towards the door, but suddenly Harry appeared and stopped me.

'Daddy, I'll get the door. It's Finn from school. Can I go rollerblading with him?' His pleading look would not let me say no.

'You didn't tell me you had a friend.' I felt a prick in my heart.

'There wasn't time, but I promise I'll tell you everything tonight.'

'OK, but don't go too far.'

'Thank you, Daddy.' He kissed me on the cheek and ran to his friend.

I looked out the window, but all I saw was their disappearing figures. I turned to Lucas. He smiled at me and said *I love you* with his lips, then returned to talking with Sven.

'Will you invite your mother?' Emma came over to me.

'I don't know how.'

'I don't think you need to worry. She would like you to be happy.'

'Probably...' I sighed.

'Come with me.' She offered me her hand.

I hesitated but took it. We went to the office, where Emma closed the door and handed me the phone.

'Call now. Don't wait.'

'But I don't know what to say.'

'You can do it. I'm here.'

I grabbed my phone and looked at the screen. I took a deep breath and dialled. I walked over to the window and began nervously plucking at the curtain.

'She's not answering.' I turned to Emma and tried to hang up, but she held my hand.

'Wait a bit longer.'

I waited, the sound of the ringing getting louder and louder in my ear with every second.

'Hello, Tom?' Mum's panting voice sounded.

'Mum!' Emma and I exchanged glances.

'Sorry, I was taking the rubbish out and barely heard the phone.'

'Mum...' I started. 'Up till now, we haven't talked about this... You know you are very important to me, but I have to tell you something.' I closed my eyes. 'Lucas proposed to me, and we want to get married. This wedding can't take place without you.' I blurted out the words.

There was silence; all I could hear was my heart beating hard.

'Honey, that's wonderful,' she said after a moment. 'I'm really happy.'

'But—'

'There is no but. You are my son, and how could I leave you on a day like this.'

I leaned against the window and couldn't contain my emotions. Emma came over and rubbed her hand on my back.

'Tom, don't cry. It's wonderful news, and I'll be able to spend time with Harry too. It means a lot to me. Really.'

'Thank you, Mum.' I wiped the tears from my cheeks.

'But you have to invite Judith too. She wouldn't forgive us,' she laughed.

'OK, Mum,' I said, joining her.

After Harry got home, I sought an excuse to check on him in the evening. Finally, I opened the door slightly and poked my head in.

'Do you have a moment for me?'

'Come in.' He waved his hand.

I sat down next to him on the bed.

'Will you tell me about your friend?'

'Yes, Daddy. Finn always stayed away from everyone. He sat alone during breaks. Once, I sat next to him in the cafeteria and started talking. He's got two dads, like me.' Harry tilted his head and grinned.

'Really?'

'Yes, I'm not the only one.'

Until now, I had been afraid that the other kids would make things difficult for him if Lucas and I walked him to school together. However, this was the Netherlands, not Poland, and once again, I could see that Harry and I were safe here.

'I'm happy.'

'We've become friends since then.'

'That's great. Maybe someday you'll invite him to join us. I'd like to meet him.'

'I was just about to ask you that. You're ahead of me.'

'Because I'm your daddy.' I laughed.

'Thank you.' He leaned in and kissed my cheek.

*

Two weeks later, the evening before the wedding, Emma barged into our apartment like a police officer on a raid.

'I'm sorry, lovebirds, but Tom isn't sleeping here tonight. I'm taking him home.'

'But Emma—'

'There is no but. It's bad luck.' She turned to me. 'Tom, let's get what you need, and you guys will see each other tomorrow. Trust me; this is how it has to be.'

'Are you serious?' I smiled incredulously.

'Shall I call Sven, or are you coming voluntarily?' Her face tried to make a stern grimace, but it was too hard for her. Lucas and I exchanged vague smiles.

'Come on! We don't have time,' she said.

'Can we at least say goodbye?' Lucas grimaced.

'You'll see him tomorrow morning. Tom, ready? We have to go.'

Surprised, I gathered my things, glancing at Lucas, whose expression was as confused as mine.

'Tom, take your phone.' Lucas tried to hand it to me.

'Oh no! No phone calls!' exclaimed Emma. 'Tomorrow, after the wedding, everything will go back to normal, but for now you have to trust me.'

'Emma, you're scaring me. Where are you taking him?'

'He's staying with me. It's a ritual to keep your marriage happy.'

'And Harry?' I asked.

'Harry is in on it. He'll sleep at my parents' place.' Her roguish smile spread across her face.

'But when you—'

'There's no time! Let's go,' she urged.

Outside the building, I looked at our window, where Lucas drew a heart on the glass with his finger. I sent him a kiss and got in the car with Emma. Sven was waiting at the wheel.

'Hi, Sven. Where are you kidnapping me to?'

'Sorry, Emma insisted. It's some superstition or something.'

'Don't downplay the seriousness of the situation. This is to make their marriage successful.'

'It'll be fine without it,' Sven groaned.

'You know nothing. Go now. The longing will cement their marriage forever. I saw it in a film.' She turned to me and giggled. 'Don't worry, Tom. Your mother will come to you in the morning. I've arranged everything.'

I nodded. 'I don't doubt it.'

At Emma and Sven's apartment, they took me to a small guest-room, where they'd prepared a bed for me to sleep in.

'Make yourself comfortable.' Sven set my bag down.

'Are you hungry?' Emma asked.

'I can't eat anything. It's the nerves.' I grimaced.

'I see. I'll check on you later.' She winked at me.

As I took my pyjamas out of my bag, a small piece of folded paper fell onto the floor. I picked it up and opened it. I recognised Harry's handwriting immediately.

I'll see you tomorrow, Daddy. I'd like to wish you a good night. I love you. Harry.

I smiled to myself and pressed the letter to my heart.

Just before midnight, I heard Emma knocking on the door.

'Can I come in?' she whispered.

'Yes, I'm awake.'

'Tom, you need to rest. You'll have bags under your eyes tomorrow.' She sat down next to me. 'And we wouldn't want that.'

'We're both getting married for the second time, but the stress is the same. Stupid, huh?'

'It's normal, but when you stand in front of each other and look into each other's eyes, the stress will disappear. God, Tom, I'm so glad. Lucas has been waiting for this for a long time. He's so happy, and so are you, aren't you?' She looked into my eyes.

'Yes, I'm very happy, even if it's different.'

'Different?'

'When you get married for the first time, your emotions quiver in a dance of mad joy. You can't tame them. They break out into the world, which is spinning around you, and you feel like someone special. The second wedding is different. Of course, all these powers and feelings are still there, but their intensity is not the same as the first time. They are tamer and more mature.'

'Maybe you're right,' Emma mused. 'I've never experienced it.'

'And may you never have to.'

'Tom, I just remembered something. Harry asked me if he should call Lucas "Dad" after the wedding.'

'What did you tell him?'

'That Lucas would be very happy. However, before he does it, he has to feel it in his heart.'

'And what did Harry say?'

'He said he had felt it for a long time but was ashamed to say it.'

I felt my heart grow. I'd talked to him a few times about it, but he always said he didn't know yet. *I wish I could hug him right now*, I thought.

'Try to sleep, Tom. Tomorrow is your big day.'

After Emma left, I rolled over, and my mind took me back to the day Chris and I were getting ready for the wedding. I remember the stress gripping my throat while I said my vows. I was afraid of getting the words wrong. Then relief and tears of emotion. Falling asleep, I involuntarily whispered, 'Yes.'

Emma woke me up in the morning. As I got dressed, my heart beat like crazy. *It's almost time!* I thought as I buttoned up my shirt with trembling hands. Half an hour later, standing in front of the mirror, I was ready. I looked at my reflection, trying to find the man from years ago, but I failed. The baggage of experience was imprinted on his face, and carefree joy had grown, giving the emotions a different colour.

'There's someone here for you.' Emma looked into the room, opened the door wider, and I saw Sue.

'You look beautiful,' Mum said, and kissed me.

'You've come!' I rushed into her arms. 'Thank you,' I whispered.

'You didn't think I'd leave you alone, did you? Everyone's waiting. Are you upset?' She adjusted my tie.

'I shouldn't be, I've done it before.' I laughed nervously. 'I'm nervous, just like I was the first time.'

'It'll be fine.' She patted my shoulder. 'Tom, Harry asked me to give you this. He said, "He will know." She took a small box from her purse and handed it to me. When I opened it, the dragon medallion flashed inside, and it immediately brought a smile to my face.

'Thank you, Mum.' I squeezed the medallion tight then slipped it into my jacket pocket.

'Tom, listen. I know it's a little late, but will you let me walk you down the aisle? I would like that very much.'

'Mum...' Gathering tears took my voice away. I hugged her and smelled her lily of the valley perfume – the same as when I first met her years ago.

'Don't cry, son. You'll have red eyes in the photos.' She took a handkerchief from her bag and gently collected my tears, and after a moment, she wiped her own cheek.

'Let's not keep Lucas waiting any longer. Let's go.'

I took my mother's hand and we walked to the car.

*

In the wedding hall, I sat in the front row with my husband. Harry, in a navy-blue suit, his hair gelled, waited beside Lucas, who shifted impatiently from foot to foot, exhaling loudly. I got up and walked over to them.

'Emma, why is it taking so long?' Lucas said.

'Relax.' I took his hand. 'He's on his way, and soon you'll be the happiest man on earth. Tom is talking to his mum; give them a minute.'

'Do you think—'

Lucas didn't have time to finish what he wanted to say because the door opened. Everyone immediately stood up, holding their breath. Sue entered with Tom, holding his arm. The joy that painted their faces was addictive, and the glow emanating from them followed them down the aisle. They walked with a calm, even step. Tom returned the guests' smiles with adorable shyness, and Sue proudly led her son to Lucas, who tried unsuccessfully to hold back tears.

'I entrust you with my son. Take care of him,' Sue said with emotion.

'Thank you, Mum,' he whispered.

'I have two sons now,' she added, and kissed Lucas, then took a handkerchief from her purse and handed it to him.

She sat beside me, Sven, Lucas's sister and Harry, who had a serious expression on his face. He was nervous about the task that had been assigned to him. In the next row, Tracy, Tom and Harry's therapist, adjusted the fascinator in her hair now and then; I think it was slipping. Tom's neighbour, Judith, constantly whispered in the ear of her partner, who was always smiling. The attention of most of the men, including Lucas's boss, was directed at the cleavage of a beautiful woman named Lia. From what

I remember, she was a stewardess, a friend of Lucas's. There was also a Frenchman named Pierre, from Tom's work.

As Lucas and Tom faced each other and said their vows, we could see their love filling the hall. God, how they loved each other. I felt like time slowed down, just as it did at my wedding. For a moment I stopped hearing any sound. It was just me and my partner saying the words of a vow. Then Harry got up and, avoiding the eyes of those gathered, approached Lucas and handed him the rings on a tray. He followed them seriously with his eyes as they both slipped them onto their fingers, and after a moment, a wide grin quickly spread across his face, and they both kissed him.

Immediately after, to thunderous applause, the couple exchanged a kiss. The guests got up and came one by one to congratulate them.

I remember Tom telling me about butterflies once. That day I had the impression that they were flying into the room through an open window. I could have sworn I heard their wings beating. Colourful butterflies gathered above us in a joyful dance, rhythmically fluttering their wings.

Copyright © 2023 by James Ally

All rights reserved, including the right to reproduce this book or portions thereof in any form whatsoever.

Copyedited by Toby Selwyn

Cover concept by James Ally

Cover design by Ken Dawson

A catalogue record for this book is available from the Polish Library.

ISBN

PB: 978-83-964631-2-8

eBook: 978-83-964631-3-5

To find out more about the author and his book, please visit:

www.jamesally.com

Printed in Great Britain
by Amazon

41732712R00172